Praise for
How To Be a Woman

"Caitlin Moran is the profane, witty, and wonky best friend I wish I had. She's the feminist rock star we need right now; *How To Be a Woman* is a hilarious delight."

—Ayelet Waldman, author of *Bad Mother*

"Caitlin Moran is a feminist heroine for our times. I can't wait to give this book to my daughters."

—Zoë Heller, author of *The Believers* and *Notes on a Scandal*

"Caitlin Moran is so fabulous, so funny, so freshly feminist. I don't want to be like her—I want to *be* her. But if I can't, at least I can relish her book. You will, too."

—Peggy Orenstein, author of *Cinderella Ate My Daughter*

"The U.K. version of Tina Fey's *Bossypants*. . . . You will laugh out loud, wince, and—in my case—feel proud to be the same gender as the author."

—Emma Gilbey Keller, VanityFair.com

"Ingeniously funny. . . . In her brilliant, original voice, Moran successfully entertains and enlightens her audience with hard-won wisdom and wit. . . . She doesn't politicize feminism; she humanizes it."

—*Publishers Weekly* (starred review)

From the British Reviews

"Moran's view is that being a woman in today's society is too serious a business to be treated seriously. So, while she tackles some of the most pressing issues facing women today—abortion, aging, sexism, and high heels—she does so with a Wodehousian command of language and many, many jokes about cystitis. . . . 'Simply the belief that women should be as free as men, however nuts, deluded, badly dressed, fat, receding, lazy, and smug they might be.'"

—*Sunday Times*

"A must-read for all humans."

—*Evening Standard*

"Totally brilliant."

—*Independent on Sunday*

"Like *My Secret Garden* as written by Lady Gaga. . . . [Moran is] a rockstar feminist. . . . This is what feminism needs right now."

—*The Guardian*

"Hugely entertaining and exhilarating. . . . A book with the power to amuse, inspire, and even enrage readers of any age and gender, but it should be compulsory reading for teenagers."

—*Irish Times*

"A huge, provocative, hilarious, and powerful hoot."

—*Daily Telegraph*

How To Be a Woman

Woman

CAITLIN
MORAN

HARPER PERENNIAL

NEW YORK • LONDON • TORONTO • SYDNEY • NEW DELHI • AUCKLAND

HARPER ● PERENNIAL

First published in Great Britain in 2011 by Ebury Press, an imprint of
Ebury Publishing, A Random House Group Company.

HarperCollins books may be purchased for educational, business,
or sales promotional use. For information, please e-mail
the Special Markets Department at SPsales@harpercollins.com.

FIRST U.S. EDITION

Library of Congress Cataloging-in-Publication Data
is available upon request.

ISBN 978-0-06-212429-6

20 21 DIX/LSC 30 29 28 27 26 25 24 23 22 21

CONTENTS

Prologue: The Worst Birthday Ever 1

Chapter 1: I Start Bleeding! 15

Chapter 2: I Become Furry! 39

Chapter 3: I Don't Know What to Call My Breasts! 53

Chapter 4: I Am a Feminist! 67

Chapter 5: I Need a Bra! 85

Chapter 6: I Am Fat! 99

Chapter 7: I Encounter Some Sexism! 115

Chapter 8: I Am in Love! 137

Chapter 9: I Go Lap-dancing! 157

Chapter 10: I Get Married! 169

Chapter 11: I Get into Fashion! 189

Chapter 12: Why You Should Have Children 211

Chapter 13: Why You Shouldn't Have Children 229

Chapter 14: Role Models and What We Do with Them 241

Chapter 15: Abortion 263

Chapter 16: Intervention 279

Postscript 289

Acknowledgments 303

How To Be a
Woman

PROLOGUE

The Worst Birthday Ever

Wolverhampton, April 5, 1988

Here I am, on my 13th birthday. I am running. I'm running from the Yobs.

"Boy!"

"Gyppo!"

"Boy!"

I'm running from the Yobs in the playground by our house. It is a typical playground of Britain in the late eighties. There's no such thing as safety surfaces, ergonomic design, or, indeed, slats on the benches. Everything's made of concrete, broken bottles, and weeds.

As I run, I'm totally alone. I can feel the breath in my throat catching, like vomit. I've seen nature documentaries like this before. I can see what's happening here. My role is, clearly, that of weak antelope, separated from the pack. The Yobs are the lions. I know this never really ends well for the antelope. Soon my role will turn into a new one: that of lunch.

"Yah, pikey!"

I'm wearing Wellington boots, National Health Service glasses that make me look like Alan Bennett, and my dad's *Withnail*-style army coat. I do not, I admit, look very feminine. Diana, Princess of Wales is feminine. Kylie Minogue is feminine. I am . . . femi-none. So I understand the Yobs' confusion. They do not look as if they have dabbled much in either (a) the iconography of the counter-culture or (b) the inspirational imagery of radical gender-benders. I imagine they were confused by both Annie Lennox and Boy George when they appeared on *Top of the Pops*.

If they weren't so busy chasing me, I would probably say something to this effect. Maybe I would tell them that I have read *The Well of Loneliness*, by famous trouser-wearing lesbian Radclyffe Hall, and that they need to open their minds to alternative modes of dress. Perhaps I would mention Chrissie Hynde, too. *She* wears masculine tailoring.

"Yah, pikey!"

The Yobs stop for a moment and appear to confer. I slow to a trot, lean against a tree, and hyperventilate wildly. I am knackered. At 182 pounds, I am not really built for hot pursuit. I am less Zola Budd—more Elmer Fudd. As I catch my breath, I reflect on my situation.

It would be amazing, I think, if I had a pet dog. A well-trained German shepherd, who would attack these boys—almost brutally. An animal really in tune with the fear and apprehension of its owner.

I observe my pet German shepherd, Saffron, 200 yards away. She is joyfully rolling in a slick of fox shit and waving her legs in the air with joy. The dog looks so happy. Today is working out really well for her. This is a much longer, and faster, walk than usual.

Although today is obviously not working out very well for me, I am nonetheless surprised when—having finished their tête-à-tête—the Yobs pause for a minute, and then start throwing stones at me. That seems a bit extreme, I think. I start running again.

You don't have to go to this bother to oppress me! I think, indignantly. I was already pretty subjugated! Honestly—you had me at "pikey."

Only a few of the stones actually hit me and, obviously, they don't hurt: this coat has been through a war, possibly two. Pebbles are nothing. It's built for grenades.

But it's the thought that counts. All this time spent on me, when they could be engaging in other, more worthwhile pursuits— like abusing solvents, and fingering girls who are actually dressed *as* girls.

As if reading my mind, after a minute or so the Yobs begin to lose interest in me. It looks like I'm yesterday's antelope now. I'm still running, but they're just standing still—throwing the occasional rock in my direction, in an almost leisurely way, until I'm out of range. They don't stop shouting, however.

"You bloke!" the biggest Yob shouts, as a final thought at my departing back. "You . . . *bummer!*"

I get home, and cry on the doorstep. It's honestly too crowded to cry in the house. I've tried crying in the house before—you explain why you're crying to one person between the sobs, and then you're only halfway through before someone else comes in and needs to hear the story from the top again, and before you know it, you've told the worst bit six times and wound yourself up into such a hysterical state you have hiccups for the rest of the afternoon.

When you live in a small house with five younger siblings, it's actually far more sensible—and much quicker—to cry alone.

I look at the dog.

If you were a good and faithful hound, you'd drink the tears off my face, I think.

Saffron noisily licks her vagina instead.

Saffron is our new dog—"the stupid new dog." She is also a "dodgy dog"—my dad "procured" her in one of the deals he periodically conducts at the Hollybush pub, which involve us sitting outside in the van for two hours, while he occasionally brings us crisps, or a bottle of Coke. At some point, he'll suddenly come bowling out at a rapid lick, carrying something incongruous like a bag of gravel or a statue of a concrete fox with no head.

"It's gone a bit serious in there," he would say, before gunning off at top speed, pissed.

On one occasion, the incongruous thing he came out carrying was Saffron—a one-year-old German shepherd.

"Used to be a police dog," he said proudly, putting her in the back of the van with us, where she promptly shat all over everything. Further investigation revealed that, while she had been a police dog, it was only a week before the police dog trainers realized she was profoundly psychologically disturbed, and scared of:

1) loud noises
2) the dark
3) all people
4) all other dogs
5) and suffers stress incontinence

Still, she is my dog and, technically, the only friend I have who isn't a blood relation.

"Stay near, old friend!" I say to her, blowing my nose on my sleeve and resolving to become cheerful again. "Today will be truly notable!"

Having finished crying, I climb over the side fence and let myself in through the back door. Mum is in the kitchen, "getting the party ready."

"Go into the front room!" she says. "Wait in there! And DON'T LOOK AT THE CAKE! It's a surprise!"

The front room is packed with my siblings. They have materialized from every nook and cranny in the house. In 1988, there are six of us—there are eight by the time the decade is out. My mother is like some Ford car production line, producing a small, gobby baby every two years, as regular as clockwork, until our house is full to bursting point.

Caz—two years younger than me, ginger, nihilistic—is lying across the sofa. She doesn't move when I come in. There is nowhere else for me to sit.

"AHEM!" I say, pointing at the badge on my lapel. It says, "It's my BIRTHDAY!!!!" I am forgetting all about crying now. I have moved on.

"It'll be over in six hours," she says, flatly, immobile. "Why don't we just stop the charade now?"

"Only six hours of FUN left!" I say. "Six hours of BIRTHDAY FUN. Who KNOWS what could happen! This place is a MAD-HOUSE, after all!"

I am, by and large, boundlessly positive. I have all the joyful ebullience of an idiot. My diary entry for yesterday was "moved the deep-fat fryer onto the other worktop—it looks BRILLIANT!"

My favorite place in the world—the south beach at Aberystwyth—has a sewage pipe on it.

I truly believe the new, stupid dog is our old dog, reincarnated—even though our new dog was born two years before the old dog died.

"But you can see Sparky's eyes in there!" I will say, looking at the stupid new dog. "Sparky NEVER LEFT US!"

Rolling her eyes in disdain, Caz gives me her card. It is a picture of me, in which she has drawn my nose so that it takes up approximately three-quarters of my head.

"Remember: you promised you'd move out on your 18ᵗʰ birthday, so I can have your room," it says inside. "Only five years to go now! Unless you die before then! Love Caz."

Weena is nine—her card is also based around me moving out and giving her my bedroom: although she has robots saying it, which makes it less personal.

Space really is at a premium in our house, as evidenced by the fact I still have nowhere to sit. I am just about to sit on my brother Eddie when Mum comes in, holding a plate of burning candles.

"Happy Birthday TO YOU!" everyone sings to me. "I went to THE ZOO. I saw a FAT MONKEY—and I THOUGHT IT WAS YOU!"

Mum crouches down to where I am on the floor and holds the plate out in front of me.

"Blow them out and make a wish!" she says brightly.

"It's not a cake," I say. "It's a baguette."

"Filled with Philadelphia!" Mum says cheerfully.

"It's a baguette," I repeat. "And there's only seven candles."

"You're too old for a cake anymore," Mum says, blowing out the candles herself. "And the candles count for two years each!"

"That would be 14."

"Stop being so fussy!"

I eat my birthday baguette. It's lovely. I love Philadelphia. Lovely Philadelphia! So cool! So creamy!

That night—in the bed I share with my three-year-old sister, Prinnie—I write up my diary.

"My 13ᵗʰ birthday!!!!" I write. "Porridge for brekkie, sausage and chips for dinner, baguette for tea. Got £20 all in all. 4 cards and 2 letters. Get green (teenage) ticket from library tomorrow!!!!! Man next door asked us if we wanted some chairs he was throwing out. We said YES!!!!"

I stare at the entry for a minute. I should put everything in, I think. I can't leave out the bad stuff.

"Some boys were shouting rude thinks [sic] in the field," I write, slowly. "It's because their willies are getting big."

I have read enough about puberty to know that burgeoning sexual desires can often make teenage boys act cruelly toward girls.

I also know that, in this case, it really was *not* suppressed desire that made those boys throw gravel at me while I ran up a hill—but I don't want my diary to pity me. As far as my diary will know, *I* had the philosophical upper hand there. This diary is for glory only.

I stare at the entry for my 13th birthday. A moment of unwelcome clarity washes over me. Here I am, I think, sharing my bed with a toddler and wearing my dad's old thermal underwear as pajamas. I am 13 years old, I am 182 pounds, I have no money, no friends, and boys throw gravel at me when they see me. It's my birthday, and I went to bed at 7:15 p.m.

I turn to the back page of my diary. This is where I have my "long-term" projects. For instance, "My Bad Points."

My Bad Points
1) I eat too much
2) I don't exercise
3) Quick bursts of rage
4) Loseing [sic] everything

"My Bad Points" were written down on New Year's Eve. A month later, I have written my progress report:

1) I no longer eat gingernuts
2) Take dog for a walk every day

3) Trying
4) Trying

Underneath all these, I draw a line and write my new list.

By the Time I'm 18
1) Loose weight [sic]
2) Have good clothes
3) Have freinds [sic]
4) Train dog properly
5) Ears pierced?

Oh God. I just don't have a clue. I don't have a clue how I will ever be a woman.

When Simone de Beauvoir said, "One is not born a woman—one becomes one," she didn't know the half of it.

In the 22 years that have passed since my 13th birthday, I have become far more positive about being a woman—indeed to be honest, it all picked up considerably when I got some fake ID, a laptop, and a nice blouse—but in many ways, there is no crueler or more inappropriate present to give a child than estrogen and a big pair of tits. Had anyone asked me in advance of my birthday, I think I would have requested a thesaurus or maybe pajamas, instead.

At the time, I was—as you can see—far too busy fighting with my siblings, training my dog, and watching the classic musicals of MGM to ever have made space in my schedule for becoming a woman until my hand was forced, eventually, by my pituitary gland.

Becoming a woman felt a bit like becoming famous. For, from being benevolently generally ignored—the baseline existence of most children—a teenage girl is suddenly fascinating to others and gets bombarded with questions: What size are you? Have you done it yet? Will you have sex with me? Have you got ID? Do you want to try a puff of this? Are you seeing anyone? Have you got protection? What's your signature style? Can you walk in heels? Who are your heroes? Are you getting a Brazilian? What porn do you like? Do you want to get married? When are you going to have kids? Are you a feminist? Were you just *flirting* with that man? What do you want to *do?* WHO ARE YOU?

All ridiculous questions to ask of a 13-year-old simply because she now needs a bra. They might as well have been asking my dog. I had absolutely no idea.

But—like a soldier dropped into a war zone—you have to get some ideas, and fast. You need reconnaissance. You have to plan. You have to single out your objectives and then *move*. Because once those hormones kick in, there's no way to stop them. As I rapidly discovered, you are a monkey strapped inside a rocket; an element in a bomb timer. There isn't an exit plan. You can't call the whole thing off—however often you may wish you could. This shit is going to happen, whether you like it or not.

There are those who *try* to stop it, of course: the teenage girls who try to buy themselves time by aggressively regressing back to their five-year-old selves and becoming obsessed with "girliness," and pink. Filling their beds with teddies, to make it clear there's no room for sex. Talking in baby talk, so they aren't asked adult questions. At school, I could see some of my contemporaries were choosing not to be active women—out there, making their own fate—but to be princesses, just waiting to be "found" and married, instead. Although obviously I didn't analyze it like that at the time. I just noticed Katie Parkes spent every math lesson drawing hearts on her knuckles in pen and showing them to David Morley—who, by rights, should have been experiencing his first stirrings of sexual excitement when looking at my exemplary long division instead.

And at the most dysfunctional end, of course, there are the kamikaze girls who wade into war with their pituitary—trying to starve it or confuse it into defeat, with anorexia, or bulimia.

But the problem with battling yourself is that even if you win, you lose. At some point—scarred and exhausted—you either accept that you must become a woman—that you are a woman—or you die. This is the brutal, root truth of adolescence—that it is often a long, painful campaign of attrition. Those self-harming girls, with the latticework of razor cuts on their arms and thighs, are just reminding themselves that their body is a battlefield. If you don't have the stomach for razors, a tattoo will do, or even just the lightning snap of the earring gun in Claire's Accessories. There. There you are. You have dropped a marker pin on your body, to reclaim yourself, to remind you where you are: inside yourself. Somewhere. Somewhere in there.

And—just as with winning the lottery, or becoming famous—there is no manual for becoming a woman, even though the stakes are so high. God knows, when I was 13, I tried to find one. You can read about other people's experiences on the matter—by way of trying to cram, in advance, for an exam—but I found that this is, in itself, problematic. For throughout history, you can read the stories of women who—against all the odds—got being a woman *right*, but ended up being compromised, unhappy, hobbled, or ruined, because all around them society was still wrong. Show a girl a pioneering hero—Sylvia Plath, Dorothy Parker, Frida Kahlo, Cleopatra, Boudicca, Joan of Arc—and you also, more often than not, show a girl a woman who was eventually crushed. Your hardwon triumphs can be wholly negated if you live in a climate where your victories are seen as threatening, incorrect, distasteful, or—most crucially of all, for a teenage girl—simply uncool. Few girls would choose to be right—right, down into their clever, brilliant bones—but lonely.

So while *How to Be a Woman* is the story of all the times that I—uninformed, underprepared, fatally deluded as to my ability to "style out" a poncho—got being a woman wrong, in the 21st century, merely recounting experience doesn't seem to be enough anymore. Yes, an old-fashioned feminist "consciousness-raising" still has enormous value. When the subject turns to abortion, cosmetic intervention, birth, motherhood, sex, love, work, misogyny, fear, or just how you feel in your own skin, women still won't often tell the truth to each other unless they are very, very drunk. Perhaps the endlessly reported rise in female binge drinking is simply modern women's attempt to communicate with each other. Or maybe it is because Sancerre is so very delicious. To be honest, I'll take bets on either.

However, while chipping in your two cents on what it's *actually* like—rather than what we *pretend* it's like—to be a woman is vital, we still also need a bit of analysis-y, argument-y, "this needs to change-y" stuff. You know. Feminism.

And this is where the second problem arises. Feminism, you would think, would cover all this. But feminism, as it stands, in the U.K. at least, well . . . stands. It has ground to a halt. Again and again over the last few years, I turned to modern feminism to answer questions that I had but found that what had once been the one most exciting, incendiary, and effective revolution of all time had somehow shrunk down into a couple of increasingly small arguments, carried out among a couple of dozen feminist academics, in books that only feminist academics would read, and discussed at 11 p.m. on BBC4. Here's my beef with this:

1) Feminism is too important to be discussed only by academics. And, more pertinently:

2) I'm not a feminist academic, but, by God, feminism is so serious, momentous, and urgent that now is really the time for it to be championed by a lighthearted broadsheet columnist and part-time TV critic who has appalling spelling. If something's thrilling and fun, I want to join in—not watch from the sidelines. I have stuff to say! Camille Paglia has Lady Gaga ALL WRONG! The feminist organization Object is *nuts* when it comes to pornography! Germaine Greer, my heroine, is *crackers* on the subject of transgender issues! And *no one* is tackling *OK! Magazine*, £600 handbags, Brazilians, stupid bachelorette parties, or Katie Price.

And they have to be tackled. They have to be tackled, rugby-style, facedown in the mud, with lots of shouting.

Traditional feminism would tell you that these are not the important issues: that we should concentrate on the big stuff like pay inequality, female circumcision in the Third World, and domestic abuse. And they are, obviously, pressing and disgusting and wrong, and the world cannot look itself squarely in the eye until they're stopped.

But all those littler, stupider, more obvious day-to-day problems with being a woman are, in many ways, just as deleterious to women's peace of mind. It is the "Broken Windows" philosophy, transferred to female inequality. In the Broken Windows theory, if a single broken window on an empty building is ignored and not repaired, the tendency is for vandals to break a few more windows. Eventually, they may break into the building and light fires, or become squatters.

Similarly, if we live in a climate where female pubic hair is considered distasteful, or famous and powerful women are constantly pilloried for being too fat or too thin, or badly dressed, then, eventually, people start breaking into women, and lighting fires in them. Women will get squatters. Clearly, this is not a welcome state of affairs. I don't know about you, but I don't want to wake up one morning and find a load of chancers in my lobby.

When Rudy Giuliani became mayor of New York in 1993, his belief in the Broken Windows theory led him to implement the "Zero Tolerance" policy. Crime dropped dramatically, significantly, and continued to for the next ten years.

Personally, I feel the time has come for women to introduce their own Zero Tolerance policy on the Broken Window issues in our lives—I want a Zero Tolerance policy on "All the Patriarchal Bullshit." And the great thing about a Zero Tolerance policy on Patriarchal Broken Windows Bullshit is this: In the 21st century, we don't need to march against size-zero models, risible pornography, lap-dancing clubs, and Botox. We don't need to riot or go on hunger strikes. There's no need to throw ourselves under a horse, or even a donkey. We just need to look it in the eye, squarely, for a minute, and then start laughing at it. We look hot when we laugh. People fancy us when they observe us giving out relaxed, earthy chuckles.

Perhaps they don't fancy us quite as much when we go on to bang on the tables with our fists, gurgling, "HARGH! HARGH! Yes, that IS what it's like! SCREW YOU, patriarchy!" before choking on a mouthful of chips, but still.

I don't know if we can talk about "waves" of feminism anymore—by my reckoning, the next wave would be the fifth, and I suspect it's around the fifth wave that you stop referring to individual waves and start to refer, simply, to an incoming tide.

But if there *is* to be a fifth wave of feminism, I would hope that the main thing that distinguishes it from all that came before is that women counter the awkwardness, disconnect, and bullshit of being a modern woman not by shouting at it, internalizing it, or squabbling about it—but by simply pointing at it and going "HA!" instead.

So yes. If there is a fifth wave, then this is my contribution. My bucketful. A fairly comprehensive telling of every instance that I had little, or in many cases, no idea . . . of how to be a woman.

CHAPTER 1
I Start Bleeding!

So, I had assumed it was optional. I know that women bleed every month, but I didn't think it was going to happen to *me*. I'd presumed I would be able to opt out of it—perhaps from sheer unwillingness. It honestly doesn't look that much use or fun, and I can't see any way I can fit it into my schedule.

I'm just not going to bother! I think to myself, cheerfully, as I do my ten sit-ups a night. Captain Moran is opting *out*!

I am taking my "By the Time I'm 18" list very seriously. My "Loose [sic] Weight" campaign has stepped up a gear—not only am I still not eating gingernuts, but I'm also doing ten sit-ups and ten push-ups a night. We don't have any full-length mirrors in the house, so I've no idea how I'm doing, but I imagine that, at this rate, my boot-camp regime will have me as slender as Winona Ryder by Christmas.

I'd only found out about periods four months ago, anyway. My mother never told us about them—"I thought you'd picked it all up from *Moonlighting*," she said vaguely, when, years later, I asked her about it—and it's only when I came across a Tampax leaflet, stuffed in the hedge outside our house by a passing schoolgirl, that I'd discovered what the whole menstrual deal was.

"I don't want to talk about this," Caz says, when I come into the bedroom with the leaflet and try to show it to her.

"But have you *seen?*" I ask her, sitting on the end of her bed. She moves to the other end of the bed. Caz doesn't like "nearness." It makes her extremely irascible. In a three-bedroom council [subsidized] house with seven people in it, she is almost perpetually furious.

"Look—this is the *womb*, and this is the *vagina*, and the Tampax expands *widthways*, to fill the . . . *burrow*," I say.

I've only skim-read the leaflet. To be honest, it has blown my mind quite badly. The cross-section of the female reproductive system looks complicated, and impractical—like one of those very expensive Rotastak hamster cages, with tunnels going everywhere. Again, I'm not really sure I want in on all of this. I think I thought I was just made of solid meat—from my pelvis to my neck—with the kidneys wedged in there somewhere. Like a sausage. I dunno. Anatomy isn't my strong point. I like romantic 19th-century novels, where girls faint in the rain, and Spike Milligan's war memoirs. There isn't much menstruation in either. This all seems a bit . . . unnecessary.

"And it happens every *month*," I say to Caz. Caz is now actually lying, fully dressed, under her duvet, wearing Wellington boots.

"I want you to go away," her voice says from under the duvet. "I'm pretending you're dead. I can't think of anything I want to do less than talk about menstruation with you."

I trail away.

"*Nil desperandum!*" I say to myself. "There's always someone I can go to for a sympathetic ear and a bowlful of cheery chat!"

The stupid new dog is under my bed. She has gotten pregnant by the small dog, Oscar, who lives across the road. None of us can quite work out how this has happened, as Oscar is one of those small yappy-type dogs, only slightly bigger than a family-size tin of baked beans, and the stupid new dog is a fully grown German shepherd.

"She must have actually dug a hole in the ground, to squat in," Caz says in disgust. "She must have been *gagging* for it. Your dog is a whore."

"I'm going to become a woman soon, dog," I say. The dog licks her vagina. I have noticed the dog always does this when I talk to her. I have not yet worked out what I think about this, but I think I might be a bit sad about it.

"I found a leaflet, and it says I'll be starting my period soon," I continue. "I'll be honest, dog—I'm a bit worried. I think it's going to hurt."

I look into the dog's eyes. She is as stupid as a barrel of toes. Galaxies of nothing are going on in her eyes.

I get up.

"I'm going to talk to Mum," I explain. The dog remains under my bed, looking, as always, deeply nervous about being a dog.

I track Mum down on the toilet. She's now eight months pregnant, and holding the sleeping one-year-old Cheryl while trying to do a wee.

I sit on the edge of the bath.

"Mum?" I say.

For some reason, I think I am allowed only one question about this. One shot at the "menstrual cycle conversation."

"Yes?" she answers. Even though she is doing a wee and holding a sleeping baby, she is also sorting out a whites wash from the washing basket.

"You know—*my period*?" I whisper.

"Yes?" she says.

"Will it hurt?" I ask.

Mum thinks for a minute.

"Yeah," she says, in the end. "But it's okay."

The baby then starts crying, so she never explains why it's okay. It remains unexplained.

Three weeks later, my period starts. I find it to be a deeply uncheerful event. It starts in the car on the way to Central Library in town, and I have to walk all around the nonfiction section for half an hour, desperately hoping it won't show, before Dad takes us all home again.

"My first period started: yuk," I write in my diary.

"I don't think Judy Garland ever had a period," I tell the dog, unhappily, later that night. I am watching myself cry in a small hand mirror. "Or Cyd Charisse. Or Gene Kelly."

The bag of Pennywise sanitary napkins my mum keeps on the back of the bathroom door has become my business now, too. I feel a sad jealousy of all my younger siblings who are still "outside the bag." The napkins are thick and cheap—stuck into my knickers, they feel like a mattress between my legs.

"It feels like a mattress between my legs," I tell Caz.

We're playing one of our Sindy games. Four hours in, and Caz's Sindy, Bonnie, is secretly murdering everyone on a luxury cruise ship. My Sindy, Layla, is trying to solve the mystery. The one-legged Action Man, Bernard, is dating both of them simultaneously. We argue constantly over the ownership of Bernard, even though he actually belongs to Eddie. Neither of us want our Sindy to be single.

"A horrible, thick mattress," I continue. "Like in *The Princess and the Pea*."

"How long are they?" Caz asks.

Ten minutes later, and six Pennywise sanitary napkins are laid out, like a dormitory, with Sindys sleeping on them.

"Well, this is lucky!" I say. "Like when we found out that a

Brussels sprout looks *exactly* like a Sindy cabbage. See, Caz—this is the *bright* side of menstruation!"

Because the sanitary napkins are cheap, they shred between my thighs when I walk, and become ineffective and leaky. I give up walking for the duration of my period. My first period lasts three months. I think this is perfectly normal. I faint quite regularly. I become so anemic my finger- and toenails become very pale blue. I don't tell Mum, because I've asked my question about periods. Now I just have to get on with them.

The blood on the sheets is depressing—not dramatic and red, like a murder, but brown and tedious, like an accident. It looks like I am rusty inside and am now breaking. In an effort to avoid hand-washing stains out every morning, I take to stuffing huge bundles of toilet paper in my knickers, along with the useless sanitary napkins, and lying very, very still all night. Sometimes, there are huge blood clots, which look like raw liver. I presume this is the lining of my womb, coming off in inch-thick slices, and that this is just how visceral menstruation is. It all adds to a dreary sense that something terribly wrong is going on, but that it is against the rules of the game to ever mention it. Frequently, I think about all the women through history who've had to deal with this ferocious bullshit with just rags and cold water.

No *wonder* women have been oppressed by men for so long, I think, scouring my knickers with a nail brush and coal-tar soap in the bathroom. Getting dried blood out of cotton is a bitch. We were all too busy *scrubbing* to agitate for the vote until the twin sink was invented.

Even though she's two years younger than me, Caz starts her period six months after me—just as I'm starting my second one. She comes crying into my bedroom when everyone else is asleep and whispers the awful words, "My period's started."

I show her the bag of sanitary napkins on the back of the bathroom door and tell her what to do.

"Put them in your knickers, and don't walk for three months," I say. "It's easy."

"Will it hurt?" she asks, eyes wide.

"Yes," I say in an adult and noble manner. "But it's okay."

"Why is it okay?" she asks.

"I don't know," I say.

"Well, why are you saying it, then?" she asks.

"I don't know."

"Jesus. Why do you bother talking? The *stuff* that comes out of your mouth."

Caz gets horrific cramps—she spends her periods in the bedroom with the curtains drawn, covered in hot-water bottles, shouting "Fuck off" at anyone who tries to come into the room. As part of being a hippie, my mother doesn't "believe" in painkillers and urges us to research herbal remedies. We read that sage is supposed to help and sitting in bed eating handfuls of sage and onion stuffing, crying. Neither of us can believe that we're going to have to put up with this for the next 30 years.

"I don't want children anyway," Caz says. "So I am getting nothing out of this whatsoever. I want my entire reproductive system taken out and replaced with spare lungs, for when I start smoking. I want that option. This is pointless."

At this juncture, it seems there is absolutely nothing to recommend being a woman. Sex hormones are a bitch that have turned me from a blithe child into a bleeding, weeping, fainting washerwoman. These hormones do not make me feel feminine: every night, I lie in bed feeling wretched, and the bulge of my sanitary napkin in my knickers looks like a cock.

I take everything off, sadly, while I get my nightie out of the drawer. When I turn around again, the dog has slunk out from under the bed and started to eat my bloody sanitary napkin. There are bits of shredded, red cotton all over the floor, and my knickers are hanging out of her mouth. She stares at me, desperately.

"Oh, God—your dog's a lesbian vampire," Caz says from her bed, turning over to sleep.

I go to retrieve my knickers, and faint.

In the midst of this hormonal gloom, however, the cavalry finally arrives, over the hill, jangling its spurs, with epaulettes shining in the sun: my green library card. Now I'm 13, I can get adult books out of the library, without having to borrow my parents' cards. And that means I can get secret books out. Dirty books. Books with sex in them.

"I've been having these dreams," I tell the dog as we walk to the library. The library is on the other side of the Green—a gigantic, desolate stretch of grass, where one must be constantly on the lookout for the Yobs. It doesn't do to boldly walk in the middle of it—this leaves one exposed. You must stick to the outer edges, near the houses, so that if you get attacked the people who live in the houses can get a good view of you getting your head kicked in without having to fetch their binoculars.

"Dreams about . . . men," I continue. I look at the dog. The dog looks back at me. I think the dog deserves to know the whole truth of what is going on here. I owe her that much, at least.

"I'm in love with Chevy Chase," I tell the dog, in a sudden, joyful burst. "I saw him in the video to Paul Simon's 'You Can Call Me Al,' from the 1986 *Graceland* album, on Warner Bros., and I just can't stop thinking about him. I had this dream where he kissed me, and his mouth felt exciting. I'm going to ask Dad if we can get *The Three Amigos* out of the video shop on Friday."

Requesting *The Three Amigos* from the video shop will be a bold move—the next video for rental has already been earmarked as *Howard the Duck*. I will have to pull a lot of fancy footwork but it will be worth it. I have not told the dog yet but the thought of kissing Chevy Chase has made me so excited that, yesterday, I listened to "You Can Call Me Al" 16 times on repeat, imagining him touching my face while Paul Simon plays the bass solo. I am so hot for Chevy. I have even imagined what my first line to him will be—the one that will capture his heart.

"Chevy Chase?" I will say, at a party very closely modeled on the ones I've seen on *Dynasty*. "Any relation to *Cannock* Chase?"

Cannock Chase is just off the A5 to Stafford. LA-born movie star and comedian Chevy is going to both get, and love, this joke.

Of course, I have had crushes before. Well, one. It didn't go very well. When I was seven, I saw an episode of *Buck Rogers* and fell in love with that dumb American space-cowboy, so obviously based on Han Solo they might as well have called him San Holo and had him ride around in the Fillennium Malcon, with Bewchacca.

As the new love-chemicals rushed through me—Bucknesium and Rogerstonin—I discovered what love is, and found that it's just feeling very . . . interested. More interested than I had been about anything before.

I was interested in absolutely everything to do with Buck. Just looking at his face was interesting. How he stood, near a door = interesting. The way he held the obviously lightweight and plastic laser gun as if it were very heavy = interesting. The theme song takes on such an unbearable load of yearning and Buck Rog-ersness that—28 years later—I still feel stirred when I hear it.

Obviously, these were all some big-assed feelings to be deal-ing with, and so I did what we always did when an event of some import was going on. I grabbed Caz—then five—and pulled her into the airing cupboard with me. Like the Mitfords used to—

except theirs was probably much larger than ours and didn't smell of Bold, mouse droppings, and farts.

"Caz," I said, pulling the door as shut as I could and assuming an expression of deep portent. "I have something incredible to tell you."

I paused, staring at her.

"I . . . am IN LOVE, with Buck Rogers. Don't tell Mum."

Caz nodded.

My burden lifted, I opened the door again and gestured for Caz to leave. I watched her cross the landing and go down the stairs. I heard her open the front room door.

"Mum. Cate's in love with Buck Rogers," she said.

I learn then, in that moment—as mortification burns across me like hot ash—that love is agony, all crushes should remain secret, and Caz was an untrustworthy, fainthearted son of a bitch.

All these facts stood me in good stead, subsequently. I learned a lot in the airing cupboard that day. Just 20 minutes later, I was stuffing frozen peas into Caz's pillowcase while whispering, portentously, "And so the war begins."

But—having crushed all feelings of love for so long—the onrush of adolescent hormones have made it now impossible to ignore them any longer. The 13-year-old girl with her hair in plaits, edging around the Green, talking to her pregnant dog, is actually crazed with lust.

"I'm going to check the novelization of *Fletch* out," I tell the dog. *Fletch* was a very average movie of the time, starring Chevy Chase. "There will be a picture of Chevy on the cover, and I am going to look at the picture of Chevy, and then copy it into my Love Book."

The Love Book is a recent invention. On the cover it says "Inspiration Book," but it is really the Love Book. So far, I have nine pictures of the Duchess of York in there, and a very small picture of Kermit the Frog, cut out of the *Radio Times*. I love the Duchess of York. In 1988, she's very fat, but married to a prince. She gives me hope for the future.

I've already planned exactly what I'm going to do with the novelization of *Fletch*. When I get home, I'm going to wrap it up in an undershirt and hide it at the back of my knicker drawer, so my parents don't see it. It's very important my parents don't think I'm starting to fall in love with people, because then they might notice that I'm growing up, and I'm kind of trying to keep it secret. I think it will cause some kind of incident.

At the library, I find the novelization of *Fletch* easily. It has a satisfyingly big picture of Chevy on the cover—I am going to wear down some pencil lead copying out *that* sweet face.

Almost as an afterthought, I put *Riders* by Jilly Cooper onto the countertop to be checked out. It's got a horse on the front. I like horses. I can hear the dog whining outside. I've tied her to a tree, but she often fusses around and kind of lynches herself with the lead a bit. It's probably time to cut her down, before she stops breathing.

Three hours later, and I cannot believe what I am reading. My first day of getting adult books out, and I have struck filth gold. Absolute filth gold. *Riders* by Jilly Cooper is more than I could ever have dreamed of—there's cocks, tits, and shagging everywhere. Clits falling from the sky. Arses two feet deep. A hurricane of nipples, blow jobs, and muff diving.

Some of it's confusing—Cooper keeps referring to one heroine's "bush," and until I get to page 130, I can't swear with absolute certainty that she's not talking about vegetation. And I have no idea what cunnilingus is—certainly no one I've ever met in

Wolverhampton can afford it. I bet they don't even have it in Birmingham. It must be a London thing.

But this aside, it is, without doubt, a Bible of lubriciousness, the Rosetta Stone of filth: the key text that will translate "new and unusual feelings" that I have been having into "masturbating furiously and compulsively for the next four years."

The first time I try—halfway through chapter 5—it takes 20 minutes to come. I don't really know what I'm doing—in the book, people "delve" around in "wet bushes" until something amazing happens. I futz around—tongue clamped between teeth in concentration—and determinedly try everything, in this absolutely unfamiliar place I have had for 13 years.

When I finally come, I lie back, damp, exhausted, hand aching, out of my mind with excitement. I feel amazing. I feel like the Fonz must feel when he walks in the room and says, "Heeeeeey," or like the Duchess of York feels when Andrew kisses her. I feel kind of clean, and light, and happy. I feel, in this cherry-blossom starburst glow—ears ringing, breath still ragged—a bit, well, beautiful.

I cannot write about what has happened in my diary—Caz and I have had a tit-for-tat diary-reading war on for years. Sometimes, she writes comments—"You're so pathetic"—in the margins, when an entry particularly disgusts or riles her.

But the gusto with which I write about the rest of the day's events does, perhaps, betray the extremity of my feelings.

"Mum bought pastry brush! USEFUL!" I write. "Cheese sarnies for tea—they're soooooooooo tastie. Dad says we can get *The Three Amigos* out. YESSSSSSSSS!!!"

Over the next few weeks, I become an amazingly dexterous masturbator. The time and effort I put into the project is phenomenal. I woo myself in a variety of different locations—in the front room, in the kitchen, at the bottom of the garden. Standing up, sitting in a chair, lying on my front, and with my left hand—I want to keep things fresh for myself. I am a considerate and imaginative lover of me.

Some afternoons, I lock myself in my bedroom and come for hours and hours and hours—until my fingertips are as wrinkled as if I'd been in the bath. This new hobby is amazing. It doesn't cost anything, I don't have to leave the house, and it isn't making me fat. I wonder if everyone knows about it. Perhaps there would be revolution if they did! I can't wait to tell everyone, except I will never tell anyone, because this is the biggest secret ever. Even more secret than periods, or the fact I have spots on my bum.

I tell the dog, of course, and the dog, as is her wont, licks her vagina—which seems appropriate, but also not quite enough. I need more disclosure. I must do what I always do.

"If you are going to try and tell me how much you enjoy wanking," Caz says, with a look very similar to when lasers come out of the eyes of Zod, in *Superman II,* "then I will have to strongly pray to God that you die in the next four seconds. I don't ever want to know anything about this."

I turn around, go back to my room, and open up page 113 of *Riders* again. The glue in the spine is shattered, so it now opens at this page quite naturally. Billy takes Janey down to the Bluebell Wood—where the nettles are peppery and damp, and August makes everything slow—and I float away again.

Under the bed, the dog whines.

Over the next few years, masturbation becomes a time-consuming but fulfilling hobby. Even though—after a few weeks—I learn that it is called "masturbation," I never call it that myself. "Masturbation" sounds too much like "perturbation," and this is, by and large, a very unperturbing development. "Wank" is similarly unsuitable—it sounds like cranking a handle, or some difficult handling of chunky machinery that requires axle grease, and shouting.

What I am doing, by way of contrast, is dreamlike, delicate and soft—apart from the occasions where I have grown my nails too long and become so sore I have to repel my own advances for a few days. I just think of it as "it"—and, soon, "it" requires more than *Riders*, however revolutionary *Riders* has been, to feed it.

I start doing what everyone of my generation is doing—the last generation before free online pornography starts being handed out, with the same largesse with which the postwar Labour government handed out milk and spectacles. I start reading the *Radio Times* and trying to work out where the dirty TV programs are.

The best sources of filth, I soon discover, along with millions of other teenagers in the late eighties/early nineties, are split evenly between "classy films and dramas on BBC2," and "late night 'youth programs' on Channel 4." There are certain key words you look for in the listings. "Jenny Agutter" is the big one. Agutter is the surefire harbinger of filth. *Logan's Run, An American Werewolf in London, Walkabout*—which might as well have been retitled *Wankabout*: wherever Agutter materializes, there will be bosoms, and neck biting, and thighs grabbed by hands, soundtracked by gasping. Even in *The Railway Children*—lovely, family-friendly *The Railway Children*—she ends up waving her undergarments at a trainful of startled Victorian gentlemen as they come out of a tunnel in a fury of steam and squealing brakes. It's as if she insists on this stuff.

I watch *An American Werewolf in London* late at night, with the sound down low, as Jenny Agutter slowly, hungrily bites David Naughton's shoulder in the shower, and I think how I, too, would like to have someone to eat—even if they did later turn out to be a werewolf and got shot in front of me in the street, like a bad dog.

I am accepting of the downs, as well as the ups, of love. I know it won't be easy. Many of the tracks on *Graceland* have also told me this. Late at night, I am in the gutter, looking at Agutter.

But it's not Agutter alone we seek. "A dark story of sexual betrayal" is always a good listings harbinger—*A Sense of Guilt* and *Blackeyes* are full of moments where I have to run across the room, quickly, and rest my finger on the off button, lest my mother come in and see me watching unsuitable things. It's very unsuitable. Hands are thrust into black stocking-tops, Blackeyes is sent to be drowned. Sex seems unbelievably complicated and nerve-wracking, but at least I'm seeing kissing, and some tits. When I see the red-haired teenager being seduced by Trevor Eve in *A Sense of Guilt*, I want to tell Caz—also a redhead—that I have finally found her another role model, aside from Woody Woodpecker, and Annie in *Annie*—but only the week before, we have had this exchange:

ME: "Guess what happened yesterday!"
CAZ: "I've decided what I want for my birthday: you not to speak to me."

On one single occasion, the sex isn't guilty, or interspecies, but just gorgeous. In *The Camomile Lawn*, Jennifer Ehle's character rackets around wartime London in an unimaginably pleasurable froth of parties, champagne, cheerful licentiousness, and fucking. There is one scene that looks the ultimate in adult aspiration: half-reclining in a zinc bath, Ehle is arranging her social life on a black Bakelite phone.

"London's great!" she trills poshly, hair damp at the nape of her neck, eyes already champagne-bright. "That's SO many paaaaahrties!"

Her tits float, like archipelagos of junket, in serene perfection. The nipples are mouse-nose pink. Later, they will be dressed in

rose-colored silk and walked out onto a balcony to smoke a cigarette with some handsome boy who sighs to touch them. Jennifer
Ehle's *Camomile* tits made having tits look like the most fun in the
world. I watch them, sitting in the front room, alone, in the dark.
My tits do not look like that in the bath. I have no clue what my
tits look like in the bath—I always cover them with a washcloth,
in case someone bursts in on me and sees them. There is still no
lock on the bathroom door.

"One of the kids might shut themselves in and *drown* themselves," my mother cautions, as I climb into the bath, still wearing
my knickers.

And then, in 1990, Channel 4 shows the biopic of the young
Cynthia Payne's life, *Wish You Were Here*, and it is my big moment
of revelation. Oh, Emily Lloyd in *Wish You Were Here*! My Beatles
of porn! My Dickens of fucking! The first character I see of my
age and background—teenage, working-class—who treats sex not
as something dark and leading to doom, but silly and fun—to be
taken as seriously as smoking a fag (which I haven't done yet, but
intend to) or riding a bicycle (which I did once, and fell off, but
hey-ho).

Alone in the front room, wrapped in a duvet, eating our favorite snack of the moment—the Cheese Lollipop: a lump of cheese
on a fork—I watch, wide-eyed, the scene that almost all my sexual
persona comes to be based on. Cynthia's dirty uncle takes her into
a shed and, after a small session of prick-teasing, starts fucking
her, up against a wall. She's in a neatly fitted 1950s cotton sun-
dress, with winged eyeliner and ankle sox on. As he grunts away,
she chews her gum and whispers, "You dirty. Old. Sod."

Ten minutes later, she's on the seafront, tucking her dress into
her knickers and shouting, "Up your bum!" at passersby, while
laughing hysterically.

Coupled with the pansexual, freak-show silliness of *Eurotrash*—

Lolo Ferrari, the woman with the biggest breasts in the world, bouncing on a trampoline; drag queens with dildos and butt plugs; gimps in harnesses; hoovering bored Dutch housewives' flats—this is the sum total of all the sex I see until I'm 18. Perhaps ten minutes in total—a series of arty, freaky, sometimes brutal vignettes, which I lash together and use as the basis for my sexual imagination.

Along with a couple of recurring dreams about Han Solo, and Aslan (which I cook up myself—I am not idle), this is the first thing that feels like a crude but true sensor into adulthood: Sex. Desire. Wanting to come. Something that will lead me in the right direction. It feels like it will—eventually—somehow—I don't know how—and only if I attend to its lessons carefully—make me dress right, say the correct things, give me the impetus to leave the house and find whatever it is that's out there for me.

At the time, I wish I could see more sex. I want more porn than I can run through, in my head, while making a sandwich. In later years, however, I come to believe that this wasn't such a bad sexual education, after all. Freely available, hardcore 21st-century pornography blasts through men's and women's sexual imaginations like antibiotics and kills all mystery, uncertainty, and doubt—good and bad.

But in the meantime, I have found this thing. I have discovered this one good thing, so far, about being a woman, and it is coming.

Twenty-two years later, on an idle night, I float around the Internet, looking for porn. I know what I like—threesomes, screaming, giant mythical lions from *The Chronicles of Narnia*—and, to be fair, I can find them all, if I look hard enough. There is almost nothing that can be conceived of, sexually, that can't be found with a rigorously specific Google search string and ten minutes to spare.

But there is one thing—one obvious, amazing thing—that is

not available. Something glaringly absent among the MILFs and DILFs and S&M and A2M. There's one thing I can't find at all, no matter how many websites I try, or how many times I punch in my debit card details. One thing that fuels all my anger about pornography, which I will come back to later.

On the other hand, there's one thing that's glaringly overavailable—something that fills YouPorn and RedTube and wank.net to the brim. One thing that the Internet is stocked with, shelf after shelf, clip after clip, and none of them more than six minutes long—the average time it takes for a man to come. This is 21st-century heterosexual porn:

Once upon a time, a girl with long nails and a really bad outfit sat on a sofa, trying to look sexy, but actually looking like she'd just remembered a vexing, unpaid parking fine. She might be slightly cross-eyed, due to how tight her bra is.

A man comes in—a man who walks rather oddly, as if he's carrying an invisible garden chair in front of him. This is because he's got a use-lessly large penis, which is erect and appears to be scanning the room for the most sexually disinterested thing in it.

Having rejected the window and a vase, the cock finally homes in on the girl on the sofa.

As she disinterestedly licks her lips, the man leans over and—inexplicably—weighs her left breast in his hand. This appears to be the crossing of some kind of sexual Rubicon because 30 seconds later she's being fucked at an uncomfortable angle, then bummed while looking quite pained. There's usually a bit of arse-slapping here, or some hair-pulling there—whatever can ring in the variety in a straightforward two-camera shoot in less than five minutes.

It all ends with him coming all over her face, messily—as if he's hap-hazardly icing a bun in one of the challenges on Minute to Win It.

The End.

There are obviously variants on this—maybe she gets double-ended by two guys or perhaps she has an equally badly dressed, dagger-nailed female friend whom she pretends to go down on in a desultory manner, for a faux lez-up—and there are, obviously, *endless* amounts of niche stuff available.

Essentially, the Internet vends a porn monoculture—a sexual East Anglia. Hedgeless and featureless and planted, as far as the eye can see, with the dull, monotonous sex-spuds described above. This is the Microsoft Windows screw; crushing every other kind of sex out of the market.

That single, unimaginative, billion-duplicated fuck is generally what we mean by "porn culture"—arguably the biggest cultural infiltration since the countercultural revolution of the 1960s; certainly more pervasive than peer rivals, such as gay culture, multiculturalism, or feminism.

It's so embedded, we don't even realize when we're looking at it, half the time. Brazilians. Hollywoods. Round, high plastic tits. Acrylic nails that make it impossible to do up a shoe buckle, or type. MTV full of crotches and tits. Anal sex being an assumed part of every woman's repertoire. Posters for makeup, or TV shows, that show women glassy-eyed, open-mouthed, and ready for a faceful of come. Knickers being replaced by thongs. High, high heels that aren't really made for walking—just lying back and being fucked in. Lindsay Lohan's prejail "sex" shoot. If 12 percent of the Internet is pornography—that's 4.2 million websites, 28,000 people looking at porn per second—then that means that 12 percent of the images of women on the Internet are of them either on all fours, rammed into some highly unhygienic PVC, or being forced around outsized male genitalia, as if their sundry openings were some manner of tube bandage.

Just as a quick comparison point: this is clearly as unhappy and detrimental to women's collective peace of mind as it would be if 12 percent of images of men on the Internet were of them having their heads horrifically blown off by alien laser guns, or being lowered down a well full of Nazi sharks, crying. After the brief promise of the sexual revolution freeing up women's sexual lexicon, it's been closed right down again, into this narrow, uncomfortable, exploitative series of cartoons. It's just . . . not very nice. Not polite. It's harshing our mellow.

It's not pornography per se that's the problem here. Pornography is as old as humankind itself. Practically the first action of the Neanderthal—on the happy day he evolved out of the monkey egg—was to draw a picture on a cave wall of a man with an enormous willy. Or, indeed, perhaps it was the first action of a *woman*. After all, we're more interested in (a) cocks and (b) decorating.

This is why museums are so wonderful: walking around, observing mankind's joyride from slime to WiFi, you see incredible ironwork, inspirational pottery, fabulous vellums, and exquisite paintings, and—across these disciplines—tons of fruity historical humping. Men fucking men, men fucking women, men going down on women, women pleasuring themselves—it's all there. Every conceivable manifestation of human sexuality, in clay and stone and ocher and gold.

The idea that pornography is intrinsically exploitative and sexist is bizarre: pornography is just some fucking, after all. The act of having sex isn't sexist, so there's no way pornography can be, in itself, inherently misogynist.

So no. Pornography isn't the problem. Strident feminists are *fine* with pornography. It's the porn *industry* that's the problem. The whole thing is as offensive, sclerotic, depressing, emotionally bankrupt, and desultory as you would expect a widely unregulated industry worth, at an extremely conservative estimate, $30 billion to be. No industry ever made that amount of money without being superlatively crass and dumb.

But you don't ban things for being crass and dispiriting. If you did, we would have to ban Big Macs first—and we would have a revolution on our hands.

No. What we need to do is effect a 100 percent increase in the variety of pornography available to us. Let's face it: the vast majority of the porn out there is as identikit and mechanical as refrigerators rolling off a production line.

And there are several reasons why this is bad for everyone—men and women equally. First, in the 21st century, children and teenagers get the majority of their sex education from the Internet. Long before school or parents will have mentioned it, chances are they'll have seen the lot on the net.

But it's not just their sex education—which is a series of useful facts and practicalities, and the basic business of what goes where, or what *could* go where, if you're determined enough—that kids are getting from the net. It's also their sex hinterland. It informs the imagination, as well as the mechanics.

This is why—however limited, patchy, or centered on Trevor Eve the pornography I scavenged in my teenage years—there was, at least, a *balance* to all the stuff I was finding—a *variety*. I had petticoats and spies and woodlands and nuns and threesomes on sun loungers and vampires and sheds and gum and fauns and the backseats of Capris, and, more often than not, even though I was reading something from the 19th century, the chicks got their kicks. The women came. The women's desires were catered to. Indeed, these *were* the women's desires.

And this was important, because the sexual imagery of your teenage years is the most potent you'll ever have. It dictates desires for the rest of your life. One flash of a belly being kissed now is worth a million hard-core fisting scenes in your thirties.

One early sex researcher, Wilhelm Stekel, described masturbation fantasies as a kind of trance or altered state of consciousness, "a sort of intoxication or ecstasy, during which the current moment disappears, and the forbidden fantasy alone reigns supreme."

You want to make sure that whatever you're thinking of in that state, it has an element of . . . joy to it.

I did a talk last year at a meeting by a feminist pressure group called Object. In a discussion about pornography—which everyone seemed to presume, automatically, had to be banned—the conversation turned to how upsetting accidentally watching hardcore pornography would be for young girls.

"*And* young boys," I pointed out mildly. "I think eight-year-old boys would be as distressed as a girl on clicking a link and seeing some hardcore anal sex."

"NO! NO!" a very angry woman shouted.

I regret to say that she looked like everyone's clichéd idea of a post-Dworkin feminist. She was wearing one of those little velvet smoking caps, covered in embroidery and mirrors.

"A BOY wouldn't be upset about that, because he's watching the MAN being IN CONTROL."

And I thought about all the eight-year-old boys I know—Tom, and Harris, and Ryan, still getting a *little* bit nervous at the skeleton pirates in *Pirates of the Caribbean*—and I thought, I don't think they'd be exhilarated by seeing a man in control. I think they'd be scared of someone who looks like an angry Burt Reynolds, bumming someone across a landing. I also think that, when they'd told their mums what I'd shown them, I'd probably be off the playdate circuit for a good six months.

And that was when I started thinking that we needed *more* pornography, not less. Eight-year-olds aren't *supposed* to see hardcore pornography, so, of course, it doesn't matter at *all* what their reaction to it is. They might as well be giving us their feedback on whiskey, and sales tax.

But when they do come of an age where they want to start viewing sexual imagery, I want Harris and Ryan and Tom to have a chance of finding some, for the want of a better word, free-range porn out there. Something that shows sex as something that two people do together, rather than a thing that just happens to a woman when she has to make rent. Something in which—to put it simply—everyone comes. In a genre where you're really not holding out for incredible SFX, or a deathless monologue, and it's solely and only some humping, that's got to be a baseline requirement. Universal hoggins.

And that's why we need to start making our own stuff. Not the anodyne stuff that's ostensibly "women-friendly" porn—all badly shot princesses, and dominatrix lady bosses getting office juniors to do a bit of extracurricular faxing.

No. I suspect that female pornography, when it really gets going, will be something wholly other: warm, humane, funny, dangerous, psychedelic, with wholly different parameters to male porn.

You only have to read Nancy Friday's *My Secret Garden*—a compendium of female masturbatory fantasies—to be able to make the enjoyably sweeping generalization that while male fantasies are short, powerful, and to the point—a bit like "My Sharona" by The Knack, say—female fantasies are some symphonic, shape-shifting thing by Alice Coltrane. In their fantasies, the women grow and shrink, shape-shift, change age, color, and location. They manifest as vapor, light, and sound, they strobe through conflicting personas (nurse, robot, mother, virgin, boy, wolf) and a zodiac of positions while, you suspect, also imagining consistently great-looking hair. NO woman ever came with an imaginary bad bouff.

But that's just the start. Imagine if pornography was not this bizarre, mechanized, factory-farmed fucking: bloodless, naked aerobics, concerned solely with high-speed penetration and ostentatious ejaculation. Imagine if it were about desire.

Because the one thing I couldn't find, that night as I glided around the Internet, was desire. People who actually wanted to fuck each other. *Had* to fuck each other. Imagine watching two people screwing at that early, white-hot stage of attraction when your pupils dilate just looking at each other, and you want to melt each other's bones so bad you're practically eating each other's clothes off the minute the door closes. I can't be the only one who's occasionally had a fuck so spectacular, all-encompassing, cinematic, and intense that, at the end of it, I've lain back—ears still ringing—and thought, CNN wanna get a hold of *that*. Now *that* REALLY needed a tickertape running underneath it.

In a world where you can get a spare kidney, a black-market Picasso, or a ticket to ride into space, why can't I see some actual sex? Some actual fucking from people who want to fuck each other? Some chick in an outfit I halfway respect, having the time of her life? I have MONEY. I'm willing to PAY for this. I AM NOW A 35-YEAR-OLD WOMAN, AND I JUST WANT A MULTIBILLION-DOLLAR INTERNATIONAL PORN IN-DUSTRY WHERE I CAN SEE A WOMAN COME.

I just want to see a good time.

CHAPTER 2
I Become Furry!

It's a cold house—a cold house, and a small one. When you get out of the bath, you wrap yourself in the towel—still damp from the last person who used it—and run downstairs, to dry in front of the fire.

It's Saturday night, so *Bergerac* is on. The sofa has six people on it, of varying sizes, packed in tight, at sundry angles. Some people are essentially lying on top of other people—only "on" the sofa in the most nugatory sense. Eddie lies across the back of the sofa, like an antimacassar made of seven-year-old boy. It looks a little bit like the Galactic Senate in *The Clone Wars*—if everyone in the Galactic Senate were eating cream crackers, Branston Pickle, and cheese.

I come into the room, towel like a cloak, and crouch in front of the fire. I still have the shower cap on, which is one of the best things in our house. It's one of our more feminine items. I always feel a little bit demure wearing it. Not as much as when I wear a pair of woolly tights on my head—to signify long, princess hair. But still, quite lovely.

As Charlie Hungerford shouts, "Jim! It was just a *misunderstanding!*" I start to put on my nightie.

"Oooooooh!" rings out a voice, suddenly, from the tightly packed sofa. It's my mother. "Is that PUBES I can see? PUBES, Cate?"

The sofa stirs into instant alertness. Everyone stops looking for the diamond thief on *Bergerac* and starts looking at my pubic hair instead—except my dad, who appears absolutely unaware of what is going on and continues to eat crackers and cheese while staring at the television. There is clearly a part of his brain that has evolved to be like this, in order to survive the horror of his daughters' puberty.

I feel like I'm not allowed to look for the pubes myself—I have to be nonchalant about it, although it is all, frankly, news to me. The contents of my underpants are a bit like my subconscious, or the field by the playground. Since my bad birthday, I've tried not to go down to any of them.

"There!" my mother says, pointing. The whole sofa cranes to see. "It's DEFINITELY a pube! AND your little legs are getting hairy! You're growing up! You're growing into a *lady*!"

My mother has a way of saying this that makes me feel that this is both the worst possible outcome to being a 13-year-old girl and also, somehow, my fault.

"Look!" I say, pulling my nightie down firmly and pointing at the television. "Look! Liza Goddard!"

The next day, I resolve to sort all this out before things get out of hand. I am simply going to remove all the hair so that the most interesting thing to look at in the front room will be, once again, *Bergerac*, and everything can get back to normal.

"I'm going to commit a crime," I tell the dog. The dog lies under my bed—nervous, baleful eyes glowing in the dark. Since the incident on my birthday, I have put the whole affair from my mind, but the dog has become even more anxious. Last week, she ate the clay model village that Caz had made. In the dog's feces the next day, we could clearly make out the tiny face of the woman who ran the Post Office.

"I'm going to steal one of Dad's razors and beautify myself," I continue. Even saying it to the dog makes me nervous. Stealing a blade, in order to address the issue of my pubic hair, is definitely the most transgressive and rebellious thing I've ever done. It feels little better than stealing a gun, in order to start my period. It's a world away from my previous biggest crime: eating more than half a packet of raw strawberry Jell-O, then claiming that it wouldn't set because the weather was "too warm."

As my mother believes in neither medicine ("Just have a poo and a hot bath, and go to bed, and you'll be *fine* in the morning") nor "beauty treatments" ("Deodorant gives you cancer, and you don't want *that*"), there are only four things in the bathroom cabinet: a dark-blue 1920s-style glass eye-bath, a bottle of calamine lotion, baby gin (gripe water), and Dad's razors. Under the cover of running a bath, I take the razor from the shelf. I am so nervous I can feel my heartbeat in the soles of my feet, on the linoleum.

As my mother doesn't believe in locks on the door, either ("They give you cancer"), I barricade myself into the room with the washing basket, get into the bath, lather myself up, and shave off my pubes. I place them on the side of the bath, by the soap. They never even had a chance to get curly. They were cut down in their infancy.

I then shave my legs, too; not really understanding which direction the razor should go in, slashing my knee and thigh. It feels like it takes around nine hours. I am amazed how much calf I have. Just after I finish one bit, I notice another outcrop, looking like a patch of marram grass on a dune. I wish some manner of leg mower had been invented, so it could be done all in one go.

I frequently think 13-year-old girls should not be allowed to use razors. It is *dangerous*. Wow. I really am bleeding quite a lot!

But, eventually, the shaving is done. I have removed the problem. I am back to normal.

"Feel all clean and silky," I write in my diary that night, sticking a fresh piece of tissue to the wounds. "Might do under my arms tomorrow!"

I turn out the light. I have to rest, in order to be fresh for stealing again in the morning.

Hair is one of the first big preoccupations of womanhood. It appears, unbidden, and so decisions must be made about it—decisions that signal to yourself, and the world, who you are. As the teenage years are where you begin the complicated, lifelong business of starting to work this out, hair is the opening salvo in decades of quietly screaming "WHO AM I?" while standing in front of an array of products in the drugstore, clutching an empty basket.

And it is hair that has the most money, and attention, spent on it. Hair in the "wrong" place: legs, underarms, upper lip, chin, arms, nipples, cheeks, and across the sundry contours of your pelvis. Against this hair, lifelong wars of attrition are waged. It informs the ebb and flow of day-to-day life—the scheduling of events. Sometimes, the entire course of a woman's life.

A man may think, I have a party next week. I'd better roughly scrub my face before I tootle out the door.

A woman, on the other hand, will call up the calendar in her head—like the midair screens in *Minority Report*—and start a cycle of furious planning, based around hair management.

Here is my friend, Rachel, and me on a Sunday night, discussing a forthcoming party.

"Party's on Friday," Rachel says, sighing. "Friday. This means we will have to get our legs waxed tomorrow, latest, in order to start undercoating self-tan on Tuesday. Can't undercoat on Monday—all the follicles will still be open, from the ripping."

We've both applied self-tan when the follicles are still open, from "the ripping." The self-tan embeds itself in each tiny, empty hole. Your legs end up looking like that freckled, ginger kid on the cover of *Mad* magazine.

"I'll make us a waxing appointment for tomorrow," Rachel says, picking up the phone. "But we should book upper lip and eyebrows for Thursday. I want minimal regrowth. I think Andrew's going to be there."

"Are you going to shag him, though?" I ask. "What about your foof?" I care for Rachel. She looks inside her undies and assesses.

"It looks like Desperate Dan's chin, so only if it's dark, and we're drunk," she says finally. "I'm not adequately prepped for a brightly lit room. Chances are, if we do shag, it *will* be drunk and dark. First shags always are. So I don't need to bother."

"But what about the next morning?" I ask. I really do care about Rachel. "If you stay over, you might have a second, sober, well-lit pre-breakfast shag. Are you going to be ready?"

"Oh, God!" Rachel says, looking back in her undies again. "I hadn't thought of that. Bloody hell. But it's £20, and I'm broke. I don't want to spunk my taxi money on a wax if there *isn't* going to be a pre-breakfast shag." She stares gloomily at her crotch. "I don't want to be hairless—but on a night bus, fuckless."

"If you *are* getting your bikini done, you'll need to do it by Wednesday—to let the terrible, disfiguring rash die down," I say. I really am being as helpful as I can.

We stare at each other. Rachel starts to get annoyed.

"Bloody hell, why can't he just call me now and say, 'Rachel, are you on for a pre-breakfast shag on Saturday?' I can't budget correctly with all these Random Fuck Factors in my week. No wonder everyone's a slag these days. Even if you don't like anyone at the party, you want to get *some* return on your wax. I hate my hair."

And all of this isn't done to look scorchingly hot, or deathlessly beautiful, or ready for a nudie shoot at the beach. It's not to look like a model. It's not to be Pamela Anderson. It's just to look *normal*. To have normal-looking legs, and a normal-looking face, and a crotch you're confident about. To not be anxiously standing in the bathroom with a roll of Scotch tape, dabbing at your upper lip and wailing, "As soon as the bright lights hit, I realized I was looking a bit Hitler! I honestly don't want to annex the Rhineland! I just want a beer and a feel!"

And of all these hair dilemmas—these decisions that you must make with your follicles, about who you are and what you want to say about yourself—it is pubic hair that is now the most politically charged arena. That palm-sized triangle has come to be top-loaded with more psychosexual inference than marital status and income combined. Over the years, pubic hair has gone from the very least of a woman's worries—when I was 17, around the time of grunge, the idea of waxing your bikini line was bizarre, marginal, for porn models only—to a pretty routine part of "self-care." Pubic hair must be confined to a very small area or, increasingly, removed completely. The industry-standard pop-video crotch shots of girls in bikinis make it very, very clear: there should be nothing there. It must be smooth. Empty. You must clean this area of fur. To see even a single hair, curling out the side, would be to have the whole world going, "Is that a PUBE I can see? A PUBE, Lady Gaga?"

While some use the euphemism "Brazilian" to describe this state of affairs, I prefer to call it what it is—"a ruinously high-maintenance, itchy, cold-looking child's vagina."

In fact, in recent years I have become more and more didactic about pubic hair—to the point where I now believe that there are only four things a grown, modern woman should have: a pair of yellow shoes (they unexpectedly go with everything), a friend who will come and post bail at 4 a.m., a fail-safe pie recipe, and a proper muff. A big, hairy minge. A lovely furry moof that looks—when she sits, naked—as if she has a marmoset sitting in her lap. A tame marmoset, that she can send off to pickpocket things, should she so need it—like that trained monkey in *Raiders of the Lost Ark*.

I am aware that my views on waxing run contrary to current thinking. As far as pubic hair is concerned, I am like someone sitting in a pub, tearfully recalling how exciting it was to go into Woolworth's and buy the new Adam Ant single on seven-inch vinyl. I am "vagina retro."

"I remember when it was all furry round here," I will say sadly in the changing rooms of the gym, surrounded by smooth, pink genitals. "Hairy toots as far as the eye could see. Wild and untamable. An arbor of nature. Playground of my youth. I used to spend hours there. Now . . . now it's all waxed and empty. All the wildlife has gone. The bulldozers have moved in. They're going to build a new Safeway there, on the vaginas."

It is now accepted that women *will* wax. We never had a debate about it. It just happened—and we never thought to discuss it.

Even though I know we are living through a time of pube disapproval, I was still, nonetheless, shocked by a recent letter to *The Times*'s sex columnist, Suzi Godson, from a 38-year-old divorcee, worried about her retro befurred moof. She said that her 29-year-old boyfriend was "shocked" by "my lack of personal grooming." Somewhat naively, I thought *The Times*'s sex columnist—a feisty-looking chick, with the peroxide hair of a sassy 1950s telephone operator—would briskly tell her correspondent's boyfriend to go to hell.

Instead, she took on a sadly chiding tone. "Things have rather changed in the genital grooming department," she began, explaining that "any woman who dares to be less rigid in her styling, as you have found, risks being labeled as bucolic, unsanitary, or possibly French. If your boyfriend has been conditioned to expect a tidy Brazilian, he may genuinely find anything else very off-putting."

Godson firmly instructed her correspondent to go for a wax, went on to describe just how much that waxing would hurt—"think of burning-hot Sellotape . . . now treble the pain"—before ending with one of the most annoying pieces of "good news" I've ever heard.

"Fortunately," she said, "the craze for Brazilians is abating. The hot new haircut is the Sicilian. It is like a Brazilian—but you are left with a neat little Sicily-shaped triangle, which at least means that you still look like a woman. Good luck!"

Sicily? The good news is that I can make my luge look like Sicily? Home of the Mafia? That's my vagina now? It's got the Godfather in it? Ha-ha! Can you imagine if we asked men to put up with this shit? They'd laugh you out the window before you got halfway through the first sentence.

I can't believe we've got to a point where it's basically costing us *money* to have a vagina. They're making us pay for *maintenance and upkeep* of our lulus, like they're a communal garden. It's a stealth tax. Muff excised. This is money we should be spending on THE ELECTRICITY BILL and CHEESE and BERETS. Instead, we're wasting it on making our Chihuahuas look like a skanky chicken breast. God DAMN you, mores of pornography that have made it into my undies. GOD DAMN YOU.

And, of course, it is pornography that's costing us all this money, time, and follicular pain. If you ask the question, "Why do 21st-century women feel they have to remove their pubic hair?" the answer is, "Because everyone does in porno." Hollywood waxing is now total industry standard. Watch any porn made after, say, 1988, and it's all hairless down there: close-ups are like watching Daddy Warbucks, with no eyes, eating a very large, fidgety sausage.

And when you first see it—*it* being hard-core pornography—there is a slight frisson to it. Completely hairless? Ooooh, that's *nasty*. Like Lucite heels, spit roasting, and anal sex, the extreme, effortful "Blimey, this isn't everyday sex, is it?" aspect is quite exciting. So long as your cast have been recruited from neither a nursery nor a zoo, anything goes, really.

But the hairlessness isn't there for the excitingness. It's not, disappointingly, there to satisfy a kink. If it were, I could argue it until the cows literally came home. Nah—it seems to me that the *real* reason all porn stars wax is because, if you remove all the fur, you can see more when you're doing penetrative shots. And that's it. This gigantic, billion-dollar Western obsession with Brazilians and Hollywoods, which millions of normal women have to time events in their lives around, endure pain and inconvenience for—and, I regret to tell you, ladies, which actually makes your thighs look bigger—is all down to the technical considerations of cinematography. It's just a lighting thing. The day-to-day existence of your foof has been dictated to by the Miyagawa of minge, or the Charles B. Lang of dong.

Given that it is simply an "industry thing," our widespread adoption of it is as bizarre as everyone, in the early days of black-and-white television, walking around in the thick pancake makeup and black lipstick the presenters used. It's like—ladies! This shit doesn't apply to us! We're not getting paid for this! We don't need to bother! Grow your little minge-fro back! Be Hair Now!

But, of course, it *does* apply to us, as I've said: because hard-core pornography is now the primary form of sex education in the

Western world. This is where teenage boys and girls are "learning" what to do to each other, and what to expect when they take each other's clothes off.

As a result, we're at risk of a situation in which every boy expects to undress a girl and find a thorough wax job, and every girl—terrified by the idea of being rejected, or thought abnormal—waxes for them. My beautician told me she has had girls of 12 and 13 coming in for Brazilians—removing the first signs of adulthood even as they appear, in a combination that—with its overtones of infantilization and impetus in hard-core pornography—is pretty creepy, whichever way you look at it.

It's now got to the point that, if you listen in on conversations in the back row of the bus, you can hear 14-year-old boys being *horrified* to discover that, on fingering a 13-year-old girl, she has pubic hair. In the 21st century, modern boys watching hardcore pornography are now as panicked by pubic hair as Victorian art critic John Ruskin apparently was in 1848, when he was so alarmed at the sight of his new wife's pubic hair that he refused to ever consummate the marriage. Bloody hell. Aside from every conceivable, dolorous psychosexual side effect, it saddens me that 13-year-old girls are spending what little money they have on getting their foofs stripped. They should be spending that money on the really important stuff: hair dye, tights, Jilly Cooper paperbacks, the Guns N' Roses back catalog, the poems of Larkin, KitKats, Thunderbird 22, earrings that make your ears go green and septic, and train tickets as far away from your hometown as you can possibly afford. TAKE YOUR FURRY MINGE TO DUBLIN, that's what I say.

Because there is a great deal of pleasure to be had in a proper, furry muff—unlike those Hollywood versions, which look like they want only for a quick squirt of Palmolive, and a buff with a lint-free cloth.

Lying in a hammock, gently finger-combing your Wookiee while staring up at the sky is one of the great pleasures of adulthood. By the end of a grooming session, your little minge-fro should be even and bouffy—you can gently bounce the palm of your hand off it, as if it were a tiny hair trampoline.

Walking around a room, undressed, in front of appreciative eyes, the reflection in the mirror shows the right thing: a handful of darkness between your legs, something you refuse to hurt. Half animal, half secret—something to be approached with a measure of reverence, rather than just made to lie there, while cocks are chucked at it like the penultimate game on *Wipeout*.

And on proper spa days, you can pop a bit of conditioner on it and enjoy the subsequent cashmere softness, safe in the knowledge that you have not only reclaimed a stretch of feminism that had gotten lost under the roiling Sea of Bullshit, but will also, over your lifetime, save enough money from not waxing to bugger off to Finland and watch the aurora borealis from a five-star hotel while shit-faced on vintage brandy.

So yeah. Keep it trimmed, keep it neat, but keep it what it's supposed to be: an old-skool, born to rule, hot, right grown woman's muff.

"But what about underarm hair?" people will say—usually 40-something men, who look uncomfortable when you use phrases such as "lovely big Hair Bear Bunch–style minge," and then downright alarmed when you bring pornography into it.

"If you don't believe in Brazilians, do you shave your armpits? Do you shave your *legs*? And pluck your *eyebrows*? You look like you pluck to *me. What about your lady mustache?*"

And then they sit back, a little smug—as if they have just put a sausage roll in the bottom of a trapping pit and are fairly confident you're about to go in after it and be captured.

But the crotch, the upper lip, and the armpit are miles apart—well, on average, 17 inches apart. What happens to them, and why, is wholly different—primarily because armpits aren't intimately associated with sexual maturity or, indeed, sexuality at all, unless you're on some seriously specialist websites.

So what you do with your armpits is just an aesthetic concern—and not really part of the Struggle. Given this, I have, over the years, experimented with different looks for my armpits. Some days, a shaved armpit just looks a bit ... boring. If I'm wearing jeans and a vest top, and I'm hanging with my homies, it's quite nice to go a bit George Michael—a bit "Faith," with a flash of four-day fuzz. There's something pleasingly musky about it—like you've been too busy living the bohemian dream, souping up your hot rod, to do something as mimsy as shave. On other occasions, I've grown it properly long—a hollow of damp curls, like it's 1969 all over again, and my entire life is made of Indian gauze, sitars, and hash.

One Glastonbury, when the hair on my head was down to my waist and dyed cherry-red, I decided to dye my armpits and foof to match and cracked out the Crazy Colours. "I shall be red in foof and maw!" I thought cheerily, slapping on the crème.

Alas, it all sweated off in the first two hours and soaked through my T-shirt, making it look like I had terrible, suppurating armpit eczema. Mind you, I got away with dye lightly that year at Glastonbury. Caz dyed her ginger eyebrows black and, in the pounding sunshine, they turned the color of aubergine. When she spotted Thom Yorke from Radiohead in the Green Field and ran up to him to tell him how much she loved him, his reception was "slightly off."

"No one wants to hear 'I love you' from someone with purple eyebrows!" she wailed afterward.

When it comes to hair—legs, upper lip, eyebrows, chin, nipple, pubic—the desirable outcome would be an expanding of the aesthetic lexicon: like when Eddie Izzard explains his transvestism as "equal clothing rights for all." He doesn't want to wear a dress every day—he might not wear stilettos for a year. But whenever the mood takes a man to wear a dress, or a woman to go furry, there's no reason why it shouldn't be part of the range. There are some women out there who are just going to look better with a mustache: that's statistics. There are a lot of armpits that will look better with a silky curl of fur than they do stripped, or plucked, depending on what outfit is being rocked at the time. A monobrow can be magnificent: my six-year-old—raised on pictures of Frida Kahlo—is militant about hers: "I love it, because it never ends."

On "dress like a character from history" day at school, she dresses as Kahlo and applies mascara to the center, "To make it even better."

She is so much saner than I was at her age.

Having shaved my first scared, lonely pube off at the age of 13, I continue to remove all my pubic hair for three further months, and then stop. There are a number of reasons.

1. As they become more numerous, picking them out of Dad's razor—so I can replace it on the shelf, ostensibly untouched—becomes more and more difficult. My fingertips are covered in a crisscross of tiny razor-blade scars, as if I've decided to replace my fingerprints with something more angular, or am attempting the least effective self-harming session ever. Cleaning out a razor is *dangerous*. A 13-year-old shouldn't be doing it.

2. It's itchy. Insanely itchy. The regrowth appears to be made of three parts asbestos, one part artisan mohair, and drives me to distraction. Three weeks in, and I'm

scratching like I've caught the pox—which is ironic, because the final reason I abandon shaving is:

3. The realization that no one is going to see what's going on there for years. YEARS. Since the terrible day of *Bergerac*, I now dress—shiveringly cold—in the bedroom. There will be no more putting my nightie on in front of my family. In front of anyone at all. As my friend Bad Paul will put it, in years to come: "What you look like undressed? That's scarcely something *you* need worry about, dear." The idea of a 13-year-old virgin shaving off her pubic hair is as ridiculous as Neil Armstrong splashing on aftershave before setting foot on the moon: any audience for the effort is entirely imaginary. I let it all grow back, in peace, and leave my father's razor next to the eye-bath and the lotion. I move on to the next incident on puberty's agenda.

The next time anyone sees me naked, I am 17, losing my virginity in a bedsit in Stockwell, South London, to a man with steady eyes, who clearly couldn't care what I do with my pubic hair, and just wants to take my green dress off and lay me down.

CHAPTER 3

I Don't Know What to Call My Breasts!

Of course, I know that adolescence is supposed to be an incredible ... unfolding. I've spent my time in the library. I've read *Gray's Anatomy*, cruising for the juicy bits. I can quote chapter and verse on adolescent neural development—on how when the sex hormones kick in, the teenage brain, essentially, explodes. White matter—wirelike fibers—establishes motorways of reason. The brain lights up like the Eastern Seaboard at dusk—lights flashing on and off in ripples; starbursts; spirals; waves. At 14, I am an experiment. Inside, I am being resurrected. I am in the middle of the kind of explosion of perspective that, in later years, I will pay a great deal of money to emulate in nightclubs, and at parties, in bathrooms—counting out tenners for pills in order to feel a tenth this remorseless, expanded, and inspired.

I read the biographies of age contemporaries and boggle. Bobby Fischer was Chess Grandmaster at 15. Picasso was exhibiting at 15. Kate Bush writes "The Man with the Child in His Eyes" aged 14—so young the child in his eyes might actually have been her own reflection. I have—as with any other teenager—the potential to take my place in the world, the equal, or better, of any adult. I could be a fucking genius.

That's the theory, anyway. And, to be fair, I am aware of it: my diary records that I am using this unprecedented expansion of my mental capacity to chew over some fairly major questions and concepts: "Wish I could cry forever. It would be such a relief." "Am I one of the *wrong* people?" "Some days, I feel like I can do ANYTHING! I know I am here to, in some small way, save the WORLD!" "Would wearing a hat make me look thinner? Seriously?" And, on March 14, 1990, "I have found the meaning of life: Squeeze. Cool for Cats! BRILLO!"

But, to be honest, I'm generally too busy firefighting all the physical stuff to pay much attention to my brain, or my potential for prodigious genius. Man, it's going nuts. There's crazy shit breaking out all over the place. Bleeding and masturbatory experimentation are the very least of it. The transformation of my body from something that does little more than poo and do jigsaws into a magical department store that will, one day, vend babies takes up nearly all my time and worry.

One morning, I wake up to find that my entire body is covered in livid red marks—raspberry-ripple streaks across my belly, thighs, breasts, underarms, and calves. At first I presume it's a rash and walk around for two days smothered in Sudocrem—baby-rash ointment—in the hope that it will soothe them. When my mother notices her supplies are running low, she accuses two-year-old Cheryl of having eaten it again and I, nobly, don't correct her.

But when I examine the marks more closely—door locked, using an angle-poise lamp, listening to "Cool for Cats" very loudly for moral support—I see that they aren't welts at all, but indentations. My skin has torn as I've grown—these are stretchmarks, covering nearly every soft part of my body. Puberty is like a lion that has raked me with its claws as I try to outrun it. Or, as I put it to Caz that night, "I am going to have to wear tights and turtlenecks for the REST of my LIFE. Even in summer. I'm going to have to pretend I'm just always very cold. That's going to have to be the thing everyone knows about me. That I'm cold."

Caz and I have hit a rare moment of peace in our relationship. Two days ago, we spontaneously hugged each other. My mother was so shocked and alarmed she took a photo of us, to mark the occasion. I still have it now—both of us in matching bathrobes, barefoot, faces pressed together in expressions of 98 percent goodwill, 2 percent festering aggression. Our mother thinks that we have, finally, bonded—brought together by the combined responsibility of being the eldest two siblings of seven children—able to now settle our differences as the adults we are swiftly becoming.

Why we're *actually* hugging is because we've just had a two-hour-long conversation about what to call our vaginas.

"I can't say it," I say to Caz. We're in the bedroom—me on my bed, her on the floor. We're listening to "Cool for Cats" for the ninth time that morning. The tape is already wearing thin—Chris Difford's voice now wobbles a bit as the Indians send signals from the rocks above the pass. Caz is knitting a sweater in order to have something to wear.

"I think I'd rather pretend I don't have one at all than say 'vagina,'" I continue. "If I injure myself and end up in a very formal hospital where they don't allow slang words and they ask, 'Where is the pain?' I think that, rather than say 'In my vagina,' I would just reply, 'Guess!' and then faint. I hate the word 'vagina.'"

"It was so much easier last year," Caz agrees sadly.

Until last year, all the Moran children were laboring under the illusion that the word "navel" didn't refer to the belly button but, in fact, the female genitalia. Any injury to the area would result in the shriek, "I banged my NAVEL!" and communal sympathy. One corollary of this was finding the phrase "naval officer" almost unbearably amusing. When Prince Andrew married Sarah Ferguson and was referred to as "a naval officer" during the ceremony on BBC1 by Jonathan Dimbleby, we became so hysterical we had to lie upside down, on the stairs, until the blood went back into our heads.

Additionally—for a short period in 1987—our little sister Weena mispronounced "vagina" as "china," and we used that word for a spell. Then in the autumn, T'Pau released the number one single "China in Your Hand," and, once again, we all had to lie upside down on the stairs until our circulations went back to normal. Entering a shop where it was playing was borderline dangerous. We would have to run out, with our hoods up, shaking.

So now, in 1989, we have no word for "vagina" at all—and with all the stuff that's going on down there, we feel we need one. We sit in silence, thoughtfully, for a moment.

"We could call them Rolfs," Caz says eventually. "Like Rolf Harris? They look like his beard."

We stare at each other. We both know that Rolf Harris is not the answer we are looking for.

The problem with the word "vagina" is that vaginas seem to be just straight-out bad luck. Only a masochist would want one, because only awful things happen to them. Vaginas get torn. Vaginas get "examined." Evidence is found in them. Serial killers leave things in them, to taunt Morse—like they're the shelf in the hallway, where you leave your keys and spare change. No one wants one of those.

No. Let's clear this up right now—I don't actually have a vagina. I never have. Indeed, I reckon very few women ever have. Queen Victoria, obviously. Barbara Castle. Margaret Thatcher. With the pubic hair styled, of course, in an exact replica of that on her head.

But everyone else—no. Because I'm scarcely the only one. No one I know would refer to their vagina as their "vagina." They have slang names, pet names, made-up names—family names for the front parlor that have been passed down from generation to generation. When I asked on Twitter for people's childhood appellations, I got over 500 replies in 20 minutes—a great percentage of them totally, dementedly barking. It was like I'd opened up a Pandora's Box of Minge. The first one I got set the tone: "My childhood best friend's mum referred to it as 'ducky,' and periods as 'duck's disease.'"

This is, clearly, a train of thought uninterrupted—possibly for generations—by any outside influence. It's lexical inbreeding.

The range was immense. Some were quite lovely and/or amusing: your flower, your tuppence, pickle, tissy, Mary, flump, putt, tuchas, minny, pum-pum, tinkle, fairy, foof, my lady, woo-woo, bits and pieces, muffin, cupcake, and pocket.

Then there were ones that were clearly the result of some family in-joke: Valerie, Aunty Helen, pasta shell, bumgina, fandango, Yorkshire pudding ("She would cry, 'I've got sand in my Yorkshire!'"), Under Henge, and Birmingham City Centre.

And then there were the downright bizarre and/or worrying: your difference, your secret, your problem, Sweet Fanny Adams (nickname of a murdered Victorian child; not a great day at the Vagina Imaginarium, all told), and vent. I can only presume "vent" was the product of a family that kept snakes and wanted to use the same word across species, to save time.

Across the range, it was interesting to note the appearance of la-la, tinky, and po—meaning almost the entire cast of Teletubbies appear to be based on familial slang words for "vagina." I suppose you have to get your inspiration from somewhere.

I, personally, have a cunt. Sometimes it's "flaps" or "twat," but, most of the time, it's my cunt. Cunt is a proper, old, historic, strong word. I like that my fire escape also doubles up as the most potent swear word in the English language. Yeah. That's how powerful it is, guys. If I tell you what I've got down there, old ladies and clerics might faint. I like how shocked people are when you say "cunt." It's like I have a nuclear bomb in my underpants or a mad tiger, or a gun.

Compared to this, the most powerful swear word men have got out of their privates is "dick," which is frankly vanilla and, I believe, you're allowed to use on children's TV if something goes wrong. In a culture where nearly everything female is still seen as squeam-inducing and/or weak—menstruation, menopause, just the sheer, simple act of calling someone "a girl"—I love that "cunt" stands, on its own, as the supreme, unvanquishable word. It has almost mystic resonance. It is a cunt—we all *know* it's a cunt—but we can't call it a cunt. We can't say the actual word. It's too powerful. Like Jews can never utter the tetragrammaton—and must make do with "Jehovah" instead.

Of course, I knew all the thinking behind calling my cunt a cunt was useless when I had my two daughters. There's no point in telling them all that "mystic resonances of Jehovah" stuff when they're being chased around the nursery by a teacher with a broom, enraged by them casually saying the biggest swear word in the English language, just before midmorning snack-time.

When Lizzie was just a few days old—around the time the first kilo of morphine wore off and I could focus again, but, to be frank, still a good two weeks before I could sit down without screaming "HOLY MARY I THINK IT'S BROKEN!"—my husband and I stared down at our beautiful little daughter. Blue-eyed, kissy-mouthed, and soft as a velvet mouse, she had just done a dump so enormous, it had filled every crevice of her lower body.

My husband approached her nethers tentatively with a wet wipe, and then slumped back, looking defeated.

"Not only have I got to clean all . . . this out," he said, looking on the verge of mania, "but I don't even know what I'm cleaning. What are we going to call it? We can't call it 'cunt.'"

"Her NAME is Lizzie!" I said, shocked.

"You know what I mean," my husband sighed. "I'm not using that word. That's what you've got. You've got a cunt. It's not what she's got. You've got . . . Scooby. She's got Scrappy Doo. It's totally different. Oh God—it's all up her back as far as her hat. I'm wiping shit off a hat. I'm not sure I like parenthood. WHAT ARE WE GOING TO CALL HER VAGINA?"

Over the next few weeks, we brainstormed over the issue, like ad executives blue-skying the ad campaign for a new ham-flavored yogurt.

"It looks like a ladybird," my husband said during one particularly fanciful moment. "We could call it her ladybird!"

"Yeah, but by that token, it looks equally like a Volkswagen Beetle," I pointed out. "We could call it Herbie. And when she reaches adolescence and goes boy-crazy, we can say, 'Herbie goes bananas' to each other over and over again, as you build the door-less turret we can lock her in."

Another week, my husband came up with "Baby Gap"—"It's her baby gap!"—which was not only a great joke, but also meant that putting her in a T-shirt or sweater with the Baby Gap logo on it prompted valuable minutes of roflment.

In the event, though, that name lived fast and died young—we used it so many times all the fun fell off it. The words began to feel old and stale, like overchewed gum.

We knew we needed something less gimmicky, but it was only when Lizzie started talking—at around 12 months—that the word finally came to me.

She'd fallen over and hurt her "baby gap." As I pulled her onto my knee and described out loud to her what had happened—in the manner that you do when you are teaching a child to speak—I reached out into the dark of my subconscious and came back with—

"Bot-bot. You've hurt your bot-bot!" I said, palming her tears off her face.

"Bot-bot" is what my mother had referred to all our genitals as, before we hit adolescence: "bot" for the back and "bot-bot" for the front. One word fits all. We were too poor for anything more . . . specialized.

And now here it was, coming into service for another generation. A round, tidy, stout little name for a round, tidy, stout little bot-bot.

Of course, when she gets older, Lizzie will find herself in exactly the same place Caz and I were, in 1989. As a teenage girl, you have to find something a bit more . . . rock'n'roll. Once your adolescence kicks in, there's no way you can refer to the place that will be the epicenter of most of your decisions and thought processes for the next 40 years as your "bot-bot." Scarlett O'Hara was not running around Atlanta after Ashley and then Rhett because of her bot-bot. There is no bot-bot element to the paintings of Georgia O'Keeffe. Madonna is not showing us her bot-bot in *Sex*.

Often—after walking into a woodland clearing and partaking of a ceremonial pipe among tribefolk—I have reflected that working out what to call your genitals is a formal rite of passage for a girl. As significant as menarche, or assessing if you can style out dungarees or not. When "fingering" starts at school—I believe around 12 these days; it appears to be the slightly more grown-up version of a toddler's implacable desire to jam their fingers into DVD players—it's important a girl starts thinking exactly where she's being fingered. Although "inside me" is a fair enough starting point, it is, essentially, a direction or a command—not a name.

These days, in a world where adolescents get all their sex education from pornography, Adam may have named the animals, but Ron Jeremy names the vaginas. As one might expect, when one leaves the choice of words to porn stars who are improvising the dialogue during a double-penetration scene, not much thought, delicacy, or aesthetic goes into it.

As a result, there is a whole generation of girls growing up whose go-to phrase for their genitalia is "pussy." Personally, I dislike "pussy." I've heard "pussy" referred to in the third person too many times in porn films for it to seem like a joyful or fun word.

"Your pussy likes that, doesn't it?" "Shall I give this to your pussy?"

It's got all that unpleasant physical-disconnect bullshit—women separated from their vaginas—that I find un-hot in bad pornography, PLUS it gives the constant, unsettling impression that the gentleman might actually be referring to the woman's cat, which is sitting just out of camera shot, glaring balefully.

One day, I think idly, all the cats who are watching porn being made will rise up, revolted by all the uncouth dialogue ostensibly being aimed at them, wander onto the set, and ostentatiously vomit up a hairball in the middle of some bumming.

But, let's be honest, "pussy" is the least of it. There is a panoply of slang words that are, in their ways, just as truly awful as "vagina." Let's bullet point!

- Your sex: sounds like a preemptive attempt to shift blame.
- Hole: a bad thing that can happen to stockings or tights. My Johnnylulu is a GOOD thing that happens to stockings and tights.
- Honeypot: inference of imminent presence of bees.
- Twat: an unpleasant mélange of cow-pat, stupidity, and punching. No.
- Bush: the band of the same name are tiresome. The vegetation has spiders. No.

- Vag: sounds like the name of a busybody battleaxe, à la "Barb" and "Val." Suggestion also of chain-smoking Marlboro Lights, and borderline addiction to bingo. No.

On the other hand, ones I do like:

- Minge: sounds a bit like a slightly put-upon cat. Sometimes mine feels like that.
- Flaps: amusing.
- Foof: pampered, slightly ridiculous French poodle.
- The Saarlac Pit: endless resonance, not least because, however much it wants Han Solo inside it, it never quite gets him.

Of course, once you start with the silly names for your number one vestibule, there's no real reason to stop.

"It's all going off at West Midlands Safari Park and Zoo," I will say ruefully, sitting on the toilet during an attack of cystitis. "The tree has been struck by lightning in Tom's Midnight Garden."

On other, happier days, one can comment, "The mist is really rolling in on the Mull of Kintyre tonight."

But what of your wabs? After all, it's not like it's any easier to think of something to call your breasts. They sit on your rib cage from the age of 13 onward, and yet there's scarcely a word you can refer to them with that isn't going to make either you or someone else uncomfortable.

A couple of years ago, the voluminously lipped sex-minx du jour Scarlett Johansson revealed that she calls her breasts "my girls."

"I like my body and face," she said, echoing the thoughts of all but the blind, "and I love my breasts—I call them 'my girls.' "

Not for the first time in her career,* Johansson had raised a vexing issue. What, exactly, can a grown woman of sense and wit call her tits? She has come up with the perfect answer—"my girls" is playful, possessive, feminine—but no one else can now refer to their hurdy-gurdies as "my girls," as people will think you are referring to Scarlett Johansson's tits, rather than your own.

"I dunno, do my girls look odd in this top?" you might say.

"Well, my girls would look fantastic in that top, because Scarlett Johansson's got the kind of rack that could bring about world peace," a friend would reply. "But *yours* look lopsided, and your nipples are all over the place. To be honest, they look like Marty Feldman's eyes."

In tabloid world, of course, things are easy. The word is "boobs." Or, rather, BOOBS! "Keeley the Page 3 girl has great BOOBS!" says Shayne Ward. "Cheryl has the best BOOBS in Girls Aloud!" Even if one uses a different word when in conversation with a *Sun* journalist, they put it through their soaraway spell check and it still comes out as "boobs" anyway. I was once interviewed by them at the time I was referring to my tits as "jugs"—it was the height of Britpop; I was just doing what I thought Blur would approve of—and, sure enough, the piece appeared the next day as " 'I love my BOOBS,' says Caitlin Moran."

Personally, I don't have boobs. Not one. It felt as odd as reading, " 'I love my STRIPY PREHENSILE LEMUR TAIL,' says Caitlin Moran."

"Boobs" are too Benny Hill. Boobs are perfectly spherical, bouncing, jokey—you might as well refer to your "pink chest

---

*In *Lost in Translation*, she presented us with the question, "Is it ever right not to have sex with Bill Murray during a trip to Japan?" to which anyone with any sense was able to answer, "No—you must always have sex with Bill Murray when you are on a trip to Japan."

clowns" while making a trombone-y "wah wah wah waaaaaaah" sound and have done with it.

Boobs are also, by and large, white and working class—you don't really get Bangladeshi boobs, or boobs from Bahrain. There are no "boobs of Lady Antonia Fraser." Boobs are what Jordan and Pamela Anderson and Barbara Windsor have—except when Barbara had a breast cancer story line in *EastEnders*, when they quickly became "breasts." "Boobs," of course, can't get cancer, or lactate, or be subject to the subtle erotic arts of the Tao. Boobs exist only to jiggle up and down on the chests of women between the ages of 14 and 32, after which they get too droopy, and then presumably fall off the face of the earth, into space; maybe to eventually become part of the giant rings of Saturn.

For exactly the opposite reasons, "breasts" will not do, either. You never hear the word "breasts" in a positive scenario. Breasts are bad news. Much like vaginas, breasts exist to be examined by doctors and get cancer, but breasts also rack up impressive horror points for being hacked off chickens and cooked in white wine, and as being the word of choice for awkward men about to have very bad sex with you ("May I touch your left breast with my finger?") and aging pervs ("Her magnificent breasts were unleashed from the flimsy fabric.")

"Bosom" sounds a bit Benny Hill. "Cleavage" doesn't work, obviously—"I have a pain in my cleavage"—and neither does "embonpoint," because it sounds both embroidered and pointy, and so would cease to exist when you took your bra off. "Tits" seems nicely down to earth for day-to-day use—"Give me a Kit-Kat, I've just banged my tit on the door"—but struggles to make a satisfactory transition to nighttime use, where it seems a little too brusque. Personally, I quite like the idea of "the guys"—but then that's also how I refer to my seven brothers and sisters, and as potential confusion there could lead to an even greater incidence of mental illness than we already have, I'll probably have to leave it be.

I did go through a phase of referring to my upper palaver by the names of celebrated duos—"He made me get my Cagney & Lacey out!" "And it was all going so well until the Scarecrow and Mrs. King here refused to fit into the top." "Actually I call them Simon and Garfunkel because one's bigger than the other."—but then I had a baby. The midwife looked very sternly at me trying to wedge the business end of "Sonny Bono" into my newborn's mouth, while "Cher" lay, traumatized and bleeding nearby.

The English language has yet to get its head convincingly around the problem of the average woman's bristols. Indeed, given what alarmed, ignorant, giggling fools we are, there's every chance that this is a problem that could hang around for a while. Maybe we should give up on spoken language during the interregnum and just refer to them as "(.)(.)."

Certainly the solution to mine and Caz's problem was realizing that—when it came to both breasts and vaginas—language wasn't really necessary. After a short period of referring to them, jointly, as "Upstairs, Downstairs"—which had the additional benefit of making them sound like a classy BBC production that inspired fond memories in many—it dawned on us that we could simply point at the relevant areas, while mouthing *"there,"* extravagantly. *"There"* and *"there"* worked by way of a holding operation until we finally felt worldly and louche enough to use the words "tits" and "cunt"—for me, 15, and for Caz, around 27, as I recall. But, man, what a maid-of-honor's speech that was.

CHAPTER 4
I Am a Feminist!

In *The Female Eunuch,* Germaine Greer suggests that the reader take a moment to taste her menstrual blood. "If you haven't tasted it yet, you've got a long way to go, baby," she says.

Well, I cannot help but agree. You have to try everything once—even eating sweet-and-sour prawns from a dodgy-looking takeaway van in Leicester, or wearing a puffball skirt. I have, of course, tasted my own menstrual blood. By and large, I'd prefer a bag of Doritos, but it was all right: better than most stuff you can buy on an Amtrak snack car, and certainly an ethically sound product. My welfare of me has been exemplary. I always have clean, deep hay to sleep on.

Personally, however, I will not be urging you to taste your menstrual blood right now, as I'm very aware you might be on a bus or sitting on a bench in a playground, making desultory small talk with a woman called Barb. As with so many "empowering" things—doing a parachute jump, learning belly dancing, getting a tattoo—tasting your menstrual blood would be, let's face it, just another thing to add to the "to do" list, along with getting that curtain rod mended, de-fleaing the cats, and sewing the button back on your coat that, now you come to think of it, fell off in 2003.

No, ladies, rest easy. You will not have to taste your menses today. Not on my watch.

What I AM going to urge you to do, however, is say "I am a feminist." For preference, I would like you to stand on a chair and shout "I AM A FEMINIST!"—but this is simply because I believe everything is more exciting if you stand on a chair to do it.

It really is important you say these words out loud. "I AM A FEMINIST." If you feel you cannot say it—not even standing on the ground—I would be alarmed. It's probably one of the most important things a woman will ever say: the equal of "I love you," Is it a boy or a girl?" or "No! I've changed my mind! I don't want bangs!"

Say it. SAY IT! SAY IT NOW! Because if you can't, you're basically bending over, saying, "Kick my arse and take my vote, please, patriarchy."

And do not think you shouldn't be standing on that chair, shouting, "I AM A FEMINIST!" if you are a boy. A male feminist is one of the most glorious end-products of evolution. A male feminist should ABSOLUTELY be on the chair—so we ladies may all toast you, in champagne, before coveting your body wildly. And maybe get you to change that lightbulb, while you're up there. We cannot do it ourselves. There is a big spiderweb on the socket.

I was 15 when I first said, "I am a feminist." Here I am in my bedroom, saying it. I am looking in the mirror, watching myself say it: "I am a feminist. I am a feminist."

It is now nearly three years since I wrote my "By the Time I'm 18" list, and I am slowly piecing together a vague plan of who I should be. I still haven't gotten my ears pierced, lost any weight, or trained the dog, and all my clothes are still awful. My second-best top is a T-shirt with a cartoon of an alligator holding a beer, with HAVE FUN IN THE FLORIDA SUN! written underneath it in neon pink. It looks wholly incongruous on a depressed, fat, hippy girl with waist-length hair, walking around Wolverhampton in the rain. It looks, to be frank, like an ongoing act of immense sarcasm.

I still don't have any friends, either. Not one—unless you count family, which obviously you don't, because they just come free with your life, wanted or not, like the six-page Curry's brochure that falls out of the local paper, advertising Spectrum 128k home computers and "ghetto blasters." No. Family doesn't count at all.

But on the plus side, I am not alone because—as with a million lonely girls and boys before—books, TV, and music are looking after me now. I am being raised by witches, wolves, and unexpected guest stars on late-night chat shows. All art is someone trying to tell you something, I realize. There're *thousands* of people who want to talk to me, so long as I open their book or turn on their show. There are a trillion telegrams with important information and tips. It may be bad information or a misconstrued tip—but at least you are getting *some* data on what it's like out there. Your CNN ticker tape is running full blast. You are getting input.

Books seem the most potent source: each one is the sum total of a life that can be inhaled in a single day. I read fast, so I'm hoovering up lives at a ferocious pace, six or seven or eight in a week. I particularly love autobiographies: I can eat a whole person by sundown. I'm reading about Welsh hill farmers and round-the-world yachtswomen, World War Two soldiers and housekeepers in prewar Shropshire mansions, journalists and movie stars, screenwriters, Tudor princes, and 17th-century prime ministers.

And every book, you find, has its own social group—friends of its own it wants to introduce you to, like a party in the library that need never, ever end. When I first meet David Niven's *The Moon's a Balloon*, it keeps on mentioning Harpo Marx, until—when I finally bump into him, on the "Autobiographies: M" shelf—we get on like a house on fire. I'm soon up to speed with how Marx spends his afternoons: at the Algonquin Round Table in New York, which is by way of a prewar Valhalla for cocktail-drinking dandies with typewriters. Robert Benchley and Robert E. Sherwood and Alexander Woollcott—who stirs in me a lifelong affection for camp, waspy men who show their love with increasingly vile insults ("Hello, Repulsive").

Finally, through Woollcott, I come face-to-face with the holy Dorothy Parker, who I feel has been waiting for me forever, in 1923, with her lipstick and her cigarettes and her glorious, whiplash despair. Dorothy Parker is monumentally important because, it seems to me at the time, she is the first woman who has ever been capable of being funny: an evolutionary step for women as major as the development of the opposable thumb or the invention of the wheel. Parker is funny in the 1920s and then—I am led to believe—no other women are funny until the eighties. Parker is the Eve of female humor.

Robert Johnson invented the blues, at midnight, at a crossroads, after selling his soul to the devil. Dorothy Parker invented amusing women, at 2 p.m., in New York's best cocktail bar, after tipping a busboy 50 cents for a martini. It's hard not to draw conclusions as to which is the brighter sex.

But Parker also worries me, because half the funny stuff she writes is about killing herself: funny doesn't seem to be working out as well for her as it does for, say, Ricky Gervais. And it cannot be ignored that it takes nearly 60 years for any women to be funny again after her. The trail she blazed stayed notably untrodden. I start to worry that women are, as the rumor has it, not as good as men after all.

In the same month I read Parker's "Résumé"—"Razors pain you/Rivers are damp/Acids stain you/And drugs cause cramp/Guns aren't lawful/Nooses give/Gas smells awful/You might as well live"—I start reading Sylvia Plath, who everyone agrees is one of the few women who can write as well as a man, but who also keeps trying to kill herself: always crashing in the same car, or overdosing. This is worrying. I'm in the middle of being obsessed with Bessie Smith, whose life is raddled with heroin. I adore Janis Joplin, who sixties herself to death. And, increasingly, people are being horrible about the Duchess of York, just because she's ginger.

I can't help but note that most of the women who hold their own with the men seem unhappy and apt to die young. Lazy, popular opinion has it that this is because women are fundamentally unsuited to putting their head over the parapet and competing on the same terms as men. They just can't handle the big-boy stuff. They simply need to stop trying.

But when I look at their undoing—despair, self-loathing, low self-esteem, exhaustion, frustration at repeated lack of opportunity, space, understanding, support, or context—to me it seems as if they are all dying of the same thing: being stuck in the wrong century. All these earlier ages are poisonous to women, I begin to think. I knew it before—but just as quiet, accepted fact. I know it again now—but this time as loud, outraged fact.

They are surrounded by men, without a team or a den mother to cheer them on. They are the sole pair of high heels clacking through a room of brogues. They are loaded with all the wearisomeness of being a novelty. They are furious and exhausted from having to explain to the men what the women have known all along. They are astronauts in the Mir Space Station, or hearts sewn into early transplant patients. They can pioneer, yes, but it's not sustainable. Eventually, the body rejects them. The atmosphere proves too thin. It doesn't work.

And so, finally, just when I need her, I find Germaine Greer. I know roughly what she's about, of course—whenever my mother hazards a guess at what might be wrong with the car, my father replies, sighingly, "All right, Germaine Greer. Give it a rest"—but I've never actually encountered Greer. I've never read anything she's written or seen her speak. I presume she is a stern, shouting thing, always pointing out the "right" thing to do: like a nun, but angry.

Then I see her on TV. I don't know what program it is—my diary doesn't say—but it notes the day with a garland of exclamation marks. "I've just seen Germaine Greer on TV—she's NICE!!!!!!!" I write. "FUNNEEEE!!!!!"

Greer uses the words "liberation" and "feminism" and I realize—at the age of 15—that she is the first person I've ever seen who doesn't say them sarcastically or tempered with invisible quote marks. She doesn't say them like they are words that are both slightly distasteful and slightly dangerous, and should be handled only at the end of tongs, like night soil, or typhus.

Instead, Greer says, "I am a feminist" in a perfectly calm, logical, and entitled way. It sounds like the solution to a puzzle that's been going on for years. Greer says it with entitlement and pride: the word is a prize that billions of women, for the span of human history, fought to win. *This* is the vaccine against the earlier pioneers' failure. This is the atmosphere that would sustain us all in space: the piece of equipment we've all been missing. This is what will keep us alive.

A week later, and I, too, am saying, "I am a feminist," into the mirror. I am smoking a pretend cigarette made of rolled-up toilet paper. I blow imaginary smoke away, like Lauren Bacall, and say, "I'm a feminist, Humphrey Bogart."

The word feels even more exciting than swearing. It is intoxicating. It makes my head swim.

I know I am a feminist now, because—after seeing Greer on TV and liking her—I have just read *The Female Eunuch*. I haven't been drawn to it *solely* for its promise of emancipation—I must admit, I am also looking for sex scenes. I know it is—as Eulalie McKecknie Shinn refers to the poetry of Balzac in *The Music Man*—"a SMUTTY book." Look: the cover has tits on. There should *definitely* be shagging inside.

However, while there are rude bits, what is most notable, for someone raised on rock music, is that Greer writes about being a woman the way men sing about being men. When Bowie describes Ziggy in "Ziggy Stardust"—"He was the nazz/with God-given ass/He took it all too far/But boy could he play guitar"—it might as well have been Greer talking about herself. She is the nazz, with God-given ass. She writes paragraphs like piano solos, and her rendering of feminism is simple: everyone should just be a bit more like her. Scornful of any useless inherited bullshit. New; fast; free. Laughing, and fucking, and unafraid to call anyone out—from a boyfriend to the government—if they are stupid or wrong. And LOUDLY. LIKE ROCK MUSIC.

Subsequently, *The Female Eunuch* is like someone running into the room—my room—shouting, "Oh, my God!" and triggering a gold-glitter cannonade. Greer has the unstoppable velocity of someone working at the top of her game. And she has the heart-in-mouth glee of knowing she is saying stuff no one's said before. She knows *she* is the new weather front; the coming storm.

I don't understand half of what she is on about. At the age of 15, I have yet to come across anything I could call sexism in the workplace, men's loathing for women, or, indeed, what had driven me to the book in the first place: a penis looking to be stimulated and caressed. Half of it confuses the hell out of me: the combination of her anger toward men and her belief in women letting themselves down, and being weak, is pretty alien to my way of thinking. By and large, I just think we're all "the guys," trying to get on as best we can.

I don't really get massive generalizations—and I bet the rest of the world doesn't, either, I think.

But there is no doubt that this book—the world in this book— is a total thrill. Germaine makes being a woman—the sex wholly sidelined, reviled, silenced, and crushed—suddenly seem like an amazing thing to be. In the 20th century—an age in thrall to the new—women turn out to be the newest thing of all; still packed up in cellophane, still folded up in the box, having played dead for the length of history. But now we are the new species! The new craze! We are the tulip—America—the Hula Hoop—the moon shot—cocaine! Everything we do is going to be, implicitly, amazing.

I feel fandom—that slightly lazy, wholly thrilled decision to simply believe everything your hero says and does; to follow in their fluorescing slipstream without question. This is a hero who would not hurt me—who will not, suddenly and shockingly, reveal that they probably hate me—like Led Zeppelin's roadies handing out laminates to underage groupies decorated with an eye, a bird, and a sailor: "I swallow semen."

As a soft teenage girl, this is a rare hero who will be good for my soul.

In later years, of course, I would grow Greer-ish enough to dis-agree with Greer on things that she said: she went off sex in the eighties, opposed the election of a transsexual lecturer at Newn-ham Ladies College, got a bee in her bonnet about transgender males-to-females, and, most important, had a go at *Guardian* col-umnist Suzanne Moore's back-combed hair ("bird's nest hair and fuck-me shoes"), which saddened me: I love a bouff.

But at 15, by the time I have finished reading *The Female Eu-nuch*, I am so excited about being a woman that, had I been a boy, I think I would have switched sides.

*

But, of course, you might be asking yourself, "Am *I* a feminist? I might not be. I don't know! I still don't know what it is! I'm too knackered and confused to work it out. That curtain rod really still isn't up! I don't have *time* to work out if I am a women's libber! There seems to be a lot to it. WHAT DOES IT MEAN?"

I understand.

So here is the quick way of working out if you're a feminist. Put your hand in your underpants.

    a.   Do you have a vagina? and
    b.   Do you want to be in charge of it?

If you said "yes" to both, then congratulations! You're a feminist.

Because we need to reclaim the word "feminism." We need the word "feminism" back real bad. When statistics come in saying that only 29 percent of American women would describe themselves as feminist—and only 42 percent of British women—I used to think, What do you think feminism IS, ladies? What part of "liberation for women" is not for you? Is it freedom to vote? The right not to be owned by the man you marry? The campaign for equal pay? "Vogue," by Madonna? Jeans? Did all that good shit GET ON YOUR NERVES? Or were you just DRUNK AT THE TIME OF SURVEY?

These days, however, I am much calmer—since I realized that it's technically impossible for a woman to argue against feminism. Without feminism, you wouldn't be *allowed* to have a debate on a woman's place in society. You'd be too busy giving birth on the kitchen floor—biting down on a wooden spoon, so as not to disturb the men's card game—before going back to hoeing the rutabaga field. This is why those female columnists in the *Daily*

Mail—giving daily wail against feminism—amuse me. They paid you £1,600 for that, dear, I think. And I bet it's going into your bank account, and not your husband's. The more women argue, loudly, against feminism, the more they both prove it exists and that they enjoy its hard-won privileges.

Because for all that people have tried to abuse it and disown it, "feminism" is still the word we need. No other word will do. And let's face it, there has *been* no other word, save "Girl Power"— which makes you sound like you're into some branch of Scientology owned by Geri Halliwell. That "Girl Power" has been the *sole* rival to the word "feminism" in the last 50 years is a cause for much sorrow on behalf of the women. After all, P. Diddy has had four different names, and he's just *one man*.

Personally, I don't think the word "feminist" on its own is enough. I want to go all the way. I want to bring it back in conjunction with the word "strident." It looks hotter like that. It's been so wrong for so long that it's back to being right again. They have used it to abuse us! Let's use it right back at them! I want to reclaim the phrase "strident feminist" in the same way the hip-hop community has reclaimed the word "nigger."

"Go, my strident feminist! You work that male/female dialectic dichotomy," I will shout at my friends in bars, while everyone nods at how edgy and real we are—the word thrilling us as much as champagne, handbrake turns, and *Helter Skelter.*

The fact that it's currently underused and reviled makes it all the hotter—like deciding to be the person who single-handedly revives the popular use of the top hat. Once people see how hot you look in it, they're *all* going to want to get one.

We need the only word we have ever had to describe "making the world equal for men and women." Women's reluctance to use it sends out a really bad signal. Imagine if, in the 1960s, it had become fashionable for black people to say they "weren't into" civil rights.

"No! I'm not into civil rights! That Martin Luther King is too *shouty*. He just needs to chill out, to be honest."

But then, I do understand why women started to reject the word "feminism." It ended up being invoked in so many bafflingly inappropriate contexts that—if you weren't actually aware of the core aims of feminism and were trying to work it out simply from the surrounding conversation—you'd presume it was some spectacularly unappealing combination of misandry, misery, and hypocrisy, which stood for ugly clothes, constant anger, and, let's face it, no fucking.

Take, for instance, the "What I'm Really Thinking" column from the *Guardian*, which, in 2010, ran the secret thoughts of a cleaner:

> Sometimes . . . I ponder the ironies of the job: for example, that all the ironing consists of men's clothing. In a bid to escape domesticity, women are refusing to iron their husband's shirts. Congratulations: your act of feminism means that the job is shunted onto a different woman, assigning her to a different rank.

I've seen this idea put forward a hundred times—that a *proper* feminist would do her own hoovering. Germaine Greer cleans her own lavvy, and Emily Wilding Davison threw herself under that horse, hands still piney fresh from Mr. Muscle oven cleaner. On this basis alone, how many women have had to conclude, sighing as they hire a cleaner, that they can't, then, be feminists?

But, of course, the hiring of domestic help isn't a case of women oppressing other women, because WOMEN DID NOT

INVENT DUST. THE STICKY RESIDUE THAT COL-
LECTS ON THE KETTLE DOES NOT COME OUT OF
WOMEN'S VAGINAS. IT IS NOT ESTROGEN THAT COV-
ERS THE DINNER PLATES IN TOMATO SAUCE, FISH-
STICK CRUMBS, AND BITS OF MASHED POTATOES. MY
UTERUS DID NOT RUN UPSTAIRS AND THROW ALL
OF THE KIDS' CLOTHES ON THE FLOOR AND PUT
JAM ON THE BANISTER. AND IT IS NOT MY TITS THAT
HAVE SKEWED THE GLOBAL ECONOMY TOWARD DO-
MESTIC WORK FOR WOMEN.

Mess is a problem of humanity. Domestica is the concern of all. A man hiring a male cleaner would be seen as a simple act of employment. Quite how a heterosexual couple hiring a female cleaner ends up as a betrayal of feminism isn't terribly clear—unless you believe that running a household is, in some way:

a. an inarguable duty of womenkind—that, in addition, can

b. only ever be done out of love, and never for cash, because that somehow "spoils" the magic of the household. As if the dishes know they've been washed by hired help, instead of the woman of the house, and will feel all sad.

This is, clearly—to use the technical term—total bullshit. Everything else in this world you can pay someone to do for you. There are places that will bleach your anus for you—lest you consider the skin tone too dark. That's right. For cash, someone will apply peroxide to your bumhole and make it look like Marilyn Monroe. If you have mines in your field, you can pay someone to risk their life removing them. If you want to watch people pound each other's nasal cartilage to a pulp with their fists, you can go to see cage fighting. There are people out there carting night soil, working as mercenaries, and masturbating pigs into jars.

And yet, somehow, in the midst of all this—and of all the jobs we get chippy about—it's still wrong for a woman in North London to employ someone to clean the house.

When I was 16, I *was* a cleaner: I cleaned the house of a woman with an enormous amount of wooden paneling on Penn Road, Wolverhampton, and I was thrilled that someone with my qualifications (nil) could earn money chucking Comet around someone's faucets and chipping lime scale off a kettle with a fork. Twenty years later, I now have a cleaner myself.

And having a cleaner is nothing to do with feminism. If a middle-class woman is engaging in antifeminist activity by hiring a woman to do the cleaning, then surely a middle-class man is engaging in class oppression when he hires a male plumber? Feminism has had exactly the same problem that "political correctness" has had: people keep using the phrase without really knowing what it means.

My friend Alexis recently came across a "gentleman of the road" sitting in a shop doorway and drinking from a can of Kestrel at 9:07 a.m.

"Ha-ha-ha! I'm not being very politically correct!" the hobo said, brandishing his can by way of a toast.

Of course, getting pissed at 9 o'clock in the morning outside the Primark on Western Road, Brighton, has absolutely nothing to do with political correctness. With the best will in the world—dude, you're a tramp, getting wankered. You are not cocking a snook at Gloria Steinem, Barack Obama, and the BBC. Yet a huge number of people would agree with the tramp's definition of "political correctness," i.e., all vaguely risky fun being "banned" by the "politically correct brigade," rather than the *actual definition* of political correctness: formalizing politeness. Codifying courtesy in areas where, previously, really awful things—like using epithets such as "Paki," and me being called "Tits McGee" by a builder when I was 15—used to happen.

There's a whole generation of people who've confused "feminism" with "anything to do with women." "Feminism" is seen as absolutely interchangeable with "modern women"—on one hand, a cheering reminder of what feminism has done, but on the other, a political, lexical, and grammatical mess.

Over the last few years, I've seen feminism—to remind ourselves: the liberation of women—blamed for the following: eating disorders, female depression, rising divorce rates, childhood obesity, male depression, women leaving it too late to conceive, the rise in abortion, female binge drinking, and rises in female crime. But these are all things that have simply INVOLVED WOMEN and have nothing to do with the political movement "feminism."

In the most ironic twist of all, feminism is often used as the stick—actually, a stick is inappropriately phallocentric, maybe a "furry cup"—to stop women behaving as freely, normally, and unselfconsciously as men. Even—in some extreme cases—suggesting that acting as freely, normally, and unself-consciously as men is destroying *other* women.

Like with bitching. There is currently this idea that feminists aren't supposed to bitch about each other.

"That's not very feminist of you," people will say if I slag off another woman. "What about the sisterhood?" people cry when Julie Burchill lays into Camille Paglia, or Germaine Greer has a pop at Suzanne Moore.

Well, personally, I believe that feminism will get you so far—and then you have to start bitching. When did feminism become confused with Buddhism? Why on earth have I, because I'm a woman, got to be *nice* to everyone? And why have women—on top of everything else—got to be particularly careful to be "lovely" and "supportive" to each other at all times? This idea of the "sisterhood" I find, frankly, illogical, I don't build in a 20 percent "Genital Similarity Regard Bonus" if I meet someone else wearing a bra. If someone's an arsehole, someone's an arsehole—regardless of whether we're both standing in the longer bathroom queue at concerts or not.

When people suggest that what, all along, has been holding women back is *other women* bitching about each other, I think they're severely overestimating the power of a catty zinger during a cigarette break. We have to remember that snidely saying, "Her hair's a bit limp on top" isn't what's keeping womankind from closing the 30 percent pay gap and a place on the board of directors. I think that's more likely to be down to tens of thousands of years of ingrained social, political, and economic misogyny and the patriarchy, tbh. That's just got slightly more leverage than a gag about someone's bad trousers.

I have a rule of thumb that allows me to judge—when time is pressing and one needs to make a snap judgment—whether some sexist bullshit is afoot. Obviously it's not 100 percent infallible but, by and large, it definitely points you in the right direction.

And it's asking this question: "Are the men doing it? Are the men worrying about this as well? Is this taking up the men's time? Are the men told not to do this, as it's "letting our side down"? Are the men having to write bloody books about this exasperating, retarded, time-wasting bullshit? Is this making *Jon Stewart* feel insecure?"

Almost always, the answer is: "No. The boys are not being told they have to be a certain way. They're just getting on with stuff."

Men are not being informed that they are oppressing other men with their comments. It is presumed that men can handle perfectly well the idea of other men bitching about them. I think, on this basis, we can presume women can cope with other women being bitchy about them, too. BECAUSE WE ARE ESSENTIALLY THE SAME AS MEN WHEN IT COMES TO BEING VILE ABOUT EACH OTHER.

This isn't to say we should all start behaving like bitches toward each other and turn every day into a 24-hour roasting session, in which people's lives, wardrobes, and psyches are destroyed before our eyes. All along, we must recall the most important Humanity Guideline of all: BE POLITE. Being polite is possibly the greatest daily contribution everyone can make to life on earth.

But at the same time, "Are the boys doing it?" is a good way to detect spores of misogyny in the soil, which might otherwise seem a perfectly fertile and safe place to grow a philosophy.

It was the "Are the boys doing it?" basis on which I finally decided I was against women wearing burkas. Yes, the idea is that it protects your modesty and ensures that people regard you as a human being, rather than just a sexual object. Fair enough. But who are you being protected *from*? Men. And who—so long as you play by the rules and wear the correct clothes—is protecting you *from* the men? Men. And who is it that is regarding you as just a sexual object, instead of another human being, in the first place? Men.

Well. This all seems like quite a man-based problem, really. I would definitely put this under the heading "100 percent stuff that the men need to sort out." I don't know why *we're* suddenly having to put things on our heads to make it better. Unless you really, genuinely like all the gear and would wear it even if you were alone watching *EastEnders*, in which case carry on. My politeness accepts your choice. You can be whatever you want—so long as you're sure it's what you actually *want*, rather than one of two equally dodgy choices foisted onto you.

*

Because the purpose of feminism isn't to make a particular *type* of woman. The idea that there are inherently wrong and inherently right "types" of women is what's screwed feminism for so long—this belief that "we" wouldn't accept slaggy birds, dim birds, birds that bitch, birds that hire cleaners, birds that stay at home with their kids, birds that have pink Mini Metros with POWERED BY FAIRY DUST! bumper stickers, birds in burkas, or birds that like to pretend, in their heads, that they're married to Zach Braff from *Scrubs* and that you sometimes have sex in an ambulance while the rest of the cast watch and, latterly, clap. You know what? Feminism will have all of you.

What is feminism? Simply the belief that women should be as free as men, however nuts, dim, deluded, badly dressed, fat, receding, lazy, and smug they might be.

Are you a feminist? Hahaha. Of course you are.

CHAPTER 5
I Need a Bra!

Of course, feminism will only take you so far—and then you need to go shopping. I'm not talking about *Sex and the City* shopping here—that belief that it's a fun and revelatory experience, a bit like meditating, but with one leg stuck in a pair of size 12 jeggings in Topshop. Personally, I find the idea that women are supposed to "love" shopping bizarre—nearly every woman I know wants to cry after 45 minutes of trawling the high street looking for a shirt and hits the gin with alacrity upon the sad occasions when jeans have to be found.

No. By "shopping," I mean just going out and getting a thing you actually need—like knickers. Because at the age of 15, I need underpants. I need underpants very badly. I might be ready to smash the patriarchy and get my I AM A STRIDENT FEMINIST tattoo, but not if it involves showing anyone the contents of my underwear drawer. Who am I kidding? I don't even have an underwear drawer. Everything I own—underpants, two undershirts, two pairs of tights, a skirt, three T-shirts, and a single, tatty sweater—are all in a cardboard box under the bed. I don't really have "underwear" at all.

What I have, instead, is heirlooms. At age 15, I have become too big for anything you could buy from the tiny olden-days clothing shop on Warstones Road—where children's undies were kept in a huge wall of wooden drawers, and the correct-size ones would be handed to you in a paper bag, as if they were a quarter pound of boiled sweets, or some lamb chops.

So—as we are currently too poor to buy new, adult underpants—I become the recipient of the the Moran Underwear Bequest instead: four pairs of my mum's old, classic briefs. The kind a five-year-old would draw on a washing line. They have been blasted through with Bold on a boil wash so many times that the once-cheerful pink stripes are now pale shadows: like the gray outlines people are supposed to leave on walls near the epicenter of an atomic explosion.

In addition, the elastic of the waistbands is only sporadically attached to the main body of the underpants—it hangs from the overstretched rubber like bunting. It was like there was a party in my undies, to which absolutely no one was invited.

Although not a *particularly* vile child, wearing my mother's old underpants hadn't caused me any squeamish thoughts. After all, compared to the fact that I was sleeping in the bed my nanna had died in—indeed, right in the middle of the massive indentation her body left in the mattress; I am wearing her ghost as a nightie—it is chicken feed.

That is, it is chicken feed until the day I am sitting in the garden with Caz.

We are engaged in quietly and lovingly drawing a mustache, beard, and monobrow on the sleeping two-year-old Cheryl with a piece of charcoal.

Everything is quite idyllic until Caz nods down to Cheryl and says—with the mixture of distaste and shit-stirring that makes all my adolescence with her so much fun—"Mum was probably wearing your knickers when she conceived her, you know. Dad probably TORE them off her to make Chel. He was being ALL SEXY AT YOUR UNDIES."

Obviously, I then hit Caz. I hit her with all my strength, so that she fell over backward.

"You PREVERT!" I shout. "Prevert" is our new word. We all read a great deal—but also, possibly, too quickly. We have also recently taken to using the word "paradigm," pronounced as spelled. Autodidactism has its drawbacks. Or backdrawers, as we would probably have speed-read and never been corrected.

"You DICK FACE!" Caz screams, kicking out at me like a kangaroo. Were it a film, the picture my mother took just three weeks ago—of us hugging on the landing, in bathrobes—would cross-fade in, quietly burning down to ash. Our *entente cordiale* is over for another year.

But my upset was just for that afternoon. I had no choice other than to sit back down and just carry on wearing those undies, as I would for another four long, bad-underpants years. I just didn't have any other options. It's one of the many reasons why being very, very poor sucks. You have to live in underpants that give you nightmares.

Underwear—knickers and bra primarily, but also including slips, hosiery, and "control-wear"—are the specialist clothing of being a woman. They are the female equivalent of a fireman's jumpsuit and helmet. Or the large shoes of a clown. We need this stuff, for the "work" of being a woman. It's technically necessary. I mean, every woman is different but, more often than not, we must have a bra to get us through the day—particularly if that day is to involve running for a bus or wearing a low-cut dress. Otherwise one might have to do that thing of breaking into a trot while clutching one's bosom—lest one's breasts bounce so violently they appear to go round and round, like a stripper's tassels, and inadvertently hypnotize a passerby. I have done that. It was bad.

Similarly, while *Wish You Were Here*'s Judith Chalmers famously wears no knickers at all—not even up the Acropolis—I think most of us know the risks inherent in this. Yes. Spiders could climb up your legs and make a nest inside you and lay eggs in your precious. Emma Parry at school knew a girl whose cousin had had that happen to her in Leicester. When the baby spiders came out, they were hungry and ate her bum hair. Don't look at me in horror—I am just reporting what was very big news in Wolverhampton in 1986. I was surprised it wasn't picked up nationally at the time.

I think we can all see, quite clearly, that the stakes are too high for a woman to live without undies.

Because all through the four and a half years I wore my mother's knickers, I knew I was failing a major part of the curriculum in being a woman: women are supposed to look good in underwear. Chicks have to rock underpants. They should be acing bras. There is a widely held supposition that, really, when you come down to it, a woman in her underwear is a woman at her best.

And to be fair, often, she is. It's one of those inimitable talents of the softer, gentler, and rounder sex—we really can fill out a pair of knickers and a bra very well. If you've got some half-decent tits in a half-decent bra, it doesn't matter if the rest of you looks like a child's teatime blancmange that fell on the floor and got attacked by the cat—everyone will be looking at the tits in the bra. Their magic is out of all proportion to their abilities: very much not healing the sick or working complex equations, very much just sitting in a bra and, occasionally, wobbling in an exciting manner.

Indeed, the panoply of underwear—across the ages and cultures—is notable for the extraordinary, odds-bucking fact that nearly all of it looks hot. We just, to paraphrase Will Smith in *Men in Black*, make this shit look good.

The magic of good underwear—underwear so good you want to call it "lingerie" in a French accent—is endless. When you get the really good stuff—the Olympic standard gear; the stuff dealers only sell to their "special customers"—straight girls can have their heads turned by other straight girls in it.

Once, I ended up in a strip club with my friend Vicky. It's a long story. Indeed, it's most of Chapter 9. But when, at around 1 a.m., a stripper called Marina gave us a private dance, my head was swimming after just three minutes. I was in some kind of Imperial Lingerie Swoon. Marina's incredible Snow-White arse was wrapped, like a present, in cerise-colored satin—the ribbon ties trailing down her thighs. As she swayed from side to side, drunk, laughing, it was impossible to think of anything other than how you could hear the faint, faint rasp of the fabric on her skin, and how overwhelmingly tempting it was to pull on those ribbons, like an emergency brake, and bring her to a shuddering, sudden stop, right next to your face.

Marina obviously had the same idea. Woozy with vodka, she had just asked us to pull the ribbons *with our teeth* when Security came in and bellowed, "NO TOUCHING! NO TOUCHING!"

Marina sulkily pulled away from us: the girl-fun ended. I left the club reeling, my head totally shanked from the combination of sticky, demi-sec champagne and Marina's Defcon 3 lingerie drawer.

So let us hymn awhile on lingerie—recite the psalms of the smaller, higher drawers in the chest. Stockings—black, seamed, or sheer—allowing you to fuck instantly, spontaneously, standing; possibly even as you're still saying, "So do you need me to sign for this parcel?"

French knickers in peach satin, with ruffles all up the back.

Teddies in outrageous colors, flashing under corsets: kingfisher blue; rose red; gold, like the wedding ring on the floor. The frothing, cloudy egg-white joy of tulle. The way silk slip-slides over you, like a sheet of oil. Watching the blood rush through the semi-visibility of lace. The black line from calf to thigh. The hook-and-eye, with flesh swelling beneath. Torn buttons. The hem.

I have an August-blue petticoat with tiny pink roses and black suspender straps that makes me happier than nearly any-thing else I own. Not only does it embody the kind of purring, spanky, joyous 1950s soft-porn postcards I have based most of my wardrobe/sexuality on, but I also look dead thin in it. I have often noticed this with underwear: the right stuff will be the most flat-tering outfit you can wear.

Oh, if only the world knew how amazing we look, under all these clothes.

But, of course, often it can! Being able to wear underwear bril-liantly is such a key talent for a woman that there are even com-petitions to judge who is the best at it: Miss America, Miss World, Miss International, Miss Universe. You can call this "the swimsuit round" all you like—we know what it really means. It's the "bra and undies round."

I'm sure it was referred to as such up until 30 seconds before the first ever Miss World, when someone leaned across to Eric Morley and—putting his hand over the microphone as the theme music boomed out—said, "Eric, look. This feminism thing. I don't think it is 'the new skiffle.' I really think it might hang around a bit. Shall we pretend that the '—bra and pants round' is about swimming instead?"

Perhaps it is because we have formalized Being Able to Wear Bra & Underpants as a competition with incredible rewards—tour the world meeting old people and children! Have sex with footballers! Get a crown!—that, over the years, we have made wearing knickers harder and harder. Knickers have gradually become difficult. And the reason for this is that knickers have become smaller. Much smaller. Too small.

A case in point: a few months ago, I was on a crowded tube with a friend of mine, who gradually grew paler and quieter until she finally leaned forward and admitted that her knickers were so skimpy, her front bottom had eaten them entirely.

"I'm currently wearing them on my clit—like a little hat," she said.

Clearly, this is not right. Jesus Christ. Underpants like this need to be bombed back to the Stone Age. Batman doesn't have to put up with this shit—why should we? Women need, as a basic human right, to be given enough underwear for it to cling to their exteriors, like a starfish—and not slowly be pulled into the deep gravity of their inside and get internalized, due to motion friction. It's insanity.

I'm going to lay this one right on the line, right here, right now: I'm pro big undies. Strident feminism NEEDS big undies. Really big. I'm currently wearing a pair that could have been used as a fire blanket to put out the Great Fire of London at any point during the first 48 hours or so. They extend from the top of my thigh to my belly button and effectively double as a second property that I can escape to on weekends.

Lovely readers, if I have distressed you with how much you have just learned of my underwear predilections, then it is, I'm afraid, only matched by how distressed I have been to learn of the underwear predilections of others. In the 21st century, these are no longer a secret. Pencil skirts, skin-tight jeans, and leggings—they all allow us to witness an exact outline of the wearer's panties, rather like the "geo-phys" printout of an ancient drainage system on *Time Team*.

And what these results tell us is that there is scarcely a woman in Britain wearing a pair of underpants that actually fit her. Instead of having something that sensibly and reassuringly contains both the buttocks—what *I* would call a good pair of undies—they're wearing little more than gluteal accessories, or arse-trinkets. They're all in bikinis, thongs, high-cuts, or shorts.*

These tight, elasticated partitions across the mid-derrière are, in terms of both comfort and aesthetics, as cruel as the partition between India and Pakistan. There is catastrophic physical displacement. Entire body parts are split asunder, or undertake vast migrations. With my own eyes, I have seen women walking around out there with anything between two and eight buttocks—and placed anywhere between the hip and the mid-thigh. This enforced deformity is not the fault of the underpants. They are little guys, simply overwhelmed by the task that faces them. They are outnumbered. They are the Alamo.

Women, this manner of underwear cannot be an act of sanity. Why are we starving our bottoms of the resources—like an extra meter of material—to stay comfortable? Why have we succumbed to pantorexia?

It is, of course, all a symptom of women's continuing, demented belief that, at any moment, they might face some snap inspection of their "total hotness." Women wear small underpants because they think they're sexy. But in this respect, women have communally lost all reason. Ladies! On how many occasions in the last year have you *needed* to wear a tiny pair of skimpy undies? In

---

*The last, to the uninitiated, *sounds* like it would give you full coverage but merely provides a thin black strip across the middle section. Much as if your reproductive area had been the victim of a terrible crime and was being interviewed on the six-o'clock news with its identity concealed.

other words, to break this right down, how many times have you suddenly, unexpectedly, had sex in a brightly lit room, with a hard-to-please erotic connoisseur?

Exactly. With those kind of odds, you might just as well be keeping a backgammon board down there to entertain a group of elderly ladies in the event of emergencies. It's more likely to happen.

You know, when it comes to sex, you really do have to remember men are blessedly forgiving creatures. They don't care what kind of knickers you're wearing. By the time you've taken your skirt off, you could be wearing a Greggs paper bag with leg holes torn in it and it wouldn't put them off. THERE ARE MEN OUT THERE HAVING SEX WITH BICYCLES. Men don't remotely care if you're wearing sexy underpants or not.

Imagine if men suffered from this demented level of over-preparation. If they did, they would be packing two tickets for a long weekend to Prague in their boxers, lest they suddenly come across a lady who needs romance RIGHT NOW. And men aren't doing that. They really aren't.

Of course, while ostensibly both a literally and figuratively small problem, tiny undies have massive ramifications for us as a nation. It cannot have gone unnoticed that, as a country, our power has waned in synchronicity with the waning of our undies. When women wore undergarments that extended from chin to toe, the sun never set on the British Empire. Now that the average British woman could pack a week's worth of underpants into a matchbox, we have little more than dominion over the Bailiwick of Jersey and the Isle of Man. All the good that women getting the vote has done has been undone by their constant struggle against their tiny underpants. How can 52 percent of the population expect to win the War on Terror if it can't even sit down without wincing?

*

NOTE: The only time it's actually a good idea not to wear knickers at all is at a rock festival, if you're wearing a long dress. In this event, any women understandably piqued by the half-hour-long queues for the toilets can simply do a "festival wee." For this, a lady must sit down on a spare square of grass, taking care to spread her skirts about her in the manner of Miss Deborah Kerr in *The King and I*. Having ensured that the skirts are arranged suitably, she can then quietly have a wee where she sits, with no one any the wiser—and then wait for nature's gentle breezes to dry her "area."

It is the way I imagine Snow White passed water, when she was abandoned in the forest by the huntsman. Or how Galadriel from *The Lord of the Rings* wets her cabbage, as and when the need arises.

FURTHER NOTE: This plan can ONLY go wrong in the event of ants. Ants do NOT like being pissed on.

But, of course, underpants are just half of the underwear business—the bottom half. What of the top half—bras? Bras have a power all their own. Every four years, when the World Cup rolls round, the highlight of the entire event for me and my sisters is a Brazil match. Any Brazil match. Brazil vs. anyone.

"BRA!" we holler, pointing to the screen. "BRA! It says BRA on the backs of their shirts! BRA!!!!!!"

We drum our heels against the sofa, as if we are being strangled by the amusingness of it all.

"BRA!!!!!!!!" we croak, faces so hot and wet from crying we look as if we've been boiled. "BRAAAAAAAAAAAAAAAA!!!!!!!!"

Aside from finding the port of Brest in a world atlas in 1991, it is the funniest thing that ever happens to us.

The bra is, perhaps, the rudest item of women's clothing. If you do not doubt this, try this simple test: throw a bra at a nine-year-old boy. He will react as if he has had a live rat wanged at his head. He will run, screaming, away from you—he cannot handle the rudeness of bras.

Thank goodness we ladies can—for a good bra can be one of the greatest aids a woman will ever know. At 35, my breasts are, still, like peaches. But the kind of peaches you find in the bottom of your handbag—after you'd forgotten you'd put them there for a snack. Peaches that have the obvious indentation mark of your keys on one end and a bus ticket stuck to the sticky bit. The kind of peaches you'd look at doubtfully in a market, 10 for £1, and say, "I suppose I could make smoothies out of them . . ."

It's breast-feeding, man. Breast-feeding two really colicky babies. Since the day the second child had some screaming fit on the M1, and I tried to pacify her by climbing into the back, sitting next to her with my seat belt on, and doglegging my breast around and into her mouth, like some kind of lactating U-bend, my tits are bust. And they—God bless them—know that. If they were a character in a film, they'd be the girl who falls over when they're being chased by the Baddies and shouts, "Go on without me! I've had a good life!" My breasts wish the rest of me well, but they are just not going to make it.

But you know what? It's okay! It really is. First of all, I'm not an international supermodel, so I could have tits that look like Yosemite Sam's face for all the world will care. No one will ever judge me on them! Ha! The patriarchy can try to make me as insecure about my wabs as it likes! That's its hobby! Apart from darts. But it simply can't make me! Because I know the only people who are ever going to see them naked are going to approach them in an attitude of immense gratefulness, i.e., hungry children and men who are about to get laid.

And all the rest of the time, I have my faithful friend, Bra, to help me out. Oh, Bra. I love you, Bra. You are like the lingerie equivalent of ketchup—everything is great with you. With the right bra, you can put whatever is left of your mammaries into it—maybe with the help of a spade, or a loved one—and it will mold the raw material into two lovely lady-lumps.

These days, I simply coil up my shattered tits like a fire hose and rely on a fierce piece of engineering from Rigby & Peller to put them in roughly the anatomically correct place. On their own, I'd just be kicking them in front of me, like an overly long dress. But with Bra, I can place them anywhere. Indeed, when I adjust my bra straps, it is rather in the manner of a mammarian game of Pin the Tail on the Donkey. "Pin the Breasts on the Thirty-Something Woman." If I don't have my contact lenses in, they could end up anywhere. I fully expect to leave the house one day, hungover and in a hurry, with my tits on my head.

On the other hand, if you live by the bra, you must die by the bra. As one would expect from an item capable of such powerful magic, sometimes the bra is prone to suddenly turning evil and attempting to destroy you. Think of it as a little like Saruman in *The Lord of the Rings*, but with a little bow in the middle. Sarumam.

In *Cougar Town*—the Courteney Cox sitcom about a 40-something divorcee attempting, every week, to get a foot-and-a-half of 20-something cock before midnight—there's a line where she explains to her younger friend why she doesn't like going out clubbing anymore.

"I have better wine than this at home," she says, holding up what even on TV looks like a very lackluster Pinot Grigio, "and at this time of night, all I want to do is take my bra off."

For people who've never worn a bra—men, children, animals, Agyness Deyn—it is almost impossible to describe the sheer, raw pleasure that comes with taking off certain bras. I once had a bra—teal-colored, full-cup, slight padding, beautiful, extremely expensive—so cruelly tight, I rang the shop I bought it from on day three, in tears.

"Is it supposed to hurt so much?" I asked, trying to repress a sob.

"You just need to break it in," the woman said sternly, like an army drill sergeant instructing his new recruits to piss on their boots to soften the leather. I did, eventually, domesticate that bra—but on the first 20 occasions I wore it, I reached 6 p.m. every evening and went *tearing* upstairs to take it off, sighing like a spaceman getting out of a spacesuit. I would *hurl* it to the floor and rub the red welt that it had left, like a monk tending the after-effects of a hairshirt.

The relief of taking off a bad bra is immeasurable. It's like a combination of putting your feet up, going to the bathroom, having a drink of cold water on a hot day, and sitting on the steps of a trailer having a smoke. Bad bra removal is a measure of your friendships. If you would feel comfortable going round to someone's house at the end of a long day and saying, "I'm just going to take my bra off," you know you are intimate friends.

Of course, on occasion, bad bra removal has to happen in a more urgent location. I have seen women taking bras off in cabs on their way back from clubs; women taking off bras in cabs that are still *outside* clubs.

I once saw it happen at a bus stop outside Bar Rumba on Camden High Street.

I understood.

To any idiot who says, "You a feminist? Do you burn your bras, then, huh? HUH? You burn your bras, you feminist," you must reply calmly, "Fool. FOOL. Bra is my friend. My bosomest buddy. My inti-mate. Except for that balcony-cup Janet Reger one that was an inch too small and cut off the circulation to my head. Yeah. That one, I covered in gas and torched it outside the American embassy."

CHAPTER 6

I Am Fat!

So now it's 1991, and I'm 16, and I'm sitting on St. Peter's cathedral lawn with Matthew Vale, smoking.

Matt is—by both his own and several independent adjudicators' assessments—the coolest adolescent in Wolverhampton. He's got the entire Byrds back catalog and a lot of baggy charity-shop sweaters, and when he dances he has proper moves; some of which he's copied off the Supremes. One of his earliest lectures to me was how you should "always have a plan" when you walk onto a dance floor.

"Don't just go on there and . . . fuck around," he will say, smoking his fag. "Tell a little story." It is good advice. Matt has lots of good advice. Another piece he gives me is: "Try not to be a total dick." Once you've been told it, it's amazing to note how many people appear *not* to have been told it. It is wise counsel.

When you first meet Matt, he tells you—as he pulls his hair over his eyes—that he keeps his hair over his eyes because he had a bad acid trip and can't look anyone in the eye. "Because sometimes I worry that when people look me in the eye, they see that I'm *a demon*."

After I've known him for six months, I one day see him lying on a bed with his hair swept back. And I realize that it's *actually* because he has a little bit of a squint and doesn't want anyone to see it.

Yes, of course I fancy him. God, I fancy him. I didn't until my friend Jools saw him uptown and exclaimed on the phone afterward, "Who was HE? He. Was. FIT. AS."

Previously, I'd prided myself on our brotherly/sisterly vibe. After hearing the howling lust in Jools's voice, however, I stopped kidding myself and acknowledged that he was six foot two, and fucking buff under the baggy sweaters, and had eyes as green as a dragon's. When I thought about kissing him, I would reflect on how prettily pink, like a girl's, his mouth was. How I would have to eat it so carefully, to make it last. His mouth was so small. It filled up half of my head. I was 16 I was 16 I was 16, and he was 19, and we are on St. Peter's cathedral lawn, smoking fags.

This day we are smoking fags is late October. It is two months after we first met—on an adult education course for filmmaking, in which we were both immediately and consistently lackluster—and this is the first day out we have had together, alone. We are basically now auditioning each other as friends.

I've seen his girlfriend so I know we're not going to "happen"—unless she suddenly dies, which would be terribly, terribly, TERRIBLY sad—but we've had a very exciting day: bought Fleetwood Mac's *Tango in the Night* on cassette from the Cancer Research shop for 50p, shoplifted a deodorant from Boots, and generally represented all over the Mander Centre and across Queen Square.

I am dressed so carefully, as we sit on the cathedral lawn, exhaling. It's 1991 and I've just started earning money—as the least important person at *Melody Maker*—and so, for the first time in my life, I can buy clothes from shops, instead of jumble sales. I am wearing a turquoise tie-dyed shirt over a long skirt, Doc Marten boots, and a waistcoat. I'm 16 I'm 16 I'm 16, and these are my best clothes, and this is my best day, and a loft of pigeons flash past us, wings like linen, and it's autumn, and the sky goes on forever, and I can wait for him, I'll just wait for him, she *might* die, after all, she could die so easily; people drop dead on buses all the time.

And Matt says:

"Did you have a nickname at school?"

And I say:

"Yes."

And he says:

"Did they call you Fatty?"

So that's the first time I ever felt the world stop—although not the last, of course. Everything very cold and still and bright for one second. A flashbulb. Someone has just taken a picture of us, to show again at the end of our lives, in a slide show: "Here's some of your worst bits!" Me and Matty Vale, on the cathedral lawn, October 1991.

Because genuinely I thought he might not have noticed, hahaha. I thought I'd hidden those extra fifty pounds really carefully under my new shirt and the waistcoat, and I was talking too fast for him to see it. I thought my hair was long and shiny and my eyes were blue, and I'd kept it secret. I thought he might not have noticed that I'm fat.

I've said it—there, I've said it. Because I am 16, and I am fat. All I do is sit around eating bread and cheese and reading. I'm fat. We're all fat. The entire family is obese.

We don't have any full-length mirrors in the house, so whenever I want to see myself naked, I have to go uptown, to Marks & Spencer, and pretend that I'm going to try on a tartan skirt and go into the changing room and look at myself there.

I am a virgin, and I don't play sport or move heavy objects, or go anywhere or do anything, and so my body is this vast, sleeping, pale thing. There it is, standing awkwardly in the mirror, looking like it's waiting to receive bad news. It *is* the bad news. Teenage girls are supposed to be lithe and hot. A fat teenage girl's body is of no use to anyone, let alone the teenage girl. It is an albatross. An outsized white bird. I'm dragging it round like a sea anchor.

But I'm just a brain in a jar, I tell myself. That's my comforting thought. I'm just a brain in a jar. It doesn't matter about the other bits. That is what my body is. "The other bits." The jar. I'm clever, so it doesn't matter that I'm fat.

I am fat.

Because I am fully aware of what the word "fat" means—what it *really* means, when you say it, or think it. It's not just a simple, descriptive word like "brunette" or "34."

It's a swear word. It's a weapon. It's a sociological subspecies. It's an accusation, dismissal, and rejection. When Matt asks if they used to call me Fatty at school, he's already imagining me, pityingly, in the lower orders of the school hierarchy—lumped in with (as it's Wolverhampton, in 1986) the two Asian kids, the stutterer, the Jehovah's Witness with one eye, the kid with special needs, the boy who's obviously gay, and the boy so thin he's *constantly* asked if Bob Geldof has been round his house yet.

Matt is going to sympathize with me, which means he'll never fuck me, which means I will, sadly, die of terminal unhappiness—possibly within the next hour, conceivably before I've finished this cigarette, which, I notice, I'm now crying on.

In my family, my fat family, none of us ever say the word "fat." "Fat" is the word you hear shouted on the playground or the street—it's never allowed over the threshold of the house. My mum won't have that filth in her house. At home, together, we are safe. It's like an *eruv* for the slow and soft. There will be no harm to our feelings here because we never acknowledge fat exists. We never refer to our size. We are the elephants in the room.

But the silence is the most oppressive thing of all. Because there's a silent, shrugging, stoic acceptance of all the things in the world we can never be part of: shorts, swimming pools, strappy dresses, country walks, roller-skating, ra-ra skirts, sleeveless tops, high heels, rope climbing, sitting on a high stool, walking past building sites, flirting, being kissed, feeling confident.

And ever losing weight, ever.

The idea of suggesting we don't *have* to be fat—that things could change—is the most distant and alien prospect of all. We're fat now and we'll be fat forever and we must never, ever mention it, and that is the end of it. It's like Harry Potter's Sorting Hat. We were pulled from the hat marked "Fat" and that is what we must now remain, until we die. Fat is our race. Our species. Our mode.

As a result, there is very little of the outside world—and very little of the year—we can enjoy. Summer is sweaty under self-conscious layers. On stormy days, wind flattens skirts against thighs and alarms both us and, we think, onlookers and passersby.

Winter is the only time we feel truly comfortable: covered head to toe in sweaters, coats, boots, and hats. I develop a crush on Father Christmas. If I married him, not only would I be expected to stay fat, but I'd look thin standing next to him, in comparison. Perspective would be my friend. We all dream of moving to Norway, or Alaska, where we could wear massive padded coats all the time and never reveal an inch of flesh. When it rains, we're happiest of all. Then we can just stay in, away from everyone, in our pajamas, and not worry about anything. The brains in jars can stay inside, nice and dry.

When Matty Vale asks me if I used to be called Fatty, I am wearing my swimsuit from when I was 12 under my clothes—by way of a primitive and ultimately ineffective corset—and I have been painfully holding my stomach in since midday.

"No!" I say. I give an imperious, Ava Gardner–like flash of eyebrow and eye. "Jesus!"

I take another drag on the fag and stop holding in my stomach. He's busted me. Why bother.

No. They didn't call me Fatty at school, Matt, you hot, oblivious thing, who I'm going to spend the next two years pining after like crack cocaine, to the point where I will steal your sweater and keep it under my pillow, and then inadvertently cause you to split up with your girlfriend when I tell a terrible secret to the wrong person and our little social circle explodes in a spectacularly messy fashion.

It was Fatso.

Is the word "fat" making you wince when you read it? Does it feel like I'm being rude, or indelicate, to say it? In the last two generations, it's become a furiously overloaded word—in a conversation, when the word "fat" appears, it often alarms people, like a siren going off, and prompts a supportive, scared flurry of dismissal—"You're not fat! Of course you're not fat! Babe, you're NOT FAT!"—when the person is, clearly and undeniably, fat and just wants to discuss it.

More often than not, though, it's used as a weapon to stop the conversation dead: "Shut up, you fat bitch." Silence.

The accusation of fatness has replaced "gay" or "lesbian" as the playground taunt of choice. It's generally regarded to be the Hiroshima of accusations—the bomb that, once dropped, calls for immediate surrender from the accused. If you can counter a perfectly valid argument with "Yeah, well, at least I'm not *fat*," then you are the Allies, and you have won.

The accusation is so strong, it is still effective even if it has no basis in the truth whatsoever. I have seen size 10 women being silenced by this line—as if they feel the accuser has somehow sensed that they secretly have a "fat aura" or will become fat later in life and called them on it.

On being hit with "Yeah, well, at least I'm not *fat*" on two occasions, I tried to pervert a classic line and replied, "I'm fat because every time I fuck your dad, he gives me a biscuit."

But my audience didn't really get the ahead-of-its-time technique of subverting a cliché and just presumed I'd developed an eating disorder to cope with an unhappy experience of pedophilia instead.

It just added to my generally undesirable air. I am ahead of both the curve and my age-group weight percentile.

But giving the word "fat" such power is, of course, no good at all. Just as I have previously urged you to stand on a chair and shout, "I AM A STRIDENT FEMINIST," so I now urge you to stand on a chair and say the word "fat." "FAT FAT FAT FAT FAT."

Say it until you lose the nervousness around it, say it until it seems normal—like the word "tray"—and eventually becomes meaningless. Point at things and call them "fat." "That tile is fat." "The wall is fat." "I believe Jesus is fat." The heat needs to be drained out of the word "fat," like fever from a child. We need to be able to stare, clearly and calmly, right into the middle of fat and talk about what it is, and what it means, and why it's become the big topic for Western women in the 21st century. FAT FAT FAT FAT.

First of all, I think we should agree on what "fat" actually is. Obviously, norms of beauty come and go, and there are extremes of metabolism and build—that big-boned thing is TRUE! I only found out recently! Compared to Kylie Minogue, I genuinely have the bones of a mastodon! I would NEVER have fit into those gold hot pants because I have got TOO MUCH CALCIUM!

So given all this, it doesn't pay to ever be too proscriptive about the term "normal."

But after a lifetime of consideration, I believe I've finally nailed a sensible definition of what a good, advisable, "normal" weight is. What is "fat" and "not fat." And it is:

"Human-shaped."

If you look recognizably, straightforwardly human—the kind of reasonable figure a ten-year-old would draw, if asked to sketch a person in under a minute—then you are fine. "The body reasonably healthy and clean is the body beautiful," as the Goddess Greer puts it.

You *could* spend the rest of your life obsessing about the crenellations on the backs of your thighs, the beer-barrel swell of your belly, or the fact that, when you run, you can feel your buttocks banging against each other like a set of clackers. But to do that would be to operate on the subconscious assumption that, at some point, you will be forced to appear in front of people naked and judged out of ten, and—as we have discussed before—THIS ISN'T GOING TO HAPPEN UNLESS YOU ENTER *AMERICA'S NEXT TOP MODEL*. What happens in your bra and undies STAYS in your bra and undies. If you can find a frock you look nice in and can run up three flights of stairs, you're not fat.

The idea that you need to be better than merely "human-shaped"—this inch-perfect toning, where even an excess tablespoon of fat overhanging the knee is unacceptable, let alone a world where a size 12 is "XL"—is another piece of what strident feminists can technically dismiss as "total bullshit."

My fat years were when I was *not* human-shaped. I was a 224-pound triangle, with inverted triangle legs and no real neck. And that's because I wasn't doing human things. I didn't walk or run or dance or swim or climb stairs; the food I ate wasn't the stuff that humans are supposed to eat. No one is supposed to eat a pound of boiled potatoes covered in margarine or a fist-sized lump of cheese on the end of a fork, wielded like a lollipop. I had no connection to or understanding of my body. I *was* just a brain in a jar. I wasn't a woman.

Ironically, having unwittingly smashed my heart to bits with his fists on St. Peter's cathedral lawn, it is Matthew Vale who over the course of four months knocks fifty pounds off me, and thereby introduces me to the other half of myself: the bit with legs on it.

On Thursday and Friday nights, we take to climbing over the railings of the dual carriageway to a pub in the middle of nowhere and dancing for five hours straight to records from 1986 to 1991 only, made by white British bands, featured in *NME* and *Melody Maker:* Spiritualized, Happy Mondays, the Fall, New Order. He also gets me on ten Silk Cuts a day, which leaves me no money for lunch—useful.

Speeded-up CCTV footage would show me, over the six months on that dance floor, turning from something fairly Flump-like into something that is undeniably a human-shaped teenage girl, who can now go out and buy a dress from a normal shop. A short, flowery one, to be worn with cardi, boots, and eyeliner. I can pass for "normal," if I dress carefully, but I still never use the words "thin" or "fat," in case anyone starts paying closer attention; starts trying to work out which one I am.

But more important, on that tiny dance floor—ciggie in one hand, cider in the other, "How Soon Is Now" sounding like the Smiths are speeding past us, light-decked and vast, like the Millennium Falcon—I feel a newfound euphoria: I've found out where my body is. Turns out, it was RIGHT UNDER MY HEAD ALL ALONG! WHO KNEW? It's always the last place you look.

And now I can make it spin over here, badly, and leap over there, ridiculously, and pretend to play invisible maracas in a dance move that surely keeps me a virgin for another year, minimum, but it's *fun*, having these arms, and these legs, and this little belly.

And it's the start of a slow process—which takes in pregnancies and births and long, stoned afternoon fucks and 26-mile walks and learning to run, run really fast, so it just feels like dancing, but in a straight line—of getting to the point where, at 35, I can say I like my body as much as my head. My brain doesn't look as good in a frock, and my body is still fairly poor at making jokes out of the ridiculous occurrences in the life of Victoria Beckham, but we're all friends now. We get on, and we agree on things, such as what a "reasonable" amount of chips adds up to and whether I should run up the escalator (yes).

I don't wish now—as I often used to when I was 15 and particularly hysterical—that I could be involved in a serious car crash, in which my entire body would have to be rebuilt from scratch, but using around half the amount of raw materials then in employ.

And when I look at myself in the mirrors of the changing rooms at Marks & Spencer now, my body looks, finally, awake.

But why did I get fat? Why was I eating until I hurt and regarding my own body as something as distant and unsympathetic as, say, the state of the housing market in Buenos Aires? And why—while it's obviously not wholly *advisable* to swell up so large that, on one very bad day, you get stuck in a bucket seat at a local fair and have to be helped out by your ex-headmaster, Mr. Thompson— is being fat treated as a cross between terrible shame and utter tragedy? Something that—for a woman—is treated as somewhere in between sustaining a sizable facial scar and sleeping with the

Nazis? Why will women happily boast-moan about spending too much (". . . and then my bank manager took my credit card and CUT IT IN HALF WITH A SWORD!"), drinking too much (". . . and then I took my shoe off and THREW IT OVER THE BUS STOP!"), and working too hard (". . . so tired I fell asleep on the control panel, and when I woke up, I realized I'd PRESSED THE NUCLEAR LAUNCH BUTTON! AGAIN!") but never, ever about eating too much? Why is unhappy eating the most pointlessly secret—it's not like you can hide a six-KitKats-a-day habit for very long—of miseries?

Seven years ago, a friend of mine broke up with a pop star, reactivated her bulimia, binged and purged for nine days straight, and then admitted herself to the Priory.

I strapped my toddler into a buggy and went to visit her—out of a combination of love and curiosity as to what the Priory was like. I think I'd presumed it was like the Chateau Marmont, but with amazing prescription drugs. Full of interestingly ravaged celebrities clawing their way back to normality, in the midst of some helpfully gorgeous décor.

In the event, it turns out that, inside, the Priory actually looks, and smells, like a lower midrange family-run hotel in Welshpool. Faded swirly carpets, teak-effect fire doors, and, somewhere—judging by the smell—a perpetually boiling cauldron of mince, working as the world's biggest Glade Plug-In. It was less "Olympia, home of the gods," and more "Olympia, tube station of the exhibition center."

And, as my friend told me, sitting on the end of her bed chain-smoking, an institution full of emotionally troubled substance abusers turns out to be no fun at *all*.

"There's a pecking order," she sighed, shredding her cuticles with her opposing thumbnail. She was burning a Diptyque

Jasmine candle to cover up the evidence she'd just thrown up her breakfast, but the bile had lingered longer than she'd accounted for.

"The heroin addicts look down on the coke addicts. The coke addicts look down on the alcoholics. And everyone thinks the people with eating disorders—fat or thin—are scum."

And there's your pecking order of unhappiness, right there in a nutshell. Of all the overwhelming compulsions you can be ruined by, all of them have *some* potential for some perverted, self-destructive fascination—except eating.

Consider, for instance, David Bowie. Here was a man who took so much cocaine that he took to keeping his urine in bottles in the fridge, because he was scared that wizards "might steal it." And yet despite storing his rotting wazz next to his ham, it doesn't stop him being cool. On the contrary—who doesn't find the fact that Bowie now describes his mind as being "Swiss cheesed" from coke abuse kind of, well, adorably rock 'n' roll? He's David Bowie, man!

Or think of Keith Richards, in his Glimmer Twins days—snorting, smoking, injecting, drinking, and screwing everything in sight. Everyone loves him! Keef? So out of it that he doesn't notice when two groupies, fucking in front of him, accidentally set fire to their own hair? ROCK 'N' ROLL! For many, that's the *best bit* about the Stones!

Even though, by any way we can calculate it, he would almost certainly have been a complete nightmare to be around—paranoid, shaky, unreliable, prone to extreme moroseness or mania, and, a good whack of the time, so deeply unconscious that the primary method of moving from one location to another would have been being dragged by the ankles—we still have a slight, cultural frisson of "Huh—cool" when people get this fucked up.

But imagine if—instead of taking heroin—Keef had started

overeating and gotten really fat instead. If he'd really gotten into spaghetti Bolognese, say, or kept coming onstage holding foot-long Subway Meatball Subs and pausing in between numbers to have a bit of a chomp. Wandering down to Alphabet Street, twitching, four hours on the cluck, desperate to score Cheez Whiz. Long, crazy, wired nights after gigs, in penthouses, nubile dollies scattered across the room, and Keith in the center, sprawled across a silk-draped emperor-size waterbed, eating salt-and-vinegar Doritos sandwiches and Tunnock's teacakes off a tray.

By the time of *Their Satanic Majesties Request*, what his Satanic Majesty would be requesting was a 38-inch waistband, and everyone would have mocked the Stones for having a faintly ludicrous wobble-bot on guitar who was ruining the concept of rock 'n' roll.

But, of course, all this time, Keef would have been behaving like a total darling: waking at 8 a.m., keeping his hotel rooms tidy, thanking everyone, working a solid 12-hour day. There would be no going AWOL for 48 hours, then coming back with a dead goldfish in his pocket and a new tramp friend called Alan Fuck.

Because people overeat for *exactly* the same reason they drink, smoke, serially fuck around, or take drugs. I must be clear that I am not talking about the kind of overeating that's just plain, cheerful greed—the kind of Rabelaisian, Falstaffian figures who treat the world as a series of sensory delights and take full joy in their wine, bread, and meat. Someone who walks away from a table—replete—shouting, "THAT WAS SPLENDID!" before sitting in front of a fire, drinking port and eating truffles, doesn't have neuroses about food. They are in a consensual relationship with eating and, almost unfailingly, couldn't care less about how it's put an extra couple of pounds on them. They tend to wear their weight well—luxuriously, like a fur coat or a diamond sash—rather than nervously trying to hide it, or apologizing for it. These people aren't "fat"—they are simply . . . lavish. They don't have an eating problem—unless it's running out of truffle oil or finding a much-anticipated dish of razor clams sadly disappointing.

No—I'm talking about those for whom the whole idea of food is not one of pleasure, but one of compulsion. For whom thoughts of food, and the effects of food, are the constant, dreary background static to normal thought. Those who think about lunch while eating breakfast, and pudding as they eat chips; who walk into the kitchen in a state bordering on panic and breathlessly eat slice after slice of bread and butter—not tasting it, not even chewing—until the panic can be drowned in an almost meditative routine of chewing and swallowing, spooning and swallowing.

In this trancelike state, you can find a welcome, temporary relief from thinking for 10, 20 minutes at a time, until finally a new set of sensations—physical discomfort and immense regret—make you stop, in the same way you finally pass out on whiskey or dope. Overeating, or comfort eating, is the cheap, meek option for self-satisfaction, and self-obliteration. You get all the temporary release of drinking, fucking, or taking drugs, but without—and I think this is the important bit—ever being left in a state where you can't remain responsible and cogent.

In a nutshell, then, by choosing food as your drug—sugar highs, or the deep, soporific calm of carbs, the Valium of the working classes—you can still make the packed lunches, do the school run, look after the baby, pop in on your mum, and then stay up all night with an ill five-year-old—something that is not an option if you're caning off a gigantic bag of skunk or regularly climbing into the cupboard under the stairs and knocking back quarts of Scotch.

Overeating is the addiction of choice of carers, and that's why it's come to be regarded as the lowest-ranking of all the addictions. It's a way of fucking yourself up while still remaining fully functional, because you have to. Fat people aren't indulging in the "luxury" of their addiction making them useless, chaotic, or a burden. Instead, they are slowly self-destructing in a way that doesn't inconvenience anyone. And that's why it's so often a woman's addiction of choice. All the quietly eating mums. All the KitKats in office drawers. All the unhappy moments, late at night, caught only in the fridge light.

I sometimes wonder if the only way we'll ever get around to properly considering overeating is if it *does* come to take on the same perverse, rock 'n' roll cool of other addictions. Perhaps it's time for women to finally stop being secretive about their vices and start treating them like all other addicts treat their habits instead. Coming into the office looking raddled, sighing, "Man, I was on the shepherd's pie last night like you wouldn't believe. I had, like, MASH in my EYEBROWS by 10 p.m. I was on a total mince rush!"

Or walking into a friend's house, hurling your handbag on the table, and barking, "I have had one HELL of a day with the kids. I need six shots of cream crackers and cheese RIGHT NOW, or I am *seriously* going to lose my shit."

Then people would be able to address your dysfunction as openly as they do all the others. They could reply, "Whoa, dude. Maybe you should calm it down on the high GI-load carbs for a bit, my friend. You have gone a bit bongo-mondo. I am the same. I did a three-hour session on the microwave lasagne last night. Perhaps we should go out to the country for a bit. Get our heads together. Clean up our acts."

Because at the moment, I can't help but notice that in a society obsessed with fat—so eager in the appellation, so vocal in its disapproval—the only people who *aren't* talking about it are the only people whose business it really is.

CHAPTER 7

I Encounter Some Sexism!

So, I've lost weight, I can wear a dress, and I've got a job. I am now—as I cheerfully say to everyone—the Least Important Person at *Melody Maker*, the weekly music paper that everyone confuses with *NME*, which is far more famous but, we think, less cool. At the *NME*, they take drugs but don't really write about it. At *Melody Maker*, on the other hand, it's often the basis for a whole feature.

While the *NME* is staffed by normal, respectable men, who all go on to high-flying careers in broadcasting, *Melody Maker*'s retinue looks like the cast of *The Adams Family*. During editorial meetings, there's a distinct sense that everyone's come here because they failed the door policy at the cantina in *Star Wars*.

It is an odd, mismatched group. Everyone here is a social outcast for one reason or another. In the case of some of the staff, it's because they're antediluvian sexists with odd hair and a distinct aura of not having left the pub since 1976. With others, it's because they're so admirably, innovatively unnormal that it's clear that no other city but London, and no other employers but this publication, would have them.

Pricey's a strapping Welsh goth with his hair in two pigtails of ginger dreadlocks, who goes right down to the front at Public Enemy gigs wearing lipstick and nail polish. When the Manic Street Preachers are in town, he leaves the office with a black lace fan and a bottle of Malibu. Anyone who talks to him is astonished to discover he is (a) heterosexual and (b) from this planet.

Ben Turner is a tiny, shaven-headed man-child who appears to be around 13 years old. When I first meet him, I presume he's a kid with leukemia who wrote to the Make a Wish Foundation asking to hang out at a "real music magazine office" for the day. After a few weeks, I find out that he's, in fact, (a) a fully grown adult and (b) one of the leading authorities on dance music in Britain, who eventually goes on to defeat the imaginary leukemia I've given him and found the Bestival festival.

The editor, Jonesy, is in his late forties and looks like a rugged bison—but with incongruously glossy, glamorous, auburn hair. Viewed from behind in a bar, he is often the subject of initially lustful comments from men. When he turns around, they run away, screaming.

The Stud Brothers wear leather, swear like cunting dockers, and often come in drunk from the night before, then fall asleep under a desk. Simon Reynolds is a beautiful, pre-Raphaelite Oxford graduate into unlistenably cutting-edge dance music, who spends all his time in clubs where people have guns and is so clever, half of us are too scared to talk to him. Pete Paphides has just left his parents' chip shop in Birmingham and come to work for a magazine with an ethos of "no music too cool, too weird, or too marginal," while nursing his ABBA, ELO, Crowded House, and Bee Gees back catalogs and wearing a selection of snuggly cardigans from Marks & Spencer.

And now there's a 16-year-old from Wolverhampton in a hat, who chain-smokes and kicks people's shins if they slag off the Wonder Stuff. In the first week, I make David Bennun bleed.

Twenty years later, I run into him in Manchester at a Lady Gaga gig, and he ruefully rolls up his trouser leg and shows me the scar I left. Then he reminds me of the occasion where I threatened to push someone out of the window, 26 stories up, while most of the staff calmly carried on typing at their computers. It's not a normal workplace. We think this is why we are cool. *NME* think we're wankers for *exactly* the same reason.

This is the first time I've really been out in the world and met adults. Previously, all my socializing took place on the dance floor and in the bathroom of the Raglan, a tiny, dark pit populated by fringed, boot-wearing teenagers: essentially a playpen with a bar. Our innocence was obvious—it shone in our faces the same way our teeth glowed white under the UV light. Yes, people were having sex, and fighting, and spreading rumors, and taking drugs— but it was essentially like tiger cubs knocking each other around, claws velveted. We were all equal. There was no calculation or recrimination. Everything was forgotten after a nap.

Going into the adult world, then, is a shock. Rolling up at the office for my first day, I'm smoking a fag as I come out of the lift—so they know that I, too, am a grown-up. I offer everyone a nip of Southern Comfort from the bottle in my rucksack, for the same reason. Most demur, but Ben Stud—who's just come off the ferry from Amsterdam, from interviewing a band—says, "Handy!" cheerfully and takes a swig. He is, I notice, looking down, using a promotional Frisbee as a combined ashtray, plate for his bacon bap, and somewhere safe to keep his house keys.

I've already decided I'm going to have sex with as many people in London as I can. There's no reason not to. With my first wage check—£28.42—I've bought some new, pretty, gray-and-lace knickers from Marks & Spencer and finally thrown away my mum's now too-capacious inheritance, so I'm looking none too shabby in the knack. Although I've offered it all around town, no one in Wolverhampton seems remotely interested in taking my virginity, so I have concluded it's one of those things you can only get done in London—like natural-looking highlights, or Dirty Martinis. It's a specialist job.

So my task this month is to work out just how to be both a red-hot journalistic wunderkind *and* a red-hot piece of ass that someone, hopefully quite soon, will have sex with—but without getting a "reputation." Yes: at 16, I am having to learn how to drive the 16-wheeled vehicle that is my Flirt Truck, but without ruining my career.

Flirting in the workplace is a tricky subject for feminists. Many of the hard core don't believe in it at all: as far as they're concerned, you might as well go the whole hog and just install yourself in a window in Soho with a card reading "Model, 18, Hand Jobs" next to the doorbell.

And you know, for many, that's the right view to take. The idea that women should *have* to flirt in order to get it on is just as vexing as any other thing women are supposed to *have* to do—such as be thin, accept 30 percent lower wages, and not laugh at *30 Rock* when they have food in their mouth and it falls out a bit onto the floor and the cat eats it.

Some women just don't flirt. They don't want to and they don't have the bones for it, and it makes them feel tetchy and like they might punch someone. They feel about flirting like I do about anything that involves upper-body strength, high heels, or spatial awareness. They just want it to fuck off.

But for other women, flirting's just . . . how it comes out. It's not there as a defense mechanism, or as a result of years of being unwillingly sexualized by the goddamn patriarchy. It's not a consequence. It's an action. It comes from an almost demented joy in being alive, talking to someone who isn't boring you to death, and conspiring in an unspoken, momentary, twinkly, "I like you, and you like me. Isn't it lovely that we're being total lovelies together?" conspiracy.

If you're a natural flirt, it's not even a sex thing, really. You flirt with everyone—men, women, children, animals. Automated response ticket-booking phone lines ("Press 3 for more options? Oh darling, I don't think you have a button for the option *I'd* like").

As a cheerful born flirt, my rationale is, if you're going to spend all day having conversations with people—even if it's only on the phone, arranging the delivery of a new dishwasher—why not try to make it end with everyone feeling a bit bucked and perky? For me, flirting is the bit in *Mary Poppins* where Mary says, "In every job that must be done, there is an element of fun. You find the fun, and—SNAP! The job's a game."

But did flirting help me at *Melody Maker*? Did I further my career on the basis of my devastating sexual allure? I must be brisk here: no. Bear in mind, though, I was a tipsy 16-year-old in a huge hat, who still looked slightly scared of the lighter she was using to light her fags. At the time, my flirting skills were very, very rudimentary—as I recall, the majority of it revolved around "bold" winking, a bit like a mad pirate. I also have a suspicion that my idea of subtly indicating my interest in matters of a sexual nature consisted of little more than saying, "Cor. Sexy intercourse, huh? It's *sexy*," during otherwise perfectly normal conversations about, say, when the lift might arrive.

Almost without exception—and wholly understandably—my superiors at the magazine appeared to regard me as some kind of chimp in a dress who'd climbed in through an open window, and whom they'd decided they would leave alone to quietly play with the computers, lest it become agitated and start biting people. And even if they hadn't been looking at me with borderline horror, I wouldn't have wanted to flirt with them anyway: they were proper grown-ups! Really old! Like, in their thirties! If I ended up getting off with one of them, they might suddenly start talking to me about council tax, or cavity insulation, or grown-up stuff like that, and I would be all at conversational sea. It wasn't appealing at all.

So no. I did not further my career by flirting. Indeed, on the contrary: I suspect my burgeoning sexuality burgeoning all over the place led to the curtailment of a great many offers of work, due to worries about being accused of predating a chain-smoking Lolita. However, I wholeheartedly believe that, should they wish to, strident feminists are allowed to flirt their way to the top, without compromising their strident feminist principles one smidge.

Ladies, we are at a massive disadvantage in the workplace. Your male peers are flirting with their male bosses *constantly*. The average workplace is like fucking *Bromancing the Stone*. That's basically what male bonding is. Flirting. They're flirting with each other playing golf, they're flirting with each other going to football, they're flirting with each other chatting at the urinals—and, sadly, flirting with each other in after-hours visits to strip clubs and pubs. They are bonding with each other over their biological similarities. If the only way you can bond with them is over your biological differences, you go for it. Feel pressured to actually fuck them if you do? Then don't flirt. Find it an easy way to just crack on? Then crack on—and don't blame other women for doing it.

Well, not to their faces, anyway. Bitching in the bathroom is always allowed, of course.

So I am learning about flirting. Not for business—just for fun. God, it's tricky. I've only ever flirted with teenage boys before, who don't really notice it half the time, God bless them. Actually, now I come to think of it, it must have been more than half the time—I am still a virgin. They were obviously not picking up on this stuff at all.

I'm just too subtle, I think at a party a few weeks later. I'm still wearing a huge hat—since I floated the idea in my diary that it might make my body look smaller, by way of perspective, I've never taken it off—a metric meter of eyeliner, and I'm fairly tipsy. Well, I'm doing a "sexy dance" at the bar to "Respect" by Erasure. That's fairly relaxed. "I need to be less subtle. It's not working."

The next time a man comes up to me, we talk about Erasure for five minutes, float the possibility of my moving to the left slightly so he can get served, and then I stare at the man silently.

"You okay?" he asks finally, looking a little perturbed, holding out a fiver to the barman for his beer.

"I was just wondering what it would be like to kiss you," I reply, giving him an intense stare from underneath the hat. At the time I'm not aware of it, but looking back now I suspect I looked like a slightly cross-eyed clam, looking for unwary plankton.

Ten seconds later, and we're kissing. He's stuffing his tongue down my throat like I've been on a hunger strike and he's about to force-feed me with a tube, and I'm doing my level best not to cough him back out again. I am euphoric. My God! Who knew it was this easy! That you can just ask for some sexual contact—and get it! I see now that my previous tactic in Wolverhampton—simply hanging around boys, hoping they might trip over, fall on my face, and then get off with me "while they're there"—was hopelessly amateurish. *This* is the way forward—simply putting in a kissing order, like at Argos!

The next few weeks are revelatory. I essentially put my career on hold to go round getting kissed as much as possible. I learn a great deal about it. I find that, by and large, the best kissers are also the best conversationalists: they kind of . . . listen to what you're doing and reply. One man kisses me right out of my shoes in an alleyway in Soho, and I spend the next three days so high from the experience that I write a six-page poem full of terrible metaphors about stars, anemones, and quicksand. On another kissing night with another man, we both manage to smoke cigarettes all the way through our session, although I do have to demur over his chewing gum: I fish it out of his mouth and dramatically chuck it over my shoulder, saying, "Chew on *me*, instead," in a sultry Wolverhampton accent.

But the music and media industry is a tiny world—essentially a village congregating in the same five or six bars and venues every night. I start to get a "reputation" back at *Melody Maker.* Things start happening in the office I feel uncomfortable with. One writer fills that week's gossip column with barely concealed references to the fact I got off with another writer. A bloke from the art department spends one of our editorial pub sessions making comments about someone else I got off with's premature ejaculation problems—"I hope that dress is wipe-clean."

Then one of the section editors calls me over to his desk and tells me that the feature I've just filed *could* be a cover story, "So why don't you sit on my lap while we talk about it?"

Wow, I think. This is some sexism! Some sexism is happening at me! Even in an office full of forward-thinking liberal outcasts, there are still some people who are judging me for being a sexually active woman! In some respects, it's almost exciting—after all, the last time I was being judged on issues of my sexuality, it ended with the Yobs throwing stones at me on my birthday. If I've gone from being wholly undesirable (then) to being looked down upon as a slag (now), this is, surely, a bit of a promotion? Becoming a woman has to be done one step at a time, and this is, in its own way, considerable progress.

On the other hand, I'm initially stumped about what to do about it. I've read novels about the patriarchy judging sexually active women, but those books don't give me a great deal of advice on what to do next. By and large, those women end up dying on moors, being excluded by the society of Atlanta, or swallowing arsenic, before their daughter is sent off to work in the cotton mills. The coping tactics of grown women in the 19th century give me little to work on, and so—without any better role models—I simply regress into the coping methods of my childhood. As the eldest of eight children who regularly punch each other, my tactic at *Melody Maker* is just to go a bit . . . gonzo. I require the guy from the art department with his "wipe-clean dress" comments to buy me a double, for "injury to feelings." The writer who defamed me in the gossip column is told to stand on a chair in front of the whole office and apologize to me, while I point at him and say, "That column didn't even have any *jokes* in it." I can think of no worse insult.

And when the section editor asks me to sit on his lap, in order to discuss my "promotion," I think, merely, more fool you, dude, and plonk down on him, heavily, then light a fag.

"Lost your circulation yet?" I ask cheerfully, as he sweats and coughs.

I get my first front cover. He spends ten minutes in the conference room, banging his thighs until he gets the circulation back in his legs.

On the one hand, I can see why I have become a bit of a running gag in the office. I am, let's be fair, acting like a sexed-up lady Pac-Man—running around flapping my mouth open and closed, gobbling up people's faces. It's certainly worth a good 100 gags or so. Hell, I'm making about 50 on the topic myself.

But the jokes aren't "amused" jokes. There's an odd air to the comments; there's a kind of . . . poking, pinching, mean quality to them. And I notice that these jokes aren't being made about the men in the office who are kissing me. There's a kind of *crushing* element to them. It feels like these jokes are coming from a dark place. A darkness is what I sense, as I walk out of the office for the day, smoking a fag to prove I'm a grown-up, and still one of them. An uncomfortable darkness.

These days, sexism is a bit like Meryl Streep in a new film: sometimes you don't recognize it straightaway. You can be up to 20 minutes in, enjoying all the dinosaurs and the space fights and the homesick Confederate soldiers, before you go, "Oh, my God—under the wig! THAT'S MERYL."

Very often, a woman can have left a party, caught the bus home, washed her face, got into bed, read 20 minutes of *The Female Eunuch*, and put the light out before she puts the light back on again, sits bolt upright, and shouts, "Hang on—I'VE JUST HAD SOME SEXISM THROWN AT ME. THAT WAS SOME SEXISM! WHEN THAT MAN CALLED ME "SUGAR TITS"—THAT WAS SEXISM, AND NOT AN HONEST MISPRONUNCIATION OF THE NAME 'ANDREA'!"

It never used to be like this, of course—before the second wave of feminism, political correctness, and women having Mace in their handbag, sexism used to be both overt and everywhere. You knew it when you met it. It was all, "Know your limits, women," "Make us a cup of tea, love," "Look at the rack on THAT," and wolf whistles from any passing male over the age of 12.

Benny Hill chasing a blonde round and round a desk, making "honk honk" gestures with his hands, wasn't "light entertainment" back then. It was a simple fact of life. Sexism—like ashtrays, Bay City Rollers, and the smell of BO—was everywhere: no matter how inappropriate the setting. I rewatched *Gregory's Girl* recently—Bill Forsyth's lovely, fluffy, heartwarming film about the girl who's good at football and wants to play on the school team—and was amazed to note a scene where the guy teaching cookery gropes schoolgirl Susan's arse and she just saunters away, and neither she nor the film has any comment to make. In *Gregory's Girl*!

The film that I'd remembered as being essentially *Vindication of the Rights of Women* for anyone who, at the time, slept under a Holly Hobby duvet!

And no one even *thought* to complain at the time—because if you were cheerfully and publicly touching up a schoolgirl, it was just good, healthy British perving. Wench-handling. Part of our heritage, like cheese rolling, and drowning malformed babies in cider barrels.

And, of course—like half-timbered buildings and Stonehenge—there is still plenty of this old-fashioned sexism around today. I asked on Twitter if anyone had experienced any outrageous sexism recently, and while I was expecting quite a few amusingly stereotyped clangers, I wasn't expecting the deluge that started 30 seconds after I inquired, and which carried on for nearly four days afterward.

In the end, I had nearly 2,000 replies—which, as they stacked up, very rapidly turned into a gigantic debate among women who'd all presumed their cases were more isolated than they were.

Here are the ones that made me actually gasp:

"I had a boss who said, 'We all have a wank thinking about Rosie—but I'm the only one who's got an office to do it in.'"

"A guy jumped out of a car and stuck his hand up my skirt to see if I was wearing stocking or tights as I stood at a bus queue."

"I once worked in a Ford garage where the rest of the staff would shout TITTIES as I walked across the workshop."

So that's old-fashioned sexism: as slow-moving yet obvious as the giant boulder in *Raiders of the Lost Ark*. And in some ways, however ghastly, depressing, and enervating it is, I miss it. It is an increasingly complex world out there, after all. Over the years, all kinds of sexism variables have sprung up, muddying the waters. Now, there are *female* chauvinist pigs, and men trading in "ironic sexism," whereby calling you Tits McGee and telling you to go and "make us a friend egg sandwich" is technically not sexism but "a laugh," which you must "laugh" along to.

These days, a plethora of shitty attitudes to women have become diffuse, indistinct, or almost entirely concealed. Fighting them feels like trying to combat a moldy mildew smell in the hallway, using only a bread knife. Because—like racism, anti-Semitism, and homophobia—modern sexism has become cunning. Sly. Codified. In the same way a closet racist would never dream of openly saying "nigger" but might make a pointed reference to someone black having natural rhythm or liking fried chicken, so a closet misogynist has a vast array of words, comments, phrases, and attitudes that he can employ to subtly put a woman down or disconcert her, but without it being immediately apparent that that is what he is actually doing.

Take, for instance, a small dispute in the office. You have had a difference of opinion about a project. A male colleague has taken it quite badly and stomped off. When he returns, he places a packet of Tampax on your desk.

"Given how emotional you've been, I thought you might need these," he says, with a grin. A couple of people snigger.

What are you to do? Obviously, had you more resources, you would be able to reach in to your desk drawer, pull out a pair of testicles, and place them on the desk, replying, "And given how spineless you were over our last contretemps, I thought you might need *these*," but, alas, even the most prepared woman in the world is unlikely to have a spare pair of rubber knackers in her desk.

Or how about a social situation? You've gone on holiday with another family. You all have children. You notice that the men are doing around half the amount of housework and child care that the women are—they have an amazing ability to sit in an armchair, serenely playing Angry Birds on their iPhones, while the wives run around peeling potatoes and rescuing wailing, shit-encrusted toddlers from disused wells.

"I'm just not as good at that stuff," the men say, almost mournfully, as the women stand in the kitchen, stressed, knocking back shots of whiskey from 4 p.m. onward.

Again, ideally, you'd be prepared for this: perhaps having taught your older children to quote *The Female Eunuch* from memory in exchange for a Milky Way. Or maybe you'd have an iPhone app called "Division of Domestic Labor Tracker, 1600–Present Day," which you could fire up and leave on the table, next to the beer, for the men to have a look at. But again, who has the time for these delightful schemes?

When I asked the ladies of Twitter for their instances of sexism, it was, in the end, the more codified examples that were disturbing. Kate, who explained that she "no longer wears a white top and black skirt to meetings, since a queue formed in front of me at a coffee break. They all presumed I was a waitress." Or Hannah, who—on being made redundant—was comforted by her boss with the comment "Don't worry, love—at least you still have great legs."

Of course, the reason these instances are so pernicious and damaging is the element of doubt involved. Are they being sexist on purpose or is it just some accidental sexism, due to carelessness and stupidity? The "great legs" comment, for instance—that could just be an extremely cloddish attempt at condolence, rather than the implied assumption that the only thing that matters for a woman is looking good and that, as long as she still looks nice in a short skirt, she'll be *fine* in the workplace, although, obviously, buggered when she gets older and starts wearing comfy shoes and slacks.

Are you going to look like a screaming, humorless harridan if you call people out on this? Should you just shruggingly let it pass when someone your inferior sees you standing next to a tea urn and asks you for "Milk, no sugar—and you got any HobNobs?"

In short, *how can you tell when some sexism is happening to you?*

Well, in this matter, what ultimately aids us is to simply apply this question to the issue: Is this polite? If we—the entire population of the earth, male and female alike—are just, essentially, "the guys," then was one of the guys just . . . uncouth to a fellow guy?

Don't call it sexism. Call it "manners" instead. When a woman blinks a little, shakes her head like Columbo, and says, "I'm sorry, but that sounded a little . . . uncivil," a man is apt to apologize. Because even the most rampant bigot on earth has no defense against a charge of simply being rude.

After all, you can argue—argue until you cry—about what modern, codified misogyny is; but straight-up ungentlemanliness, of the kind his mother would clatter the back of his head for, is inarguable. It doesn't need to be a "man vs. woman" thing. It's just a tiff between the guys.

Seeing the whole world as "the guys" is important. The idea that we're all, at the end of the day, just a bunch of well-meaning schlumps trying to get along is the basic alpha and omega of my worldview. I'm neither "pro-women" nor "anti-men." I'm just "Thumbs up for the six billion."

Because I don't think that "men"/maleness/male sexuality is the problem here. I don't think sexism is a "man vs. woman" thing. The Man is not The Man simply because he's a man. Sometimes, The Man is a woman—particularly if you go to the kind of late-night clubs I do, although that's a different issue altogether. Men don't do this shit to women just because of their "female-ness." AND I DON'T THINK IT'S ABOUT SEX.

As I start to watch men and women interacting in the adult arena—in work, relationships, and marriages but mainly, to be fair, in the pub—I don't come to believe, as many people, including the Goddess Greer, do, that men secretly hate women. That men hate women because there is something about penis and testosterone that wants to wage war on vagina and estrogen.

No. Even though I'm quite drunk half the time, and often wearing so much eyeliner that I am technically blind, I don't see it as man vs. woman at all. What I see, instead, is winner vs. loser.

Most sexism is down to men being accustomed to us being the losers. That's what the problem is. We just have bad status. Men are accustomed to us being runners-up or being disqualified entirely. For men born prefeminism, this is what they were raised on: second-class citizen mothers; sisters who needed to be married off; female schoolmates going to secretarial school, then becoming housewives. Women who disengaged. Disappeared.

These men are the CEOs of our big companies, the big guys on the stock markets, the advisors to governments. They dictate working hours and maternity leave, economic priorities and societal mores. And, of *course*, they don't feel equality in their bones—sexism runs deep in their generation, along with a liking for boiled puddings, spanking, and golf. Their automatic reaction is to regard women as "other." The entrenched bias against the working, liberated female will only die out when they do.

Even those men born postfeminism, raised on textbooks and marches and their own mothers leaving each morning for the office, however much they might believe in the *theoretical* equality of women and respect those around them, are scarcely unaware of the great sweep of history that went before. A quiet voice inside—suppressed but never wholly silenced—says, "If women are the true equals of men, where's the proof?" And it is not just a voice inside men. It is inside women, too.

Even the most ardent feminist historian, male *or* female—citing Amazons and tribal matriarchies and Cleopatra—can't conceal that women have basically done fuck-all for the last 100,000 years. Come on—let's admit it. Let's stop exhaustingly pretending that there is a parallel history of women being victorious and creative, on an equal with men, that's just been comprehensively covered up by The Man. There isn't. Our empires, armies, cities, artworks, philosophers, philanthropists, inventors, scientists, astronauts, explorers, politicians, and icons could all fit, comfortably, into one of the private karaoke booths in SingStar. We have no Mozart; no Einstein; no Galileo; no Gandhi. No Beatles, no Churchill, no Hawking, no Columbus. It just didn't happen.

Nearly everything so far has been the creation of men—and a liberal, right-on denial of it makes everything more awkward and difficult in the long run. Pretending that women have had a pop at all this before but just ultimately didn't do as well as the men, that the experiment of female liberation has already happened but floundered, gives strength to the belief that women simply aren't as good as men, full stop. That things should just carry on as they are—with the world shaped around, and honoring, the priorities, needs, whims, and successes of men. Women are over, without having even begun. When the truth is that we haven't begun *at all*. Of course we haven't. We'll know it when we have.

I see the wrongness of this presumption in the office. *Melody Maker* is filled with good, liberal men. Whatever sexism I've experienced, it was with the people the rest of the office considered to be sad nutters: by and large, this group of rock critics are as feminist a bunch of men as I'll ever know. One of them ends up being my husband and teaches me more about the bullshit men project on women than any woman ever does. In his cardigan, with his carrier bag full of Field Mice and ABBA records, a 23-year-old Greek boy from Birmingham ends up rivaling Germaine Greer as my feminist hero.

But this is all in the future. Here, in 1993, I am sitting in the

office on a desk, smoking. I am watching liberal men tie themselves in knots trying to square their ardent belief that women are
equal to men with the evidence that there just aren't that many
great records made by women. Every six weeks or so, in an editorial meeting, the guys look around at the music scene of the
time—all grunge or Blur or whatever—and despair, "Jesus, we've
got to get some women in the paper! We've just got to get . . .
some women!"

And so we'd get Sonya from Echobelly, say, to take part in a
"debate" on the future of Radio 1. Or Louise Wener from Sleeper
to review the singles. Or—in an emergency—just print a picture
of Debbie Harry somewhere. A conscious effort had to be made
because in those days, there were no birds.

You couldn't find a woman making music for love nor money.
This was a pre–Spice Girl, pre-Gaga era, remember—when it was
presumed that there was no mass market for women making pop
music. And that's presuming they could make music in the first
place. Legendary enfant terrible and rock critic Julie Burchill, of
all people, summed up the presumptions of many when she said,
"A girl in a dress with a guitar looks weird—like a dog riding a
bicycle. Very odd. Hard to get past it."

What we were all thinking, but were too embarrassed to say,
was that women simply had less to say than men. It had, after all,
been over 70 years since women had been given the vote and yet,
as far as the music scene was concerned, we had little more than
a handful of female geniuses to show for it: Joni Mitchell, Carole
King, PJ Harvey, Patti Smith, Kate Bush, Madonna, Billie Holiday.
Few enough to be regarded as freakish anomalies rather than the
first outriders on a forthcoming storm. There was still no female
rock band to rival Led Zeppelin, or Guns N' Roses. No female
hip-hop artist to rival Public Enemy or the Wu-Tang Clan. No
female dance artist to rival Richie "Plastikman" Hawtin or the

Prodigy. And what all-female band would you put up against the might of the Beatles? The Runaways? The Go-Gos? The Slits? The disparity was laughable. But we could never, ever mention it. The truth sounded sexist.

Creativity, we silently fretted, should really have begun the moment legislation changed. All manner of female incredible-ness—pent up for centuries—should have been unleashed; flat-tening trees for thousands of miles around, like a pyroclastic blast.

But they didn't. Because simply being able to vote isn't the same as true equality. It's difficult to see the glass ceiling because it's made of glass. Virtually invisible. What we need is for more birds to fly above it and shit all over it, so we can see it properly.

In the meantime, we had Echobelly on the cover.

"Do you want to go and interview her?" the editor asked. The unspoken follow-up sentence was "Because you're a girl."

"No," I said. I knew they were awful.

So why, then, *didn't* we do anything?

Based on my own personal experiences, 100,000 years of male superiority has its origins in the simple basis that men don't get cystitis. Why wasn't it a woman who discovered the Americas in 1492? Because in a pre-antibiotic era, what woman would dare risk getting halfway across the Atlantic, then spend the rest of the voy-age clamped to the toilet crying and occasionally shouting, "Can anyone see New York yet? Get me a hot dog," out of the porthole?

We are, physically, the weaker sex. We're not as good at hefting stones, killing mammoths, and rowing boats. In addition, sex often had the added complication of getting us pregnant and leaving us feeling "too fat" to lead an army into India. It's not a coincidence that efforts toward female emancipation only got going under the twin exegeses of industrialization and contraception—when ma-chines made us the equal of men in the workplace, and the Pill made us the equal of men in expressing our desire. In more primitive times—what I would personally regard as any time before the release of *Working Girl* in 1988—the winners were always going to be those both physically strong enough to punch an antelope to the ground and whose libido didn't end up with them getting pregnant, then dying in childbirth.

So to the powerful came education, discussion, and the conception of "normality." Being a man and men's experiences were considered "normal": everything else was other. And as "other"— without cities, philosophers, empires, armies, politicians, explorers, scientists, and engineers—women were the losers. I don't think that women being seen as inferior is a prejudice based on male hatred of women. When you look at history, it's a prejudice based on simple fact.

Oddly, however, I don't feel like I can talk about sexism with other women. It feels too tender a point to discuss with them. All the women I know are strong feminists working in male environments—journalists, editors, PRs, computer programmers—but they are too busy at this point—1993—just *getting on* with stuff to have big debates about it. Besides, it is the beginning of Britpop, the dawn of the Ladette. As young women essentially at play—with no children, no child care worries, no sudden stalling of their careers in their thirties, as the men inexplicably start to sail past them—things still feel hopeful. In this era of Doc Martens and beer and minimal makeup, sexism seems to be dying so fast it would be counterproductive to draw attention to it. We all, naively, presume it is a problem of another age, and that things are getting better and better by the day. We don't know what's coming toward us—Brazilians, and another decade and a half of unequal pay. In an era of PJ Harvey, we cannot imagine the Pussycat Dolls.

But I do have conversations about the patriarchy. And I am having them with gay men. At 18, I am discovering what generations of women have long known: that the natural ally of the straight woman is the gay man. Because they are "other"—losers—too.

"Do you think they won't notice you're a woman?" Charlie says.

We're in a shabby café in Camden, eating spaghetti Bolognese. I live in London now—queuing up in Barclays Bank, Queen Square, Wolverhampton, on my 18th birthday, the very first hour I could legally get an overdraft and move out. I have a house in Camden where I am the world's most disorganized tenant: the phone is so regularly cut off that people start leaving messages for me in the nearby pub, the Good Mixer, instead. I leave a lit candle on top of the television and it melts right through to the cathode tube. Not that it matters. The electric's been cut off, too. I haven't watched the TV in months.

Coming to this café every lunchtime and eating spaghetti Bolognese, £3.75, still feels like the height of sophistication and grown-up-ness. Look at me! Eating out! Eating *foreign*! With a *homosexual*!

"Because they always do, you know," Charlie says. "They notice you're a woman straightaway. I used to think they didn't notice I was gay, too. But they do."

"It's not that there's anything terribly wrong," I say, almost apologetically. "I mean, they're not keeping me in a Rape Cupboard or anything. It's just . . ."

I sigh.

"It's just . . . oh, everything I say seems a bit weird and wrong," I say. "I'm not *normal*. I just feel like a twat. Yes, I'm reclaiming the word. Shut up."

I am still smarting from a conversation I had today at *Melody*

Maker. The big new thing is an American movement called "Riot Grrrl"—a hard-core, punk-feminist scene where band members eschew talking to the mainstream press, disseminate fanzines, ban boys from the mosh pit, and scrawl revolutionary slogans on their bodies in lipstick and marker pen.

Courtney Love is a figurehead—and through her, Kurt Cobain and Nirvana are allied. As I now work for *The Times* as a rock critic, I mentioned in conversation that I think Riot Grrrl bands should do interviews with the mainstream press, since the kind of girls who really *need* a hard-core feminist movement—in council blocks, listening to Radio 1, fantasizing about New Kids on the Block—are unlikely to come across a photocopied Riot Grrrl fanzine being handed out outside a Sebadoh gig. Any revolution worth its salt needs to get its message across to as many people as possible. Ipso facto, Huggy Bear should do an interview with me.

Halfway through this speech, I am shouted down by a male editor, who dismisses everything I say out of hand and concludes his argument with the statement "You wouldn't know what it's like to be a fat teenage girl, being shouted at in the street by arseholes."

At the time, I *am* a fat teenage girl, being shouted at in the street by arseholes. I am rendered silent with astonishment that I am being lectured on a radical feminist youth movement by a middle-age, straight white man.

"It's like he thinks he understands *everything* better than me—even *me*!" I tell Charlie, getting indignant again. "It's boiling my piss—a piss that, incidentally, I am having to queue up for *twice* as long as he is at any gig."

"Oh, I get it all the time," Charlie says cheerfully. "It's mainly conversations about how difficult it is to be a gay man—explained to me by a straight man. The problem is, straight men don't know that much about us, do they?"

"We're very mysterious," I agree, as spaghetti dangles from my mouth.

"Well, we are, aren't we?" Charlie says. "I mean, think of all those films or TV shows where there's one woman, or one gay, in a script otherwise full of straight men, written by a straight man. Or a book. Fiction and film is full of these imaginary gay men and straight women, saying what straight men imagine we would say and doing what straight men imagine we would do. Every gay I ever see has an ex-lover dying of AIDS. Fucking *Philadelphia*. I've started to think I should get an AIDS boyfriend, just to be normal."

"Yeah—and all the women are always just really 'good' and sensible, and keep putting the men, with their crazy ideas and their boyish idealism, into check," I say mournfully. "And they're *never* funny. WHY CAN'T I EVER SEE A FUNNY LADY?"

"Imaginary *Jewish* women can be funny," Charlie points out. "But they also have to be neurotic, and never get a boyfriend."

"Maybe I should convert," I say gloomily. "I'll go down to the synagogue and get one of those candlesticks, and you go down to the Elton John Aids Foundation and pull. Then we'll be proper."

"Still, we've got it easy compared to the lesbians," Charlie says, getting the bill. "There isn't a single lesbian in Britain, apart from Huffty."

As I chuck my fags into my bag, I have an idle, stupid thought. I know what I need to do next, I think. I need to get a boyfriend. A boyfriend would make everything better.

CHAPTER 8

I Am in Love!

A year later, and I am in love. He's the One. Obviously, I thought the one before him was the One, and the one before that was the One, too. Frankly, I'm so into the idea of being in love that *anyone* out of about three million could be the One.

But, no—this, now, is *definitely* the One. The very One. I am walking down Monet-gray pavements in Hampstead in March, hand in hand, and I am so in love. Admittedly I feel terrible, and he's a total arsehole, but I am in love. Finally. By sheer force of will. I've got a person, all of my own.

"You walk funny," he says in an oddly needling way. "You don't walk like a fat girl."

I have no idea what he means. I let go of his hand. I'm in love. Christ, it's miserable.

So yes, he's a boy in a band—the first boy in a band I could get. Insanely talented, very beautiful, but also very lazy, and definitely troubled. His band gets nowhere because he refuses to do "shitty gigs" he thinks are beneath him. He writes four or five songs a year but then spends months discussing each one, as if they had been number one for weeks and changed the world, instead of sitting on C90 tapes, unmixed and unfinished, scattered across my floor.

He says he hates his mother—when I ask him why, he tells a long story that ends with him throwing the lid of a tub of Flora margarine at her during an argument and her fainting. I don't understand that, either, but I agree with him that she sounds awful.

But why are they eating Flora? I wonder. If I were as rich as them, I'd eat butter every day.

Even though we are going out with each other, and he's moved into my flat, I don't think he likes me. When I write, he sits next to me on a chair and explains at great length how he's more talented than me. When we're with friends, he'll make a joke and—when I laugh—snap, "Why are you laughing? You don't understand what I'm talking about."

My family hate him: when my brother Eddie comes to stay with us, he accidentally spills a bottle of strawberry-flavored Yop on my boyfriend's suede jacket, and my boyfriend goes absolutely mental at this 13-year-old boy. Eddie cries. We have to leave my house and sit on the steps outside, smoking fags while I apologize to Eddie over and over again.

Caz is very brisk about him: "He is a cock. You were better off when you were just cohabiting with the mice in your kitchen. He's a short man with a girl's name—and that's trouble."

His name is Courtney. And he is quite short, and very thin: he's definitely smaller than me. I feel like I'm too big for him. This is a problem. I feel like if I stood up straight, I'd crush him. I start smoking a lot of weed, to make myself smaller, and quieter.

Love is the drugs, I think, rolling a joint at 11 a.m. Love is the drugs. All you need is drugs.

Besides, I'm not an amazing catch myself. I'm a teenage girl living in a house with the electricity cut off. I wake at 2 p.m. and go to bed at dawn. I'm pretty nuts: having scored an amazing job, where I present a late-night music show on Channel 4 called *Naked City*, I've become fractionally famous and have discovered that being fractionally famous consists, by and large, of drunk people coming up to you at gigs, saying, "You're shit!" and walking away again.

Not all of them say, "You're shit!"—some of them say, "You're great!" but in a way, that's worse. Because when lots of other people have said, "You're shit!" you feel you have a duty to tell the people who say, "You're great!" that a lot of other people think you're shit and that they should maybe bear those statistics in mind before they make their final analysis. And if you're trying to say all of this while you're quite drunk—as I almost always am—then people are apt to stare at you in deep confusion after a minute or two, and then make their apologies and leave.

So I'm sort of messy and fuzzy, and by turns belligerent—"I'm great! People say so!"—and weeply—"I'm shit! People say so!" I fall downstairs drunk quite a lot. Over at Pete from *Melody Maker*'s house, I get tearful and sit under the table all night, crying. Most of all—despite waiting my whole life to leave home—I'm missing my family. At night, when I lie in bed with Courtney—someone I can have sex with! A clever boy!—I find myself thinking of my double bed back in Wolverhampton, with my sister Prinnie in it, alone now.

I may often have woken up soaked in her urine but I always felt safe there, I think, as I lie in the dark. I wish Prinnie was in the bed, instead of Courtney. Little Prinnie with her gobstopper eyes, smelling of biscuits and earth and puppies, warm. When she used to wake up in the night, I would tell her stories about Judy Garland and stroke her hair until she fell back to sleep.

When Courtney wakes up in the night, he moans about how his hair is thinning, until he falls back to sleep again—leaving me restless, depressed, and awake. I'd never known how alone you can feel lying next to someone.

But I am also absolutely determined to be in love. I figure this will probably . . . knock the edges off me. It's love as a lesson, and a penance. I don't think Courtney will kill me, so he will, therefore, probably make me stronger. I will learn from this. I listen to Janis Joplin a lot. I believe in feeling bad for love. I think it is, somehow, glorious. I am stupid. I am so stupid.

Along with underwear, love is a woman's work. Women are to be fallen in love with. When we discuss the great tragedies that can possibly befall a woman, once we have discounted war and injury, it is the idea of being unloved, and therefore unwanted, that we wince over the most. Elizabeth I may have laid the groundworks of the British Empire, but she could never marry—poor, pale, mercury-caked queen. Jennifer Aniston is a beautiful, successful millionairess who lives in a beach house in LA and will never have to stand in a queue to post a pair of boots back to Topshop's online return department with a head cold—and yet her entire thirties were written off as the decade in which she just could not keep hold of first Brad Pitt, and then John Mayer. Princess Diana—so unlucky! Cheryl Cole—lonely! Hilary Swank and Reese Witherspoon—got those Oscars, but their husbands left them!

Language tells us exactly what we think of the unattached woman—it's all there in the difference between "bachelors" and "spinsters." Bachelors have it all to play for. Spinsters must play for it all, and fast. The market demand tells you a woman's value: if she is single, she is unwanted, and therefore—should this state of affairs go on for any length of time—less desirable.

So given the importance women know is attached to them being attached, it is little wonder that women are obsessed with the idea of love and relationships. We think about them all the time. Sometimes, when I tell men about the way women think about potential relationships, they start to look very, very alarmed. Discuss the same thing with women, however, and they will give a shamed bark of recognition.

Take, for instance, the average office or workplace. Within a mixed-sex staff, there will be obvious flirtations going on, all more or less apparent to the curious observer. We know all this.

But if you had some manner of Psychic Helmet that you could put on in order to read the women's thoughts, any man donning it would be instantly terrified by the previously concealed levels of female insanity it revealed.

Look at that woman in the corner—a perfectly normal, non-psychotic section manager, with a pleasant and easy demeanor toward everyone she works with. As far as anyone is aware, she doesn't really fancy anyone in the office. She appears to be writing a long, important email. But do you know what she's really doing? She's thinking about that bloke five desks away that she's only talked to about ten times.

"If we went away for a long weekend together, we couldn't go to Paris—he went there with his ex-girlfriend," she's thinking. "I know. He mentioned it once. I remember. I'm not going to go tromping around the Louvre if he's comparing me, in my spring mac, to her, in *her* spring mac. Not that we'd be going in spring, anyway—given where we are in our relationship now, if he made the first move TODAY, the earliest we'd be going on long weekends would be"—counts up on fingers—"November, and it would be really rainy, and my hair would go all flat. I'd need an umbrella."

"But," she continues, typing angrily, "if I had an umbrella, then we wouldn't be able to hold hands because I'd have the brolly in one hand and my handbag in the other. So that would be shit. UN-LESS! UNLESS I could fit everything I needed in my pockets! Then I wouldn't have to *take* a handbag to the Louvre. But I'd be without spare tights if I got splashed, and I'd have to go bare-legged, and it would be so cold that my legs would look all purple, and I'd be tense when we went back to the hotel to fuck, and I'd be trying to hide them with a towel, and he'd think I was prick-teasing him, and go off me. OH, FOR FUCK'S SAKE. WHY IS HE TAKING US TO PARIS IN NOVEMBER? I HATE HIM."

She doesn't even fancy this bloke. She's barely even spoken to him. If he asked her out for a drink, she'd probably say no. She has no desire to have an actual relationship with him. And yet, next time he talks to her, she'll be a trifle curt with him and he—in his wildest, most opium-fueled imaginings—would never come *close* to guessing why that might be. Maybe he would shruggingly presume she was premenstrual, or just having a bad day.

He would never alight upon the simple truth: that they went on a very bad imaginary long weekend to Paris together and broke up over some tights.

I imagine possible relationships all the time. All the time. My God, in my teens I was fucking *tragic* for it. I scarcely existed in the real world at all. I lived in some kind of . . . Sex Narnia. My love life was busy, exciting, and totally imaginary.

My first serious relationship was conducted with a famous co-median of the time and took place wholly in my head. I'd never met him, spoken to him, or even been in the same room as him—and yet, during one train ride from Wolverhampton to London Euston, I had one of the most intense relationship experiences of my life: all daydreamed. We'd obviously meet at a party, I thought. We'd banter, in the manner of *His Girl Friday*, amuse each other greatly, and become writing partners before finally graduating into witty, ardent lovers.

As the train sped through Coventry, I imagined our house, our dinner party, our social circle, our pets. By the time I reached

Rugby, I was imagining the pair of us appearing on *Wogan*, talking about our new project—a ditzy rom-com, currently smashing box-office records.

"But the period of writing was not without tragedy, was it?" Terry Wogan asked, leaning forward and doing his "sensitive face."

"No, Terry," I said, tearing up. I could feel Camera One zooming in for a close-up. "Halfway through writing, we . . . we lost our first baby. I was devastated. It would have been so loved, and so wanted. Dealing with that kind of loss is just . . . it's like having a trapdoor open up in your heart."

The famous comedian put his arm around me, silently.

"Caitlin was amazing," he said, wiping his eye with his shirt cuff. "She would not give up on the script. During the days, she was a lioness. But at night—at night, we'd cry ourselves to sleep."

It became one of the most famous interviews of Wogan's career—not least because the camera caught a tear on his cheek, too, as he wrapped up the interview to go over to PJ & Duncan playing their new single, "Let's Get Ready to Rhumble."

Imagining all of this, I became so hysterical with grief that, by the time I got to Euston, I had to go into the Ladies and put my head under the cold tap. Even now—17 years later—I can still feel quite maudlin remembering it. In many ways, it's still one of the most memorable relationships of my life. In an hour-and-a-half-long train journey, I'd met the love of my life, won an Oscar, lost a baby, grieved, made Terry Wogan weep on prime-time BBC1, and inspired PJ & Duncan's second single, "Too Many Tears (For a Beautiful Lady)."

When it got to number one, at Christmas, the video featured a classy black-and-white picture of me in an ornate frame, looking noble, which PJ & Duncan sang to, in the snow.

Obviously, I know all this sounds insane. And perhaps it's a *slightly* extreme example. *Slightly*. And it did make finally meeting that comedian at a party quite tricky—a friend, noticing I was drunk, had to bodily *drag* me from the room, going, "DON'T SAY ANYTHING TO HIM! TRY TO REMEMBER IT ONLY HAP-PENED IN YOUR HEAD! YOU HAVE NOTHING ACTUAL TO REMINISCE ABOUT!"

But nearly every woman I know has a roughly similar story—in fact, dozens of them: stories about being obsessed with a celebrity, work colleague, or someone they vaguely knew for *years*; living in a parallel world in their head; conjuring up endless plots and scenarios for this thing that never actually happened.

On the days where I have to rationalize this insanity to myself, I postulate that these intense crushes are a necessary evolutionary by-product of being a woman. As our fertility window is so short—allowing maybe a handful of serious, reproductively potential relationships before menopause—these serious fantasies are by way of "test runs," allowing women to run through entire possible relationships in their heads, to see if they'd ultimately work out or not. Like a computer running through algorithms.

But this febrile ability to have intense, imaginary relationships often spills over into relationships that actually exist, blurring the line between the real relationship and the imagined one. Sometimes, this is wholly benign. Who doesn't have a friend who worships her lover with a passion that seems baffling to everyone who knows them? Before you met him for the first time, she'd talked him up like he was a cross between Indiana Jones, Barack Obama, and Jon Stewart. When you finally meet him, he's a quiet little thing who looks like a baked bean in glasses and actually says "harumph" as spelled.

"I can't believe I agreed, in advance, to a weekend away with them," you think, dolorously pouring a treble into your mug. "She is dating the Bony King of Nowhere.com."

And other times, of course, this ability to live in an imaginary relationship becomes positively unhelpful in affairs that are, for whatever reason, unsatisfactory, faltering, or nugatory.

As soon as my friends and I start dating for real, we enter an exhausting paradox—a belief that, in love, everything is not as it seems: the conviction that there is a common state of affairs whereby a man can be madly in love with you and wish to spend the rest of his life with you, but will indicate this in a variety of ways so subtle, only the truly talented and determined will discern his true desires. Like it's *The Da Vinci Code*, and when a man takes you out to dinner, gets off with you, then doesn't call for two weeks, there's a *secret challenge* he's setting you that—with enough algebra, consultation of ancient scrolls, and wailing on the phone to your female friends—you can decode and, eventually, get married, i.e., win.

"Listen to this email," a friend will say. "He's put, 'Rachel, good to see you! Great night! We should do it again sometime.' That's really noncommittal, isn't it?"

"It does sound fairly noncommittal, yes," I will agree.

"But then," Rachel will go on, using the special "slightly mad" tone of voice all women use during these conversations, "he sent it at 4 p.m."

She pauses. I make a confused sound.

"4 p.m.!" she says again. "So he would still have been at work when he sent it! So maybe he was worried someone might look over his shoulder and see it, so he's kept it deliberately a little cool. I mean, he put 'XXX' at the bottom. That's his way of making it intimate again, yeah?"

"Rachel," I will say. "You put 'XXX' on the bottom of emails to the Inland Revenue. Everyone does it."

"I looked at his Facebook page, and he's changed his favorite songs list and included 'Here Comes the Hotstepper' by Ini Kamoze. AND WE WERE TALKING ABOUT INI KAMOZE DURING DINNER!"

"Rachel, I think that if he liked you, he'd just . . . spend a lot more time with you, and say things like, 'I really like you,'" I say.

"But don't you think that's kind of . . . significant, though?" Rachel will plead. "I don't think you change your Facebook play-list FOR NO REASON AT ALL. *It's a message to me.*"

After an hour of this, I give up trying to persuade her that none of this means anything at all. There's no point in trying. Even shouting, "HE'S JUST NOT THAT INTO YOU" while sounding a klaxon doesn't work. She's in the Girl Matrix—trying to catch invisible, slo-mo bullets those of us outside the Matrix can't see.

You can always tell when a woman is with the wrong man, because she has so much to say about the fact that nothing's happening.

When women find the right person, on the other hand, they just . . . disappear for six months, and then resurface, eyes shiny, and usually about six pounds heavier.

"So what's he *like?*" you will say, waiting for the usual cloud-burst of things he says and things he does and requests of analysis of what you think it means that his favorite film is *Star Wars* ("Trapped in adolesence—or in touch with his inner child?").

But she will be oddly quiet.

"It's just . . . good," she will say. "I'm really happy."

When—four hours later—she gets really drunk, there will be one dazzling frank discussion about how good he is in bed. "Honestly, the size of his penis makes it a borderline medical emergency," she'll say with impossible cheeriness.

And then that will usually be the end of the discussion. Usually forever. You stop talking about things when you've worked them out. You're no longer an observer but a participant. You're too busy for this bullshit.

I am talking about Courtney to everyone. I am a bore. It feels like our relationship is a gigantic puzzle—a huge existential and emotional quiz that, if I apply myself to it enough, I will solve and gain the result of True Love. After all, all the ingredients for us to be the perfect couple are there: he's a man, I'm a woman, and we live in the same house. All the other stuff—compatibility, courtesy, tenderness, not wanting to kill each other—are little things I can finesse, if I think about them enough.

Caz bears the brunt of my attempts to decipher the answer. I found my phone bills from that era recently, and they show, in their column of neat figures, how I called her every night: 11 p.m. to 1 a.m., 2 a.m., 3 a.m. Hours of talking. It's amazing how much you can find to say when there's one big thing you're too afraid to say: "This isn't working."

The problem is that I am the problem. Courtney is just unhappy. I know that. I know it in my bones. When I find the way to make him happy, everything will be fine. He's broken, and I must fix him—and then the good bit of our relationship will start to happen. This is just the tricky, early bit of love, where I undo all the bad stuff and let him finally be who he is, secretly, inside. Secretly, inside, he does love me. My steadfastness will prove it. If it doesn't work, it's simply because I didn't try hard enough.

This is all proven when I find his diary while he's out. I know I *shouldn't* read it—but, in a way, I'm reading it *for us*. If it *is* a betrayal, then it's one of those *good* betrayals you hear so much about. A *love* betrayal. Because if I find out what he's *really* thinking, then this relationship will finally blossom.

The entries are fairly unequivocal. "She's mad," he writes, of me. "When is she going to start taking me to celebrity parties?

I'm stuck at home, bored. When is this going to be good for my career?"

Further entries reveal he's still in love with a girl from his hometown, who dumped him three years ago.

Decoding this as Courtney merely feeling "insecure" in our relationship, I redouble my efforts. I buy underwear from Ann Summers that makes me look like a prostitute, but in a bad way. I cook for him—a constant cavalcade of chicken soups, loaves of bread, and cakes, to make our house seem like a home. I stroke his head when he complains about how little success his band is having, crushing the music journalist thoughts in my head like, Well, if you actually *played* a couple of fucking *gigs*, you might get somewhere.

I arrange a date for us, in a restaurant. Look at me! Booking a table! Like a grown-up!—but half an hour before we're due to arrive, he rings me from a pub.

"We're having a band meeting. I might be a bit late," he says, slurring slightly.

"How late?" I ask, putting on mascara.

"Two . . . hours?" he says.

"Oh, that's okay!" I say brightly. I know which pub he's in. I go there and sit on the doorstep, waiting for him, smoking fags.

When he finally emerges, he explains he's "not hungry" anymore—"I had a ham bap"—and we get the next tube home.

Sitting on the velour seat next to him, as he rambles slightly incoherently about the "meeting," the imaginary relationship I'm having in my head with him—him being broken and misunderstood, me nursing him back to happiness with all I do and say—is starting to have another set of "imaginings" compete with it. In these new imaginings, I am screaming, "WHY are you being such an arsehole? If you don't like me, JUST SAY IT" at him, while throwing things around the room. I crush these thoughts. They are not part of my plan in which we spend the rest of our lives together, blissfully happy.

In order to hold firmly on to my dream, I buy a liter of whiskey on the way home. It's easy to imagine happy things when you're very, very drunk.

I think about trying to explain all this to the police, when they turn up at our house at 2 a.m. We're both slaughtered, and Courtney has been following me around the house, screaming at me, trying to kick the door down when I lock myself in the bathroom.

The policeman is around 55. In his stiff jacket and heavy shoes, he looks so much more adult and together than the people he is staring at: a weeping, pissed teenager in a nightie, and a 26-year-old man in a paisley shirt and jeans, trembling as he lights a fag. In my drunken state, the policeman looks like he is actually emitting a blue flashing light—but that is just from the panda car, up on the pavement outside.

"We received a call about a disturbance," he says, as his walkie-talkie crackles. "Screaming and shouting at 2 a.m. Not very nice for the neighbors. What's going on?"

This policeman does not look like my friends. He's big, and solid, and male, and logical: I can't explain to him that this is just a difficult phase in my relationship, where I'm trying to turn Courtney into someone else, while Courtney projects a lot of his insecurities on me and tries, somehow, to avenge his mother for fainting when he threw a Flora lid at her that time.

This policeman isn't going to listen to all of this—not even if he has a couple of drinks, which I have offered him, with a wobbly attempt at hospitality and normality. I am slightly surprised he turns it down—when I got locked out of my last flat and the fire brigade had to break in for me, we all had beers out on the patio afterward while I told them some gossip about Oasis.

Firemen just like to party more, I think, as I promise the policeman that we will be quieter now and that it was all just a misunderstanding.

"Just a domestic," I say to him as he leaves. It sounds like quite a grown-up thing to say. Grown-ups say this about their relationships on *EastEnders*. I'm being quite adult about the whole thing.

Days later, I escape the house with the stupid new dog—now old—and walk to the Heath. I lie under a tree—dressed in my nightie, with a coat thrown over it—and stare up at the leaves. I roll a joint—just a small one. One appropriate for 2 p.m.

The people around you are mirrors, I think. The dog is paddling in the lake. I watch her lap at the water.

You see yourself reflected in their eyes. If the mirror is true, and smooth, you see your true self. That's how you learn who you are. And you might be a different person to different people, but it's all feedback that you need, in order to know yourself.

But if the mirror is broken, or cracked, or warped, I continue, taking another drag, the reflection is not true. And you start to believe you are this . . . bad reflection. When I look in Courtney's eyes, I see a crazy, overbearing woman with unbearable good fortune who is trying to ruin him.

I pause.

I love him, but he hates me. That's what I see. I will have to tell Courtney to leave. I can't live with him anymore.

I go home.

Courtney won't leave.

"I'm not going until I can find a flat as nice as this," he says firmly. "I'm not going to go and live somewhere shitty. I'm not going to break up with you and live in fucking . . . *Cricklewood*. That wouldn't be fair."

He announces that night we won't fuck anymore: "I'm too depressed to fuck you," he says. "Fucking you will make things worse."

The mirror gets darker. I almost can't see my face.

A weekend away! That's what we need. Fresh air and the countryside. We just need to get out of London. It's London that's the problem: London, with Cricklewood in it, which Courtney fears. It is London that is destabilizing us. We'll be *fine* somewhere else.

Some friends of Courtney's are recording their new album in Wales and invite a group of us to go and stay with them for the weekend. As far as everyone's concerned, Courtney and I are still the hot couple on the block: the pop star and the teenage TV presenter, partying all night long. Only Caz knows the truth, from all those 2 a.m. phone calls. She sits opposite me now, on the train out of Paddington, heading west. I invited her at the last minute—promising her the chance to hang out with a famous band and drink as much as she likes.

"I wouldn't come if it was a band I liked," she says when I ask her. "That would be weird. But given that I think they're a bunch of tossers, I'll come. Drinking enormous amounts of famous arseholes' champagne is the duty of the true revolutionary."

We've all ordered drinks from the onboard bar—the train is the preshow party. I'm reading *Private Eye* and laughing. On my third laugh, Courtney snaps, "Stop laughing. You've made your point."

"I'm just . . . laughing," I say.

"No—that's not your normal laugh," Courtney says. He's drunker than everyone else. "You only laugh like that around other people."

Everyone has gone silent. This is awkward.

"I think she's just . . . laughing, Courtney," Caz says sharply. "Although I can understand why that might not be something *you've* heard a great deal and might *alarm* you."

I kick Caz under the table to shut up. I feel embarrassed that she is now having to deal with our secret blackness. This is private. The admin of my soul. I should be able to contain it. I just won't laugh anymore.

At Rockfield, autumn is unbearably beautiful: a Welsh autumn makes an English summer look gauche and flat. The frost spangles the mountainside. While Courtney goes off to have one of his interminable "sprucing" sessions—fiddling with his hair for hours in the mirror, pouting—Caz and I stand in the driveway, cramming blackberries into our mouths, and then chase each other around a field like kids. The air is hard, like iron. I laugh hysterically and then find myself worrying.

"*Has* my laugh changed?" I ask Caz. "Does it sound more . . . London-y?"

"That is, without doubt, the stupidest question I have *ever* been asked," Caz says. She finds a fallen branch and beats my coated arse with it until I fall to the ground, crying with laughter.

The studio is where Queen recorded "Bohemian Rhapsody"—with cries of "What would Freddie do!?" we open champagne and pour it into pint glasses. I immediately spill mine over the mixing desk and shout, "You *know* Freddie would have done that! It's like his GHOST IS INSIDE ME!" while trying to mop it up with my cardigan.

Courtney is thrilled to be in a proper studio: "Finally, I'm home!" he says, slouching in a swivel chair and playing on one of the band's very expensive Martin guitars. He starts to play a couple of their hits to them—but with new lyrics "that I've written myself."

The band listen politely, but they clearly wish he'd stop.

"Woo! It's a spontaneous happening! I can review it!" I say, trying to move the mood on.

"Not unless you've learned how to write yet," Courtney replies, strumming a G minor and puffing on a fag. I'm so embarrassed that I take Ecstasy, just for something to do with my face.

As the E warms up inside, and the rest of the room melts, I see Caz is quietly watching me. Before today, I haven't seen her for months—so long I'd almost forgotten who I am when I'm with her. Her face becomes a mirror: I can see reflected in it a teenage girl with blasted pupils, sitting alone on a chair, looking very, very tired, even though I am talking fast.

She is a true mirror, I think. I should look into her more often. I can see myself in there. I can see my good points and my bad points—but I recognize that face. I feel like I haven't seen that face in a long, long time. Not since I was a child.

We stare at each other for an age—just good, old-fashioned off-your-face staring.

In the end, Caz just raises an eyebrow at me. I know what she's saying. She's saying: "What?"

I mouth back: "I hate him."

She mouths back: "That's because he's a knob-skin. They're *all* knob-skins."

I go and sit next to Caz on the floor. We sit there for what seems like an age, watching Courtney, and the band, and some giggling girls who seem to have appeared from nowhere.

Rhythms and patterns establish themselves in the room. Circles of people curling forward, like chrysanthemum petals, over cocaine—then exploding outward, into nose rubbing and violent chat. Slow kissing in corners—then triumphal returns to the throng. People face-to-face with guitars, Beatles-style, starting a song—then suddenly stopping, with barks of laughter, before another starts again.

Caz and I have maracas. We are shaking them in a manner that can only be described as "sarcastic percussion." Every so often, someone asks us to stop—but we just start again, very quietly, a minute later. It's making us happy.

Sitting on the floor in the corner, everything else looks like a scene happening on a television. It looks like a play. Until I came over and sat with Caz, I was in the show, too. But now I'm sitting with her, I can see I'm not. I'm not in this made-up story. I never have been. I'm just a viewer, watching it at home, on TV. Just like me and Caz used to watch everything on TV. I hold her hand. She holds mine back. We keep on shaking our maracas at the TV with our free hands. I've never held Caz's hand before. Maybe it's just because we're so off our tits. Mum should have given us Ecstasy when we were little. We would have got on *so* much better.

I don't know how long we've been sitting like this when Courtney comes over and looks down at us. He's still holding the very expensive Martin guitar and strumming on it like he's Allen-a-Dale, but in a suede jacket, with receding hair.

"Hello, ladies," he says superciliously. He's grinding his teeth quite badly.

We shake our maracas at him. My pupils are blasted. Caz's are like saucers.

"Hello, Courtney," Caz says. She manages to put an admirably vast amount of hatred in every letter of his name, while still sounding ostensibly civil.

"We were all wondering—could you stop the maracas now?" Courtney continues, with exaggerated politeness.

"I'm afraid we can't," Caz replies, with equal politeness.

"Why?" Courtney asks. He speaks with icy courtesy.

There is a pause.

"Because you're a total dick," Caz says, as if she is the queen, greeting the high commissioner in Zaire at a garden party. She shakes her maraca, by way of punctuation.

Before I can stop myself, I laugh—a gigantic, unsexy honk, with a definite Wolverhampton accent.

"He is!" I say joyfully. I am in the throes of revelation. "A total dick!"

"A total dick," Caz confirms formally, shaking her maraca.

"Christ, you really can't handle your drugs, can you?" Courtney says to me. "You're embarrassing yourself."

"The thing is," I say to Caz, totally ignoring Courtney, "is that I can't even break up with him, because I was never going out with him in the first place. I've been imagining the whole thing."

"A total, imaginary dick," Caz says again. We shake our maracas in unison.

"Courtney, I'm going to go home and change the locks," I say cheerfully. Still holding hands, Caz and I stand.

"We're going to order a cab now," I say to the room. "Thank you for having us, everybody. I'm sorry I short-circuited your mixing desk with champagne. That was an error."

Courtney's shouting something, but I can't really hear him. We leave the room at a lick, running as fast as we can now, to get a cab; to get back to London; to find some chewing gum, to stop this interminable teeth-grinding. We've just ordered a cab from Reception when I realize I have left one important thing undone.

"Stay there," I say to Caz.

"Where are you going?" she yells.

"STAY THERE!" I bellow, running back down the corridor. I burst into the studio. Everyone looks up. Courtney looks at me with a combination of fury, self-pity, and a vast amount of cocaine. But he looks like he will take me back if I truly apologize. If I really mean it. If I love him. If, in my heart, I love him.

"Can we keep the maracas?" I ask.

CHAPTER 9
I Go Lap-dancing!

I have no idea what to wear to a strip club. It's one of the biggest wardrobe crises of my life.

"What are *you* wearing?" I ask Vicky on the phone.

"Skirt. Cardigan," Vicky says, lighting a fag.

"What shoes?"

"Boots. Low heel."

"Oh, I was going to wear boots, low heel, too," I say. "We can both wear boots, low heel. That's good. We'll be matchy."

Then a bad thought occurs to me. "Actually, maybe we shouldn't both wear boots, low heel," I say. "If we look too matchy, people might think we're an act. You know. Like a lesbian act. And try and touch us."

"No one would believe you're a lesbian," Vicky sighs. "You'd make a terrible lesbian."

"I wouldn't!" I say indignantly. This offends my can-do nature. "If I wanted, I could be a great lesbian!"

"No, you couldn't," Vicky says. "You're offensively heterosexual. You fancy Father Christmas. By no stretch of the imagination could Father Christmas be construed to have Sapphic androgyny. He wears Wellington boots indoors."

I can't believe Vicky is doubting my ability to be a lesbian, if I really wanted to be. She's seen how versatile I can be on a night out. Once, when we went to Bournemouth, we blagged our way backstage of a theater and convinced the star of the show—a legendary sitcom actor—that we were prostitutes, just to see his reaction. He said, "Blimey!" in a very edifying manner. My capabilities are endless. She doesn't know what she's talking about.

"Maybe I'll wear sneakers, instead," I say.

Vicky has asked me if I want to join her for a night out at Spearmint Rhino, on Tottenham Court Road. It's the year 2000, and strip clubs—for so long regarded as the holding pen for the last few sad, sweaty fucks on earth—have become acceptable again.

In Britain, the mid-nineties have been all about the rediscovery of the British working class's monochrome tropes—pubs, greyhound racing, anoraks, football in the park, bacon sandwiches, "birds"—and strip clubs come under this heading. "Ladettes" now enjoy a night out in the classier strip clubs of the metropolis. Various Spice Girls have been pictured in strip clubs, smoking cigars and cheering the acts on. Titty-bars are being marketed as an exciting, marginally loucher version of the Groucho Club—just somewhere for anyone who liked to start a night out at 1 a.m.

Partly out of journalistic hunger to cover the phenomenon, and partly because newspaper editors are invariably excited by pictures of female hacks in a strip club, the *Evening Standard* has asked Vicky to go spend an evening in the Rhino in order to see what all the fuss is about.

"It's against every single one of my feminist principles. These are arenas of abuse," I said when she called.

"The manager is giving us complimentary champagne all night," Vicky said.

"I will meet you there at 9 p.m.," I said, with all the dignity I could muster.

From the pavement outside, the club has an odd air. Looking through the doors, the place is covered in ornate gold moldings, red walls, and twinkling lights; it's overdone, ersatz glamour looking like some kind of putative Titty Disneyland. As we hesitate on the wrong side of the velvet rope, a couple of punters roll up and are ushered inside by the bouncers.

I am amazed at how confident and untroubled they seem—not guilty at *all*. I would have presumed you would make *some* excuse for visiting a strip club—saying loudly to the bouncers, "I am doing a collection on behalf of the sick children," or "Council. I've come to check your electrics," or, in a fake Mexican accent, "This Pret a Manger, yes?"

Instead, they walk in—slightly sweaty suits, slightly hawkish eyes—as if it's perfectly normal to leave the office, then relax by paying very young women to reveal their labia. What a lovely social circle I have, I reflect, not for the first time. All of my male friends would be genuinely horrified to go to a strip club. They all wear cardigans, collect vinyl, and fetishize loose-leaf tea. They would never want to pay to see a stranger's labia. Indeed, my boyfriend still says, "Thank you, that was very nice," after he's seen my labia, and we've been together for four years.

"This is like an annual convention for Bad Husband Material," I say to Vicky as we go in. "Everyone here has left a trail of sad girlfriends and wives."

Still, the free champagne is very free, and we have a table, right down at the front, by the catwalk—or "twat walk," as Vicky renames it. For the first hour, we treat Spearmint Rhino like a pub, albeit one with the occasional distraction of some tits floating over our heads. One particularly enjoyable conversation about the imminent purchase of a new winter coat is interrupted by some buttocks suddenly arriving in our sight line but, to be fair, I've had this happen to me in a Pizza Express before. After two hours, some of the "girls" come over to chat, and, as is the way of all gatherings of women, we all start gossiping: Vicky in her cardi, me in my jacket, the girls in diamante bras and itchy-looking thongs.

By 1 a.m., we're pretty tipsy, have been given a private dance that has left us both quite discombobulated—this chick has an arse like heaven—and we've been regaled with an amazing story about a very famous TV presenter and habitué of the club, which ends with the line, "So his wife found out he had herpes—on Christmas Day!"

We are in our booth rofling away, thinking, "This is just like the Groucho, but with *real* twats, instead of metaphorical ones. This is actually okay."

The PR comes over to us.

"I'm off home," she says, pulling on her coat. "You ladies are welcome to stay, if you want."

I look down the neck of the champagne bottle. There's still a good two glasses left.

"We'll stay!" I say brightly. "My personal motto is: never walk away from a loaded bottle."

The PR leaves us to carry on our evening unchaperoned. Cheerfully topping up our glasses, I'm just about to launch into a lengthy anecdote about the one time I offered to strip for a lover—sadly ruining the mood by accidentally treading in a bowl of porridge I'd left by the bed that morning—when two bouncers approach our table.

"Evening, constables," I say merrily.

"It's time for you to go, ladies," they say, looking very stern and unyielding.

"I assure you, I have only had a few weak ales," I say, slightly cross-eyed. "I'm perferly fine to remain here."

"Time to go," the bouncer says, pulling my chair back from the table. His buddy does the same to Vicky. We are hustled out in less than a minute, in a flurry of coat-grabbing and indignation.

On the pavement, we are outraged.

"Why? Why are we being thrown out?" we screech. "We're simply taking a wry, sideways look at stripping! We're COLUMNISTS! We're QUALIFIED for this! We're BONA FIDE! We've BEEN ON RADIO FOUR!"

"We know your game," they said. "You're prostitutes."

Apparently, we find out—during the next five minutes of increasingly shrill inquiry—"rough-looking" Russian prostitutes often frequent the club, picking up trade from clients whose taste is for disappointingly "normal"-looking women rather than the strippers. This is what the bouncer is convinced we are. He knows we aren't strippers—so we must then, ergo, be prostitutes. Vicky in her cardigan, and me in my sneakers.

In his world, woman-type runs on a binary system: stripper, whore. There aren't any other kinds of women. Certainly not 20-something columnists hoping to milk 1,200 words out of the event, while caning the free bar for all it was worth.

Once again, I was apt to dwell on what a thunderingly inappropriate and rude relic the strip club is.

"I TOLD you they were arenas of abuse," I said to Vicky, as we sat in a doorway smoking a fag.

"But we'll both be able to get a column out of it," she replied, eminently reasonably.

And so, really, we were not losers at all.

But, of course, in a wider sense, we were. For—given the context of the entirety of history up until about yesterday—the idea of clubs where women take off their clothes in front of men is stupendously . . . impolite.

After all, history is very much "99 percent women being subjugated, disenfranchised, and sexually objectified." Women have—there's no two ways about this—really been shafted by the simple fact that men fancy them. We can see that men's desire for women has, throughout history, given rise to unspeakable barbarity. It's caused terrible, terrible things to happen, because men have been the dominant force, with no rules or checks on their behavior. It's no exaggeration to refer to "sexual tyranny," and "total bullshit." Within living memory in this country, men could rape their wives: women were not seen as a separate sexual entity, with a right of refusal. Germany only criminalized the practice in 1997; Haiti, in 2006. It's still legal in—among other places—Pakistan, Kenya, and the Bahamas. Even in countries where it has been criminalized, there is an unwillingness to actually prosecute: Japan and Poland have been particularly criticized by human rights organizations for their low conviction rates. There are large parts of the world where women are—with either the explicit or the nonexplicit sanction of the state—deemed little more than souped-up sex toys for men.

In this context, then, it's obvious that a lap-dancing club is as incongruous in a modern society as a "Minstrel Show!" or ads for "Jew Beating—Sticks £1!"

Of course, the big difference here is that if a white man suggested starting a cleaning agency that only employed black cleaners, dressed up in plantation clothing, and being excessively cowed and deferential to their employers, the entire world would be up in arms.

"What are you playing at?" they would shout. "We're not going to bring back a 'light entertainment' version of slavery! Not even if it's for a 'social experiment' reality documentary on Channel 4!"

But what are strip clubs and lap-dancing clubs if not "light entertainment" versions of the entire history of misogyny?

Any argument in their favor is fallacious. Recently, it has behooved modish magazines to print interviews with young women who explain that their career as strippers is paying their way through university. This is thought to pretty much end any objections against strip clubs, on the basis that—look!—*clever* girls are doing it, in order to become middle-class professionals with degrees! Ipso facto Girl Power!

For myself, I can't believe that girls saying, "Actually, I'm paying my university fees by stripping" is seen as some kind of righteous, empowered, end-of-argument statement on the ultimate morality of these places. If women are having to strip to get an education—in a way that male teenage students are really notably not—then that's a gigantic political issue, not a reason to keep strip clubs going.

Are we really saying that strip clubs are just wonderful charities that allow women—well, the pretty, thin ones, anyway: presumably the fatter, plainer ones have to do whatever it is all the male students are also doing—to get degrees? I can't believe women supposedly in higher education are that stupid.

One doesn't want to be as blunt as to say, "Girls, get the fuck off the podium—you're letting us all down," but: Girls, get the fuck off the podium—you're letting us all down.

But you know what? It's not just a question of girls letting other girls down. Strip clubs let everyone down. Men and women approach their very worst here. There's no self-expression or joy in these joints—no springboard to self-discovery, or adventure, like any *decent* night out involving men, women, alcohol, and taking your clothes off. Why do so many people have a gut reaction against strip clubs? Because, inside them, no one's having *fun*.

Instead, people are expressing needs (to earn money, to see a woman's skin) in pretty much the most depressing way possible. Sit in one of these places sober—as Vicky and I did initially; it took almost SEVEN MINUTES for the first bottle of complimentary champagne to get to the table—and you see what's going on here. The women hate the men. The stripper's internal monologue as she peels off her thong for the twelfth time that day would make Patti Smith's "Piss Factory" look like "I Will Always Love You" by Whitney Houston.

And the men—oh, are you any gentler or happier? You cannot put your hand on your heart and say—as the music starts up, and she moves toward you—that you have kind feelings toward these women. No man who ever cared for or wanted to impress a woman made her stand in front of him and take her knickers off to earn her cab fare home. You spend this money on nothing at all—addiction to porn and strip clubs is the third biggest cause of debt in men. Between 60 and 80 percent of strippers come from a background of sexual abuse. This place is a mess, a horrible mess. Every dance, every private booth, is a small unhappiness, an ugly impoliteness: the bastard child of misogyny and commerce.

On the high street, a strip club looks like a tooth knocked out of a face.

In 2010, Iceland—with a lesbian prime minister and a parliament that is 50 percent female—became the first country in the world to outlaw strip clubs for feminist, rather than religious, reasons.

"I guess the men of Iceland will have to get used to the idea that women are not for sale," Gudrun Jonsdottir, who campaigned for the law change, said.

I don't think that's an idea that will do men, their bank balances, or the women they come across anything but good. Men don't HAVE to see tits and fannies. They won't DIE if they don't have access to a local strip joint. Tits aren't, like, vitamin D or something. Let's take our women off the poles.

But pole-dancing classes, on the other hand, are fine. I know! Who would have thought! There seems to be no logic to it! I know a lot of feminists regard them as a sign of the End Days—evidence that the world is now being run by some misogynist Illuminati, intent on weakening our girl-children with stripercise classes at the local gym, 11:30 a.m.—but that's clearly not the case.

I mean, on a *practical* level, they're totally useless: there aren't any poles in nightclubs, girls. You're going to spend hundreds of pounds learning all these "sexy" moves and then never have any-where to show them off in public, save the grab-pole on the bus. If you think that's a fair exchange for all your time and money, then best of British.

But practical considerations to one side, there's nothing con-trary to the rules of strident feminism in gyms and dance classes offering pole-dancing lessons, and women attending them. In a world of infinite possibility, why *not* learn to hang off a pole by your pelvic floor? It probably *will* be more useful than learning Latin. For starters, I bet it's incredibly useful if, when decorating, you need to roller a tricky corner on a landing. And who's to say that, in the event of an apocalypse, being able to take off your knickers in syncopation to "Womanizer" by Britney Spears won't make the difference between the quick and the dead?

Just as pornography isn't inherently wrong—it's just some fucking—so pole-dancing, or lap-dancing or stripping, isn't inher-ently wrong—it's just some dancing. So long as women are doing it for fun—because they want to, and they are in a place where they won't be misunderstood, and because it seems ridiculous and amusing, and something that might very well end with you leaning against a wall, crying with laughter as your friends try to mend the crotch-split in your leggings with a safety pin—then it's a simple open-and-shut case of carry on, girls. Feminism is behind you.

It's the same deal with any "sexy dancing" in a nightclub—any grinding, any teasing, any of those Jamaican dance hall moves, where the women are—not to put too fine a point on it—fucking the floor as if they need to be pregnant by some parquet tiles by midnight. Any action a woman engages in from a spirit of joy, and within a similarly safe and joyous environment, falls within the city walls of feminism. A girl has a right to dance how she wants, when her favorite record comes on.

And, frankly, from a spectator's point of view, it's better than watching people line dancing or doing the Macarena.

For exactly the same reason, we shouldn't have a problem with burlesque—lap-dancing's older, darker, cleverer sister. Yes, I know: it's stripping in front of men, for cash. Given the patriarchy and all that, I can see how many would say, "But that is like eschewing Daffy Duck and loving George Costanza from *Seinfeld*. They are both essentially *the same thing*."

But, of course, they are not. The difference between a burlesque artist putting on a single show in front of hundreds and a stripper on an eight-hour shift going one on one is immense: the polarity between being a minstrel for a bored monarch, playing whatever song the monarch asks for, and U2 playing Wembley Stadium.

With burlesque, not only does the power balance rest with the person taking her clothes off—as it always should, in polite society—but it also anchors its heart in freaky, late-night, libertine self-expression: it has a campy, tranny, fetish element to it. It's not—to use the technical term—"an easy wank."

Additionally, despite its intense stylization of sexuality, it doesn't have the oddly aggressive, humorless air of the strip club: burlesque artists sing, talk, and laugh. They *tell jokes*—something unthinkable in the inexplicably po-faced atmosphere of a lap-dancing club, which treats male/female interactions with all the gravitas of Cold War–era meetings between Russia and the USA, rather than as a potential hoot. Perhaps as a direct consequence, burlesque artists treat their own sexuality as something fabulous and enjoyable—rather than something bordering on a weapon, to be ground, unsmilingly, into the face of the sweaty idiot punter below.

Because, most importantly, burlesque clubs feel like a place for girls. Strip clubs—despite the occasional presence of a Spice-Girl, ten years ago—do not. Watching good burlesque in action, you can see female sexuality; a performance constructed with the values system of a woman: beautiful lighting, glossy hair, absurd accessories (giant cocktail glasses; huge feather fans), velvet corsets, fashionable shoes, Ava Gardner eyeliner, pale skin, classy manicures, humor, and a huge round of applause at the end—instead of an uncomfortable, half-hidden erection, and silence.

Burlesque artists have names—Dita Von Teese, Gypsy Rose Lee, Immodesty Blaize, Tempest Storm, Miss Dirty Martini—that make them sound like sexual superheroes. They explore sexuality from a position of strength, with ideas, protection, and a culture that allows them to do, creatively, as they please. They are dames, broads, and women—rather than the slightly cold-looking girls you see in strip clubs. Their personas embrace the entire spectrum of sexuality—fun, wit, warmth, inventiveness, innocence, power, darkness—rather than the bloodless aerobics of the podium.

Do you know what the final rule of thumb is with strip clubs? Gay men wouldn't be seen dead in Spearmint Rhino—but you can't move for them in a burlesque joint. As a rule of thumb, you can always tell if a place is culturally healthy for women when the gays start rocking it. They are up for glitter, filth, and fun—rather than a factory-farm wank-trigger with—and I can say this now—very acidic house champagne.

CHAPTER 10

I Get Married!

So what has my sister Caz been up to in all this time? Many things. She's cut her hair short, written three plays about an ineffectual evil overlord called Venger, had a massive crush on George Orwell, racked up an impressive collection of drum 'n' bass records, and been part of the creative barkeeping team that came up—one desperate Christmas—with the sherry cappuccino: a brave, but ultimately failed, concept. Sherry curdles in milk. We know that as a fact now. We also know that you can't then reemulsify it with cornstarch, however much you stir.

But what she's mainly been doing is going to a lot of weddings. This is unfortunate, because Caz hates weddings.

"For fuck's sake," she says, throwing herself onto a kitchen chair. "For fuck's sake."

She's wearing a cream chiffon dress and cream satin shoes, both of which are covered in mud. She has nettle stings up her legs, reeks of booze, and is drinking anticystitis medicine straight from the bottle, like a cowboy necking whiskey. Her eyes have the mad, red aspect of someone who has not only recently traveled out of hell, but been charged quite a lot to travel out of hell, too.

On a train with a malfunctioning dining car. During track maintenance. On a holiday weekend.

She throws a huge rucksack into the corner. Even from here, I
can see it has a broken tent in it.

"Who would invite 200 people to a wedding on a pig farm, in
a valley with no mobile reception?" she says, tight-jawed. "Who?
'You can camp in an adjacent field,' they said. 'In a circle with all
the bride's family. We call it the Fairy Circle! We'll be *nice and
close*. There's a *sing-along* at night!' "

She shudders. As you may recall, one of the main things about
Caz is that she really doesn't like people being close to her. If she
could have a small, portable city wall—lined with archers—she
would.

"What happened when the tent broke?" I ask, pointing at the
rucksack. The rucksack is very, very wet.

"A stoned fuckwit in the next tent tried to mend the poles
with three pencils and some tape," she replies. "Even though I
kept telling him it wouldn't work, because modern tent poles
have to *bend*. Then we had to walk to the wedding, which wasn't
in an adjacent field at all but seven fields away. My shoes didn't
like the seven fields. They didn't like that at all. Neither did my
legs, when we found the nettles. In a lane, a tractor came near us,
and we had to lean into a hedge. All of me hated that. Also, the
tractor made me nervous, so I did a sweat in my dress."

She lifts up her arms to display the stains.

"But we had some luck! Because then it started raining quite
heavily on me, which made the frizziness of my hair, rather than
the sweatiness of my armpits, the go-to visual starting point for
the entire congregation when we got there. Five minutes into the
ceremony."

Caz is now pouring her cystitis medicine into a mug, along
with three shots of vodka. Her story didn't get any better from

there. Apparently, everyone had gotten so blindingly drunk that by 3 p.m., even 50-something aunties were leaning against the buffet table saying, "I've got to sober up." It being a very "close-knit" country family, Caz was repeatedly questioned by guests as to who she "knew"—"Kind of inferring that I'd walked into the middle of fucking nowhere in the rain in order to steal a portion of very mediocre ham salad." By 4 p.m., Caz was so furiously, despairingly bored that she went and sat on the toilet for an hour.

"They were very posh Portaloos. Apparently they're the ones they use at Glyndebourne," she said. "They had music pumped into them. I listened to 'Under Pressure' by Queen five times. Then I did what Freddie would have done—walked in the pissing rain up a hill until I got reception, called a minicab, and booked myself into the Marriott, Exeter. Don't ask me if I've got cystitis. I've got cystitis."

She popped three Nurofen Plus and burst into tears. "Five weddings in four years," she wailed, taking the muddy shoes off and throwing them in the sink. "I genuinely hope no one else I know ever, ever falls in love again. People discovering true love works out badly for me."

Of course, people discovering true love works out badly for everyone, really. I mean, it's okay in the end—once everyone settles down and stops making a big fuss about it. But fairly near the beginning, there is a massive test of everyone's patience and love—a wedding.

For while there are plenty of awful things we can place at the door of men—wars, rape, nuclear weapons, stock market crashes, *Top Gear*, that thing where they put their hand down the front of their jogging bottoms and rearrange their sweaty knackers while on the bus, before touching a railing *I* then have to touch, too, all covered in their sweaty bollock-mist—weddings definitely come down to the ladies.

Weddings are our fault, ladies. Every aspect of their pantech-nicon of awfulness happened on our watch. And you know what? Not only have we let humanity down, but we've let *ourselves* down, too.

Weddings do women no good at all. They're a viper's pit of waste and despair. And nearly every aspect of them reverberates badly against the very people who love them the most: us. Our love for a wedding is a bad love. It does us no good. It will end badly, leaving us feeling cheated and alone.

Whenever I think about weddings, I want to run into the church—like Dustin Hoffman in *The Graduate*—and shout "STOP! STOP THE WEDDINGS!"

And when the organ has ground to a halt, and everyone turns around, astonished, to stare at me, and the vicar has stopped stut-tering, "Well, *really!*" in a disapproving manner, I'm going to rocket up to the pulpit—tearing my stupid bloody fascinator off as I go—light a fag, lean back, and this is the sermon I will preach.

No. 1: COST. Ladies! Being a woman is already very, very ex-pensive. Tampons, hairdressers, child care, beauty aids, women's shoes being three times more costly than men's—the combination of the things we need (Tampax) combined with the things we feel naked without (proper haircuts) is already ruinous. And that's before we factor in both women earning 30 percent less than men *and* being the ones who usually have to watch their career go all *Titanic* when the question "Who will look after the kids?" raises its head.

In the old days, the question of a dowry would often be one of the deciding factors of a woman's life: how much money her parents could settle on a marriage dictating whom a woman could and couldn't marry.

These days, of course, a woman is free to marry whomsoever she chooses. And yet marriage still often involves crippling sums of money—the average cost of a UK wedding is £21,000 (about $35,000)—which are now commonly paid for by the couple themselves, in some kind of bizarre, voluntary, ultimately useless but self-imposed dowry. Spending £21,000 at a stage in your life when you are—usually—still pretty poor and trying to buy items like "a house" and "things to eat" seems pretty baffling whichever way you slice it—not least when one in four marriages ends in divorce.

If we were inventing things from scratch, surely we would decide to throw a gigantic £21,000 celebration of love right at the *end* of the whole thing—when we're in our sixties and seventies, the mortgage is paid off, and we can see if the whole "I love you forever" thing actually worked out or not.

£21,000! Oh, it makes me cry. Personally, I wouldn't spend £21,000 on anything that didn't have either (a) doors and windows or (b) the ability to grant me three wishes. It is an absurd amount of money to spend on something. It is a figure that denotes insanity.

The money thing is a key issue here—because of what it is spent on. Aside from getting together the deposit for a house, the average couple will probably never again spend that amount of money on a single thing in their lives. And what is it that that £21,000 buys? Very little that lasts. There are the overpriced photographs in the insanely expensive album, and all the presents, of course—but spending £21,000 to get £2,000 worth of kitchenware is simply poor economics. The dress is never worn again, you never get round to "dying the shoes red and wearing them to a party!" no matter how often you convince yourself you might, and as for the rings—well, I can hardly be the only married woman on her fifth wedding band, after losing various others in swimming pools, down cracks in countertops, and, once, in a loaf of bread (it's a long story).

What the £21,000 buys you is aspect two of why weddings are so bad for women.

No. 2: THE BEST DAY OF YOUR LIFE. "It's the best day of your life." Well. The snags here are obvious. Of course it's not the best day of your life. A day that was *really* the best day of your life wouldn't involve Uncle Wrong, Aunt Drip, and someone from your office you had to invite, lest you spend the next six years being sulked at every time you pass them in a stairwell.

Clearly—with these enforced parameters—your wedding is actually like some unholy mélange of some work off-site and family therapy and should, therefore, be regarded with the same mixture of quiet stoicism, grim determination, and heavy drinking.

Also, bear this in mind, ladies—the phrasing "the best day of your life." Yes, the best day of *your* life: the bride. Not anyone else's. Let's face it—from time immemorial, the groom has quietly not given a shit about the event, from beginning to end. If you want to plunge a grown man into a combination of deep despair and barely repressed panic, simply talk to him, for a minute or more, about table arrangements, boutonnieres, flower girls' shoes, marquees, the hiring of a castle, what Madonna did for *her* wedding, and whether or not you should have a colonic a week before, to look "fresh-faced."

Weddings are essentially something that brides invite grooms along to as an afterthought—and a thought that came after working out which trios of chocolate puddings were going to be served, at that. Women start planning their weddings when they're five, for goodness' sake. When they have no idea who they're marrying and just imagine an Action Man's body with a convenient pixelation where his face is. By way of comparison, at the same age, the only future event boys are planning is how they might be able to score the winning goal in the World Cup while, at the same time, playing the guitar solo to "November Rain" by Guns N' Roses.

So it's clearly not the best day of the groom's life. And it's also not the best day of any of the guests' lives, either. Because weddings aren't fun for the guests. It's something we're wholly aware of when we're guests—300 miles from home, in a pashmina, making awkward chitty-chat with a bleary drunkard on the table clearly referred to as "The Dregs" in the placement plans—but forget the minute we start planning our own weddings.

"I can't believe Carrie dragged us all to the sodding Isle of Skye for her wedding," we moan, staring at our overdrafts. "Three bloody days in a four-star hotel. She'd better not divorce him. Indeed, I feel inclined to sew them together, so they cannot stray—like the Human Caterpillar."

"Where do you want to get married, then?" someone may ask.

"Singapore!" you cry enthusiastically. "We're inviting everyone over for a week! On day three, there's a boat trip to a deserted island—only £75 extra for each person! It's going to be AMAZING!"

I did it myself. Up until my actual wedding, I'd done everything brilliantly. I had so not been a twat about being in love. I wasn't overdramatic or attention seeking. I had recovered from breaking up with Courtney by the simple expediency of making a cheerful badge that read I WENT OUT WITH SATAN—AND SURVIVED! and wearing it to all social engagements—thus answering any and all questions about the status of our relationship just by pointing at it.

I didn't mope, and I didn't sulk—instead, I made up for a year of ill-rewarded fidelity by cheerfully going back out into the world and seeing if there was any fun left out there for me. As it turned out, there was loads. Every night was like a sexy scavenger hunt around London, being all twinkly-eyed with anyone amusing, up against the clock of the last bus home. One evening with a pop star ended with his manager having to remove him, naked, from my hotel bedroom at 3 a.m.

A week later, a teenage boy literally turned up on my doorstep—who knew they did deliveries these days?—and was so unexpectedly tender and joyful, he undid half of Courtney's evil over one sunny winter afternoon and night of exclaiming wonder.

In both instances, I was gratified to note that getting back out "on the dating scene" required—contrary to everything I'd ever been given to understand on the subject—absolutely no effort or insecurity at all. There was no "post-breakup makeover" for me. I'd put on ten pounds and given myself a terrible haircut with a pair of kitchen scissors, but I was so happy, no one appeared to notice. With the eventually unconscious pop star, I simply asked the question, "Shall we have a shag?" With the teenage boy, meanwhile, I made my move while in the deathlessly hot outfit of a burgundy-colored BHS terry cloth robe.

For a month, I rode some kind of relaxed sex galleon around London like a lady pirate—remembering, again, how every conversation with a member of the opposite sex carries with it that tiny, atom-small, atomic-bright possibility: "Hello. Are you 'it'?"

And every Thursday, I would invite over Pete from *Melody Maker*, cook him soup, and tell him all these stories—"So I rang down to room service and asked for a steak sandwich and a pair of men's pants"—while we played records and cried laughing.

Then, in the middle of February, my mood suddenly changed.

I woke one Monday morning to find an odd albatross-unhappiness had descended. It wasn't depression, or misery—it was both more restless and more hopeful than that. I felt suspended: a combination of waiting for something and missing something terribly—even though I'd never had it.

Indeed, not only had I never had it—I also had no idea what it was. The source of my blues absolutely baffled me. I spent a week wandering around my flat, deflated—clueless as to what it meant. I'd pick something up—my phone, a record, a fag—and then put them down again sadly, going, "No, that's not it."

Twice I went to the shops to buy food, and halfway around the supermarket I'd think, "When I get back, it might have happened!" I'd bustle back, full of energy and hope again, and burst into the flat—only to find it exactly as I'd left it. Whatever it was still hadn't arrived.

The disappointment was crushing.

After a week of this, on Sunday night, my subconscious—as if exasperated at my dimness—finally spelled it out for me. I went to bed drunk and dreamed I was on the escalators at Baker Street underground station, going up. The escalators seemed impossibly high. I couldn't even see the top. It was going to be a long, long time before I got to the turnstiles.

"It's going to take forever to get up there!" I exclaimed.

"It's okay," a voice said. I turned around and saw Pete standing behind me. "I'm here," he said simply.

"Oh!" I said, waking up.

"Oh!"

"I'm in love! I'm in love with Pete."

I looked around the flat.

"He's what's not here."

*

Six years and a £19.99 engagement ring later, and it's our wedding day. It was—initially—going to be in a registry office in London, followed by a reception at a pub. In boring, empty mid-October. Everyone could have gotten the bus home. It would have cost less than 200 quid. We could have knocked it all off in five hours flat. Oh, I wish we'd had that wedding.

After I'd inhaled 600 bridal magazines and taken into account a few requests from the in-laws, however, it ended up being in a former monastery in Coventry, two days after Christmas. Coincidentally, also Caz's birthday. She has always borne the brunt of the love of others.

I don't want to exaggerate but, by God, it was a bad wedding.

Here I am, at 24, waiting to come down the aisle in my red velvet dress, with ivy in my hair. I look like Lady Bacchus, except for my feet. My lifelong curse of not being able to find shoes I can walk in extends even here, on my most glamorous day: under the satin-edged velvet, I'm wearing a manky pair of Doc Marten sandals.

My father is in a suit he shoplifted from Ciro Citterio and some shoes he shoplifted from Burton—but he looks calm, wise, and not a little emotional about giving away his first child in marriage.

"Oh, my lovely daughter," he says, smelling a little of whiskey. "My kitten-cat." His eyes have the faint shine of tears in them. As the music strikes up in the next room he takes my arm and leans in to whisper something. This is where he tells me something of how he and Mum have stayed together for 24 years and had eight kids, I think to myself. This is going to be one of our great bonding moments. Oh Lord, I hope he doesn't make me cry. I have so much eyeliner on.

"Darling girl," he says, as the usher opens the door, and I see the whole congregation crane around to watch my entrance. "Darling love. Remember you're a Womble."*

I walk down the aisle so fast that, halfway down, I realize I'm going to get there way before the music finishes. I also note that I am beaming rather smugly—and I worry how the registrar will take this.

She will think I'm not serious about this! I panic. She'll REFUSE to marry me, on the grounds I'm SUPERCILIOUS!

I immediately slow down to a funereal pace and assume a look of burdened worry. Later, my sisters tell me they were convinced that I'd just got the first twinge of cystitis, and that they'd all automatically reached into their handbags for a bottle of potassium citrate, which we all carry around with us.

Still, I look fine compared to my husband-to-be. He's so nervous he's a very pale green and is shaking like a sock on a clothesline.

"I've never seen a more anxious groom," the registrar confides later. "I had to give him two shots of whiskey."

I can't remember anything about the ceremony. I spent the

---

* "The Wombles" was a 1970s childrens' TV show about a group of gentle, furry creatures—Wombles—who secretly lived on Wimbledon Common, London, recycling humans' garbage. In one of the more unlikely developments in pop history, they went on to have five hit albums and a massive single, "Remember You're a Womble." The last was such an insidious ear-worm that a whole generation took to saying "Remember You're a Womble" in order to conclude conversations, or sum up the ineffable in moments of great emotion.

At least, that's what I thought when I was a kid. Then I started leaving the house and socializing with people, and realized that, actually, in the whole world, it was only my dad who did that. Only my dad. Literally no one else but Dad.

whole thing going, "REMEMBER you're a WOMBLE?" in my head, in outrage.

An hour later, and everyone's in the bar. Many of our invited guests haven't been able to make it, because it's two days after Christmas and they're with their families in Scotland, Devon, and Ireland. My family are taking advantage of the free bar—many of them can't walk anymore, and, of the ones who can, two of them have found a memorial to a dead knight and are giving his statue a "saucy" pole dance.

My dad, meanwhile, has managed to spill candle wax all over his shirt and has—on the advice of others—taken it off and put it into a freezer in the kitchen, to harden the wax. He is now sitting at the table in his vest and jacket, drinking Guinness, looking bleary. My sister Col has disappeared—we find out later this is because Dad told her he'd considered having her put into care after that time she stole all his Disney DVDs and power tools and sold them for drugs.

"I was only joking!" he says, eyes rolling in his head. "Or was I?"

In order to "find" her, my brother Eddie tries to steal a golf cart so he can drive around looking for her. Two other siblings have to stand in front of him, saying, "NO!"

By the time the reception starts, a quiet aura of failure pervades the event. As it is two days after Christmas, the guests who have trekked to Coventry in the middle of their Christmas holidays feel too fat and lethargic for a disco, and my husband's insistence that he be the DJ results in our First Dance being, incongruously, "Ask" by the Smiths. We try, ineffectually, to slow-dance to it, on a wholly empty dance floor, as everyone watches us doing a romantic "indie shuffle." When the next song comes on—"Always on My Mind" by the Pet Shop Boys—two new people join us on the dance floor. They are my new father-in-law and our friend Dave, who has been off his face on Ecstasy for around three hours now.

Dave dances toward my father-in-law, in the manner of Stevie Nicks catching butterflies.

"Have one of my pearls," he says to my father-in-law, opening his hand and revealing £300 worth of pills.

"My father doesn't want a tictac, thanks," Pete says, firmly escorting Dave out of the room.

By 10 p.m., most people have gone to bed early—trying to salvage some aspect of being dragged to an expensive hotel in the middle of their holidays. I like to think they are all eating sausage rolls stolen from the buffet and watching *Cheers*. I am happy for them. I wish I was one of them. I talk to a sad Greek in-law, head to toe in black, still mourning someone who died in 1952. I smile weakly.

I notice she—along with all my Greek in-laws—seems to have rendered herself willingly and wholly blind to the fact that one of my bridesmaids was a six-foot-two gay man called Charlie, who was wearing silver trousers and a pink cape. They only ever mention the other bridesmaid—Polly, whose bra is visible above her strapless dress, and is rocking a tattoo of a dolphin saying "Fuck."

At 10:23 p.m., the fire alarm goes off. As everyone shiveringly evacuates onto the lawn, I notice all of my siblings are missing. Going back into the hotel to find them—like Mr. Blunden in *The Amazing Mr. Blunden*—I knock on the door of my sister's room. I find all seven siblings in here—standing on the bed, waving room-service menus under the smoke detector.

"Why aren't you evacuating?" I ask, standing in the doorway in my wedding dress.

They all turn to face me. They are all wearing balloon crowns made by the balloon animal man we'd hired to entertain the kids. Eddie is holding a balloon sword.

"It's sensed our body heat!" Weena says, stoned and panicked. "There's only supposed to be two people in here but we all bunked in, and now it's overheated the room! We're trying to cool it down!"

They carry on waving their room-service menus at the ceiling. The fire alarm stops ringing. It's 10:32 p.m. I'm married. I go to bed.

In the following 11 years, not one guest ever mentions our wedding again. We all seem to silently agree that it's for the best.

Still, at least I was a merciful bride in one respect: there was no hen night. I spent the night before eating chips with my siblings and watching *Ghostbusters* for the 50th time. In that respect, at least, I was sane. Because problem number three with the modern wedding is the Bachelorette Party.

No. 3: BACHELORETTE NIGHTS. What was, 20 years ago, simply a night in the pub, but with extra-raucous screaming—sum expenditure: £30 on Baileys—now involves a huge swath of time and money from those unfortunate and loyal enough to be bridesmaids.

Caz has borne the bad end of 21st-century hen nights, as they are called in England. For despite being the world's most reluctant wedding guest, capricious beadle-like gods have made her Chief Bridesmaid no less than four times. On one occasion, she got so tanked she gatecrashed the groom's stag night to tell him she thought he was gay. On another hen night, the bride's insistence that all the attendees wear matching "Team Ciara" sateen tour jackets led to a size 16 bridesmaid having a body dysmorphia–induced panic attack at a roller disco and getting a taxi home from London to Stevenage, hysterically hyperventilating. There was also the hen night where a "bonding" walk in the Yorkshire Dales ended up with Caz having to scramble down a 50-foot scree after a buggy that someone was slightly too pissed to be responsibly in charge of; but we all agreed later that that could have happened to anyone.

No. 4: "EVERYONE I LOVE IS HERE." Do you really want "all the people I love" in one room together? It rarely works out well. I, for instance, am very bad with other people's families. At one wedding—where I was the best man—I heard the bride's mother was a huge Richard Madeley fan and, in my cups, regaled her with my best Richard Madeley anecdote: that his favorite swear word was "fuckadoodle."*

Ten minutes later, I had it explained to me that, as a devout Christian, this was literally the first time she had ever heard the word "fuck."

I was similarly lackluster at Cathy and John's wedding, when Cathy's dad gave me a tour of their beautiful all-white house, as I trailed along behind, swigging red wine.

"And this is my favorite view," Cathy's dad said, as we reached the master bedroom and he strode over to the window. "On a clear day, you can see right down the valley."

---

*Richard Madeley is a UK daytime TV presenter of no little legend. Possessed of an extraordinary and mesmeric self-confidence, equaled only by a Foghorn Leghorn lack of guile, the true magic of Madeley is perhaps best encapsulated in the day he was charged with interviewing a group of Primordial Dwarves—people who only grow to the size of large dolls, due to a chromosomal abnormality.

"Do you find people patronize you?" he asked them; before adding in a much louder voice. "THAT MEANS THEY TALK DOWN TO YOU."

Then a bat flew in through the window and right into my face.

I don't know if you've ever had a bat fly into your face, but you don't have an enormous amount of time to work out your coping technique. You kind of . . . ride on instinct. My instinct, it turned out, was to scream "WHAT THE FUCKING?" and hurl my red wine right across the world's whitest room.

"Oh, dear," Cathy's dad said, with the restraint and politeness of his kind. "I'll get some tissues."

"FUCK!" I shouted, running down the hallway. "FUCK! I'm on this. FUCK!"

Bombing into the kitchen, I returned with a bottle of white wine and started sloshing it around, in a dedicated manner.

"White wine gets red wine stains out!" I shouted. "I saw it on the telly!"

I maniacally started pouring the white wine onto the now-scarlet rug and scrubbing it with a tea towel.

Cathy's dad came across the room—slightly faster than I thought a man of his age would be capable of—and gently prised the bottle from my hand. He stared at it—now empty—for a moment.

"Ah," he said regretfully. "The '93 Alsace Grand Cru."

There was a long pause.

"Still," he said with enormous grace, touching the bottle with his fingertips. "It was a *little* too warm to drink."

It took an hour and a half for a minicab to arrive from Tiverton. I spent the waiting time behind a barn, eating cheese to sober up.

No. 5: YOU. But, at the end of the day, who really cares how many people you make miserable by evacuating them out onto a freezing lawn in Coventry two days after Christmas, putting them in a fairy-ring sing-along, or rendering them suicidal with a bad jacket?

It's your big day, after all! The bride! You *deserve* to have a single day where it's all about YOU! THIS IS YOUR BIG DAY! IT'S THE BEST DAY OF YOUR LIFE!

There are two hitches with this. The first is that you should always be distrustful of days that are preordained to be legendary: a sad trail of disappointing New Year's Eves, Christmas Days, romantic long weekends, first shags, and birthdays should tell us this. Aside from getting my mother tanked on White Russians, the quickest and easiest way to kill the fun good times is to put a massive pressure of expectation on it in advance. Really, anything a woman is assured should be "the best day of your life" should be run from a mile. It rarely works out well. Recall that another day that is often touted as "the best of your life" is when you give birth to your children. I hardly need remind you of how likely that is to end with you calling out to a godless heaven for as much morphine as your body can handle without you actually having a cardiac arrest.

And second, I don't think this demented wedding lust does our collective image any good. It makes us look like our frame of reference for fun is very small. I feel a little like Del Boy in the classic British sitcom "Only Fools and Horses," when he falls sideways like a felled tree while murmuring "Play it cool, girls, play it cool." When I hear women talking about how their wedding is going to be/was the best day of their life, I can't help but think, You just haven't taken enough MDMA in a field at 3 a.m., love.

All weddings seem to boil down to acting like Michael Jackson at the height of his insanity—pretending to be a celebrity for one insanely expensive day. And we know why the celebrities have pet monkeys and stupid shoes and the Elephant Man's skeleton and a fun fair and swimming pools shaped like guitars.

BECAUSE THEY'RE DYING INSIDE. THEY'RE STARING INTO THE VOID. They have seen, for one second, their own ultimate, motelike inconsequentiality in a universe that is endless and responded by hiring someone to be in charge of wrangling the straw in their soft drinks. We communally pity these people as damaged idiots.

And yet women now think of it as our "reward" to spend one incredibly expensive day acting like these twats, before biting the bullet, settling down, and never having another "special" day again. Of course, a great deal of not having any more special days, ever again, comes down to the fact you've just spunked £21,000 on 16,000 vol-au-vents and a "light jazz" band—but the symbolism of it all is unbearably potent.

With stuff like this, you have to look at the men. Do *they* have one special day where they feel like kings of the world—and then go back to lives of quiet drudgery? No. They go off and please themselves constantly: as Germaine Greer pointed out in *The Whole Woman*, they fill their spare time with pleasingly nonproductive activities like fishing, golf, listening to records, playing on the Xbox, and pretending to be goblins in *World of Warcraft*. They don't have this insane, pent-up need to spend one day pretending to be Princess Diana (in the fun years, obviously. Not the throwing-yourself-down-the-stairs bit. Or the bit where Camilla came in and ruined everything).

Women, meanwhile, spend their spare time taking on the never-ending list of self-improvements or domestic tasks: housework, homework, counseling the troubled, deworming the cat, doing pelvic-floor exercises, trying to be inventive with cabbage, and exfoliating ingrowing hairs—somehow mollified by having that one "best day of their lives."

Surely, women, we would happily exchange one "special" day for a life filled with more modest pleasures?

Or perhaps we should just junk the whole idea of getting married in the first place. I'm generally against anything where you're supposed to change your name. When else do you get named something else? On joining a nunnery, or becoming a porn star. As an ostensibly joyful celebration of love, that's bad company to be in.

CHAPTER 11

I Get into Fashion!

"I bought a dress today!" I say, as my husband walks through the door. "A NEW DRESS! NEW DRESS NEW DRESS NEW DRESS!"

It is a brown Indian gauze peasant-y dress—"TWELVE POUNDS, Pete—TWELVE POUNDS!"—which I bought from the market—"IT'S FROM THE MARKET, LOVE!"—on Seven Sisters Road earlier that day. The purchase has excited me hugely—it is the first new item of clothing I've bought for nearly two years.

At the age of 24, I am still not really used to buying clothes. Not only are the clothes I covet at the time—crinolines, tippets, bonnets, red flannel petticoats, button-up black patent booties, damask ballgowns, shagreen gloves, fox-fur muffs, and calico nightdresses—not that readily available on Holloway Road—but I have also been stony-ass broke for some time.

Although I had been earning a decent wage as a journalist, it turns out I had made another one of the big miscalculations of my life: believing that income tax is, like menstruation, optional. I haven't paid a penny of tax for the first four years of my working life.

"I thought they'd ring you up if they wanted it!" I wailed to the accountant I'd just hired. "Or that they'd send you a letter, saying, 'Guess what—it's Tax O'clock!' or something. But they never said *anything*. The Inland Revenue have *not* been chatty."

My accountant went on to explain how the burden of disclosure rests with the individual, rather than the Revenue, and that I would need to supply all my bank statements, wage slips, and expense claims since 1994—but I wasn't really listening.

In part, this was because I knew a great many of my bank statements, wage slips, and expense claims got left in a Dumpster in Camden in 1996, along with an armchair I now regretted, in retrospect, discarding—but it's also because I was calculating just how poor I was going to be for the foreseeable future.

Even with my shonky math, I estimated that I was going to have to put every penny of my income into paying off my back tax for at *least* two years, and that I would have to beg Pete to support me financially in exchange for bread-and-butter pudding, jokes, and sex.

"Yesthat'sfine," Pete said, moving me into his house, giving me his spare front-door key. "Thatsoundsabsolutelyfine."

For the next 24 months, I am as poor as a church mouse, but I do get a *lot* of opportunity to work on my stand-up routines.

Two years later, and I'm still going on about the dress. I'm twirling around in it like Scarlett O'Hara in her ballgown.

"It *was* only 12 pounds!" I say guiltily. "Twelve pounds! Although it felt lovely to buy something new, I won't need another dress for *years* now! I can dress it up *and* dress it down with accessories! It really will be value for the money. That's my celebratory spending spree *finished*."

"You know," Pete says, polishing off his 914th bread-and-butter pudding, "all other women buy a lot more clothes than you.

A lot. Every lunchtime, all the women in my office come back with something new in a bag. Now you've paid off that tax, I think you could buy more clothes, to be honest. If you want. I mean, I don't care what you wear. You can wear nothing at all if you want. Can I have some more bread-and-butter pudding, please?"

The next day, while Pete's at work, I think about what he said. All the other women buy lots more clothes, I think. They have lots more clothes than me. They are doing things differently. I'm not doing what the women do.

I go upstairs to the bedroom and look in my wardrobe. Here is the sum total of my clothing at the age of 24: a black velvet floor-length goth dress, which I bought when I was 17 and now has pile-less, bald patches on the elbows from wear. Two pairs of trousers—one black, one navy. A free promotional T-shirt by the band Salad, which has the word "Salad" on it, which I like to wear while preparing, or eating, sausages. A green chenille cardigan from Marks & Spencer, which is so nice I've *twice* had to steal it back off my sister Col when she comes for a visit. A Victorian-style nightie, which I often style out as daywear. And my bathing suit.

I'm not being a proper woman, I think, staring at my wardrobe. All the other women are "putting together outfits" and "working on their looks." I am just "putting together the cleanest things." Now I've got some money again, I should sort this out.

It seems that being a woman is very expensive and time-consuming. My innocence about this is incongruous, given my age, but total. I come from grunge, and then Britpop—scenes where you boast about how little you spent on an outfit ("Three quid! From a jumble sale!" "Ooooh, pricey—I found this jacket in a *Dumpster*. On a *dead man*. Under a *fox carcass*"), and taking pride in "getting ready to go out" consists of little more than washing your face, putting on your Doc Martens/sneakers, and applying black Barry M nail polish, £1, on the bus into town.

But now it seems you find "the dress"—but then "the dress" must have "the belt," and a complementary but not overly matching bag must be found, which works with not only the correct hosiery but also something to "throw over," if you become chilly. It's like fucking *Dragon's Quest*—an endless list of things you've got to run around and try to find, possibly in a cave, or under a sage. The thing you "throw over" can't be an anorak, or a picnic rug salvaged from under the stairs, by the way, but a deconstructed cardigan, a hacking-style jacket, a £200 pashmina, or a "shrug," which unfamiliar item seems, to my untrained eyes, to be a shrunken cardigan made by a fool. It all looks bloody knackering. It's going to cut into my bread-and-butter-pudding-making time severely.

All of this comes to a head in shoes—specifically, heels. I've spent my whole life in sneakers or boots, but it's very clear that, if I am to properly make a go of my twenties, I will just have to go out and get some heels. The women's magazines I read are all unequivocal about heels: they are a nonnegotiable part of being a woman, along with the potential to lactate and the XX chromosome. Women are supposed to adore heels more than they adore their own bodies, or thoughts. They're also supposed to have a great many more shoes than body, or thoughts. Unlike your arse, or thoughts of revolution, you just can't have too many shoes!!!!!!!!!!!!

"No one messes with a woman in heels," one feature in *Elle* concludes. "They are your greatest weapons in the style wars." This shit sounds serious.

The next day, I go out—determined to give being a grown-up woman a try—and purchase my first pair of high heels. I still haven't quite got it—the heels I finally, triumphantly, purchase are sky-blue jelly sandals with a block heel from Barratts, £9.99.

They make my feet sweat so much I squeak slightly as I walk—like I've used mice as insoles, and they're all slowly being crushed to death. They're also quite painful in both the toe and the heel area—but no matter! I am in heels! I am a woman!

That night, trying to negotiate a staircase in them at a gig, I stumble and fall right on top of Graham Coxon from Blur, spilling my whiskey and Coke all down his leg.

"ARGH!" Graham shouts.

"These are my great weapons in the style wars," I say sadly. "No one messes with a woman in heels. I am a woman."

"ARGH!" Graham says again, staring at his wet leg. "You fucking idiot."

I do not give in easily, though. Thirteen years on and I now have both a great many more pairs of high heels and, indeed, a great many more anecdotes about how wearing them has ended badly for me. In fact, I have a whole box full of such shoes under my bed. Each pair was bought as a down payment on a new life I had seen in a magazine and subsequently thought I would attain, now that I had the "right" shoes. Here they are. Here are all the shoes I don't wear:

1. Silver ankle-strap wedges from Kurt Geiger. I wore them once, at an awards ceremony. I got three compliments—YES—but also noticed that my gait in them was slightly less feminine and confident than that of Dame Edna Everage, 82, who was also at the event.

2. Red velvet pumps, Topshop. Wore them once, to a birthday dinner in Soho. Despite the fact I was sitting down all evening, the shoes were so tight and painful that I had to ease my feet out of them. Subsequently, things got a bit "interesting," and when I woke up in

the morning, I was only wearing one of them. The other I vaguely remembered putting on top of a toilet cistern "to be safe," in that all-night Spanish bar round the back of the HMV Megastore on Oxford Street.

3. Gray velvet pumps, exactly the same as the red velvet pumps, save the color. "Good to have this versatile shoe in a neutral color, as well!" I thought. Man, I'm good at buying shoes!

4. Peacock-blue three-inch heels with ruffle on the front. At the party I wore them to, I ended up talking to Noddy Holder from Slade—someone who, as Wolverhampton royalty, I've spent my whole life waiting to meet. Alas, however enthusiastically I tried to immerse myself in Noddytopia, it was an undeniable fact that, by then, my feet were hurting so badly I was standing alternately on one, then the other, with tears in my eyes. Eventually I had to excuse myself from talking to my idol and sit in a corridor, massaging the balls of my feet and wincing.

5. Same again, but in white. "Good to have this versatile shoe in a neutral color, as well!" I thought. Man, I'm good at buying shoes!

6. A pair of curly-toed Turkish slippers in silver-gray and berry-red. Like 90 percent of purchases women make of unwearably batshit gear, in my head I thought, The kind of thing Kate Moss would slip into, when popping out for fags, as I handed over my debit card. And, like 90 percent of women after they have done this, I had to subsequently admit that what has a reptilian, boho edge on Kate Moss looks on me like that game where you have to put on a hat, gloves, and scarf before eating a bar of chocolate with a knife and fork. But in a bad way.

There are another six pairs—gold gladiator sandals that work by way of a toe tourniquet; brown ankle boots that, overnight, went from "grungy" to "looking like something an uptight woman called Barbara would wear"; Doc Marten T-bar shoes that were so heavy, I genuinely thought I was developing Chronic Fatigue Syndrome the first—and subsequently last—time I wore them.

And yet, my understanding is that my collection of Shoes I Don't Wear—lined up neatly in a box under my bed, looking like a terra-cotta army, size 6—is a fairly modest one, within the spectrum of Women's Unworn Shoe Collections. I have one friend who has 27 pairs of heels she can't bear to part with—and yet has worn only once or twice or not at all. *All* women have one of these caches of shoes hidden somewhere in the house.

Why are all these shoes unworn? Ladies, I'm going to put it on the line. I'm going to say what, over the last 13 years, I have gradually realized, and what we all secretly knew anyway, the first time we put heels on: there're only ten people in the world, tops, who should actually wear heels. And six of those are drag queens. The rest of us just need to . . . give up. Surrender. Finally acquiesce to what nature is telling us. We can't walk in them. WE CANNOT WALK IN THE DAMN THINGS. We might just as well be stepping out in antigravity boots, or roller skates.

The unwearability of high heels is self-evident all around us— coming to a head at the average wedding reception, a uniformly high-heeled occasion. In our minds, we see it as a serene and elegant gathering of women in their finest. One of *the* big chances of the year to pretend you're at the Oscars in your stilettos. In actuality, of course, it looks like the annual convention of the Tina Turner Impressionist Union—women staggering around in unaccustomed verticality; foot flesh spilling out over tight, unkind satin; toes going numb for days afterward.

The very few who can walk elegantly in them look amazing,

of course—walking in heels is a skill as impressive as being able to walk a tightrope or blow smoke rings. I admire them. I wish them well. I wish I could *be* them. But they are a tiny minority. For everyone else—the vast majority—we look as inversely elegant as we think we will when we purchase them. We waddle, we go over on our ankles, we can't dance, and we wince incessantly, while hissing, "These SODDING shoes. My feet are killing me."

By the time the reception kicks in, 80 percent of the women are barefoot or in tights—the edges of the marquee littered with a tide line of discarded stilettos, wedges, and kitten heels. Women spend more time shopping for shoes *for* a wedding than they actually spend wearing them *at* the wedding.

But, bafflingly, we totally accept the uselessness of heels. We accept it limply, shrugging. We are indifferent to the thousands of pounds we spend over a lifetime on shoes we only wear once, and in great pain. Indeed, we're oddly *proud* of it. Women buy shoes and gigglingly say, "Of course, they're agony—I'm just going to have to sit on a barstool all night, and be helped to the bathroom by friends, or passersby," despite it sounding as OUTRIGHT INSANE as going, "I've just bought a house—it doesn't have a roof, of course, so I'm just going to sit in the front room with an umbrella up."

So why do we believe that wearing heels is an intrinsic part of being a woman, despite *knowing* it doesn't work? Why do we fetishize these things that almost universally make us walk like mad ducks? Was Germaine Greer right? Is the heel just to catch the eyes of men and get laid?

The answer is, of course, no. Women wear heels because they think they make their legs look thinner, end of. They think that by effectively walking on tiptoes, they're slimming their legs down from a size 14 to a size 10. But they aren't, of course. There is a precedent for a big fat leg dwindling away into a point—and it's on a pig.

And most men distrust, and even dislike, a heel. They often view them with Feud Eyes. This is because:

a. A chick in heels makes a man feel shorter. In man terms, this is like making a lady feel fatter. They don't like it.

b. A woman in heels stands a statistical likelihood of ending her evening with her shoes in her handbag, barefoot and demanding a piggyback to the taxi stand in order to "keep her tights clean." Men are invariably the pig whose back is called for. On this basis alone, men fear a woman tottering toward them at the beginning of an evening, already gimlet-eyed with toe pain, and sitting down to eat with an old-lady sigh.

At 35, I've packed it in. I've finally given up on heels—apart from one pair of yellow tap shoes that are inexplicably comfortable and something from the 1930s in green velvet that I can dance in. Indeed, I've pretty much given up on women's shoes altogether. Even women's flats seem insubstantial and sloppily made, compared to men's. I've got men's riding boots, men's biker boots, men's brogues, some Doc Martens—all beautifully made, comfortable, cheaper than the ones in the women's section, and a pleasingly contrary end to a leg one expects to terminate in a spindly, painful point.

I've decided I'm now essentially on strike when it comes to women's shoes. I'm going to sit out the entire world of chick footwear until designers make some that it's possible to walk in for more than an hour, with the easy gait of Gene Kelly about to break into a routine, and no daylong pain afterward. I fully realize my demands viz. footwear are wholly a minority interest at the moment—who knows how long the aftereffects of *Sex and the City*'s decade-long Blahnik-wank will continue to rumble through society—but I'm pretty determined about this. After all, I've seen those pictures of Victoria Beckham's bare, be-bunioned feet. I don't want toes that look like thalidomide pasties. If I'm going to spunk £500 on a pair of designer shoes, it's going to be a pair that I can (a) dance to "Bad Romance" in and (b) will allow me to run away from a murderer, should one suddenly decide to give chase. That's the minimum I ask from my footwear. To be able to dance in it, and for it not to get me murdered.

Handbags

Of course, the other fashion item women are supposed to go mad for is the handbag. We've long known why—apart from shoes, a handbag is the only other item you're never too fat to fit into. No one ever got dysmorphic and weepy in a changing room trying on a tote.

By the age of 35, I've had two children, paid off half my mortgage, got drunk with Lady Gaga; I make my own guacamole, can do 30 seconds of the easy bit of the "Single Ladies" dance, have two contrary opinions about globalization, know the Heimlich maneuver, and once scored 420 in Scrabble.

But I'm also still dipping into those women's magazines, and they are making me feel genuinely bad about my life achievements. Because I don't yet have an "investment handbag."

My stance on "investment handbags" has always been that if I were going to make a £600 investment, it would probably be in Post Office bonds—and not something that, by and large, lives on the floor in pubs, or that I sometimes use to carry 5 pounds of potatoes home. But I am becoming aware that I am in a handbag minority. Normal women, says *Grazia*, the leading British women's magazine, do not buy one handbag every five years for £45 from Topshop—my personal handbag routine. Normal women have dozens of handbags: small ones, potato-less ones, £600 investment ones such as a Mulberry tote.

With mounting concern, I learned that having a £600 handbag is like having a crush on the Joker in *Batman*. You MUST do it. It is an irreducible fact of being a woman.

Things were brought to a head in the now-defunct *Observer Woman* magazine. Lorraine Candy, *Elle*'s editor in chief, tried to go a week with just high street gear. On Wednesday she wrote: "I've failed. Today, I know that I cannot brave that front row with its cool bags and sexy ankle boots without the one thing that makes my outfit work: my new Chloé bag. I feel ashamed."

I had a flush of horror as I read this: no one had ever passed judgment on my cheap handbag to my face. But then, this is a reserved country. I don't know how they would react to my £45 handbag somewhere more demonstrative—Portugal, say, or Texas. They might leap onto their chairs screaming, "MAH GAHD!" trying to hit my cheap handbag with a broom, as if it were vermin.

That night, I made a decision. One of the modern wisdoms of womanhood is that eBay has fake designer handbags that you can't tell from the real thing. But despite typing "great fake £600 handbags for £100" into the Search field, nothing came up.

Genuinely intrigued, I searched for £600 handbags for £600. Louis Vuitton, Prada, Chloé: £300, £467, £582.

God, they were horrible. Like *Guernica*, in pony skin. I tried to find one I liked. I really did. Tanned, tasseled, and oddly shapeless, many resembled Tom Jones's knackers, with handles. Others were covered in straps, buckles, and brasses, like some S&M horse.

There was a whole shelf of leather clutches with gigantic gold clasps that looked a bit as if someone melted Grace Jones in 1988, leaving behind only her blouson leather jacket and huge earrings.

On page 14 of my search results I finally saw one I liked, by Marc Jacobs. It was bright acid-house yellow, with a picture of Debbie Harry on it. But my joy in finding a £600 bag I liked was mitigated when, on closer inspection, it proved to be a canvas tote for £17; basically, the only designer item I was attracted to was a Marc Jacobs shopping bag.

I am not wholly unfashionable. I have learned some things about style over the years. A bright yellow shoe is surprisingly versatile; patterned tights are never a good idea. And if—through chaos, fate, and backed-up laundry—you end up in an outfit of alarming randomness (socks, Crocs, tuxedo jacket, and tricorne hat), you just look people in the eye and say, with crocodilian self-assurance: "I don't like to be too . . . matchy-matchy."

But if I cannot connect with the finer things in life, and all I can emotionally connect with is a jumped-up carrier bag, it's just further confirmation that I am resolutely of the underclass.

If I'm honest, the handbag I would probably like most is a big hollowed-out potato with handles on it. A giant King Edward with satchel straps. Then, in times of crisis, I could bake and eat the handbag and survive the winter. That is the way of my people.

And yet, despite all this, my handbag psychology denial rumbled on. Yes, those £600 handbags might be visually unappealing, I thought. But maybe if you *touch* them, they have some manner of £600 magic that makes it all worthwhile.

"They will all be made of butter-soft leather," I told myself, not really knowing what that meant. "You can always tell the difference close up. I should go and touch the quality."

I went to Liberty and walked around, touching the handbags, waiting for the enchantment to overwhelm me. They all just felt like handbags. I did, however, see a silvery purse that I liked. For £225.

I am classy after all! I thought, running to the till, immediately incurring a £40 overdraft fine and a rumbling schism in my marriage. "Maybe I have a secret uncle who's an earl! True breeding will out! Finally I crave expensive designer items! I'm normal! Thank you, *Grazia*!"

Five days later the silver purse was pickpocketed on Gower Street. It turns out that thieves read *Grazia*, too. They can spot expensive accessories from 500 yards away.

It also turns out that husbands do not read *Grazia*, and no matter how magnificent or loving they may be, they can't help themselves from sporadically saying "£225! For a purse! JESUS CHRIST!" as if you've just stabbed them quite violently in the balls with a fork, left the fork there, and then hung your coat on it while you go and have a bath.

My current purse cost £25 from the cobblers in Crouch End. I doubt I will be "upgrading" it anytime soon.

Anyway, let's face it: the actual handbag is neither here nor there—it's what you keep in it that's the most important thing. I have—after years of extensive study on the subject—come up with the definitive list of what you ACTUALLY need in your handbag.

1) Something that can absorb huge quantities of liquid
2) Eyeliner
3) Safety pin
4) Biscuit

This covers all eventualities. You will need nothing else.

Clothes

So that's my feet, and what I'm keeping my fags in. But what am I wearing, now? As a strident feminist, how am I dressed?

Women know clothes are important. It's not just because our brains are full of ribbons and bustles and cocktail frocks—although I believe brain scans will finally prove that at some future point. It's because when a woman walks into a room, her outfit is the first thing she says, before she even opens her mouth. Women are judged on what they wear in a way men would find incomprehensible—they have never felt that uncomfortable moment when someone assesses what you're wearing and then starts talking down to you, or starts perving you, or presumes you won't "understand" the conversation—be it about work, parenting, or culture—simply because of what you put on that day.

"Wait!" you often feel like saying. "If I were wearing my collegiate corduroy jacket, instead of this school-run dress, you would include me in your conversation about Jung! If you could see my 'politically engaged' shoes, no *way* would you talk about Barack Obama like that to me! Look! I can show you a picture of it on my iPhone! I HAVE AN OUTFIT FOR THIS OCCASION—JUST NOT ON ME!"

Of course, those instances are merely vexations—classed in with "wrong" outfits that make you feel demoralized the first time you catch your reflection in a shop window and lead to you making subsequent bad "I am fat" decisions—like panic-buying harem pants or eating a disappointing "slimline" sandwich.

In the worst-case scenario, however, a wrong outfit can ruin your life. It can lead to a judge dismissing your rape case, as evidenced by the 2008 "Skinny Jeans" case (where it was claimed a woman wearing skinny jeans couldn't have been raped, because no man could take a woman's skinny jeans off unaided); or by the Amnesty International survey that found that 25 percent of people believe a woman is still to blame for being raped if she dresses "provocatively."

Women know that a woman dressed in a relaxed, casual, or even scruffy manner in the workplace is likely to be considered far less serious about her work than a male peer dressed in exactly the same way. Chicks in jeans and sneakers don't get promoted. Men in jeans and sneakers do. How women look is considered generally interchangeable with who we are—and, therefore, often goes on to dictate what will happen to us next.

So when women fret over what to wear in the morning, it's not because we want to be an international style icon. We're not trying to be Victoria Beckham—not least because there's an absolutely gigantic pile of toast downstairs with our name on it, and we've cracked a smile in the last fortnight.

No—what we're trying to do is work out if everyone that day will "understand" what we're wearing; if we're "saying" the right thing, in a very nuanced conversation. For fashion is merely suggested dialogue—like those Best Man speeches you can download off the Internet. Women are supposed to come up with their own personalized version of this. We're supposed to speak from the heart in what we wear. We have to find capsule wardrobes, things that are "us," things we can "dress up and dress down," "classic pieces," and "jackets—with a twist." It's one of the presumed Skills of a Woman—along with being "better" at doing laundry, naturally suited to being at home all day with a baby, and not really minding that men are considered to be funnier.

Woman are just supposed to be Good at Clothes, and to look down on those who aren't—who screw up even one outfit, as evidenced by all those "Circle of Shame"/"What Was She Thinking?" spreads in every magazine and every tabloid newspaper every week. Prominent female politicians are lambasted for a single pair of "wrong" shoes. You're not allowed to say that this makes you grumpy or angry or despairing—that you personally don't give a toss what Angelina Jolie wears to step off a plane, or that Susan Sarandon is stepping into her sizzling sixties in a beret. At its best—and I love a nice frock—fashion is a game. But for women, it's a compulsory game, like netball. And you can't get out of it by faking a period. I know. I've tried.

And so, for a woman, every outfit is a hopeful spell, cast to influence the outcome of the day. An act of trying to predict your fate, like looking at your horoscope. No wonder there are so many fashion magazines. No wonder the fashion industry is worth an estimated $900 billion a year. No wonder every woman's first thought is, for nearly every event in her life—be it work, snow, or birth—the semidespairing cry, "But what will I wear?"

When a woman says, "I have *nothing* to wear!" what she really means is, "There's nothing here for who I'm supposed to be today."

Because it's not easy to find clothes you're happy in. "There's nothing here for me!" is the cry on the high street, three hours into a shopping trip, having bought only a pair of tights, a foldable chopping board, and school cardigans for the kids. "Everything is two inches too short, two tones too bright, and there's NO SLEEVES. WHY ARE THERE NO SLEEVES? IF EVERY WOMAN IN THIS COUNTRY WERE ALLOWED TO COVER HER UPPER ARMS, AS GOD INTENDED, PRESCRIPTIONS OF XANAX WOULD HALVE IN A FORTNIGHT. WHY ISN'T THERE ANYTHING FOR ME IN THIS GIGANTIC, OVER-LIT SHOP?"

But, of course, there *isn't* anything there for you—specifically for you. Before the high street, women would make their own clothes or see a dressmaker, so that everything we wore was an honest expression of who we were and what we were comfortable with—within the constraints of fashion at the time, anyway.

With the advent of mass fashion, however, not a single item of clothing sold is "for" the woman who buys it. Everything we see in Topshop and Zara and Urban Outfitters and Next and New Look is made for a wholly imaginary woman—an idea in the designer's head—and we buy it if we like it, say, 70 percent. That's about as good as it gets. We rarely, if ever, find something that is 100 percent "us," that we truly desire—although we never admit this to ourselves. Most women are walking around in things they're imagining to be that little bit better. An inch longer here. Without that braiding. In a slightly darker blue. It's the first thing we say to each other: "I wish they had it without the collar!"

Because if you *know* I don't like the collar, then you'll know who I'm *really* trying to be.

And of course, because it's all made for an imaginary woman, often none of it works for a real woman. We can all recall seasons where whole, mad ranges—neon, peach, body-con, bustles—sat, sadly, unpurchased on the hangers from May to September, waiting for the imaginary women they were designed for to come and buy them.

Often a woman is apt to stare at what is approaching on the incoming tide of fashion—one-sleeved dresses, jumpsuits, chintzy florals, "daytime" fetish-wear knickerbockers with poppers on the arse—and exclaim, "But why don't fashion designers start from considering what would make a woman look nice? I don't want to have to 'sell' this outfit! I want it to sell me! For £79.99, I want it to be doing me a favor! I WANT THE CLOTHES TO BE ON MY SIDE!"

I'd never really realized how much fashion isn't "on my side" until I did a fashion shoot for *The Times*. The idea was to get a "normal woman" to wear the upcoming season's trends: pastels, safari, op-art prints, corsets as outerwear, and decorated leggings.

"We'll make you look *gorgeous*," the editor promised. "We've got an *amazing* stylist and photographer. We'll take care of you."

The following eight hours were the worst of my life that haven't ended in an episiotomy. Previously, I'd always thought that all that lay between me and looking like Kate Winslet on the red carpet was £10,000 worth of clothes, hair, makeup, a stylist, and a good photographer. And sure enough, in resulting photos, I looked pretty good. They got some frames of me looking pretty hot in a corset, silk combat trousers, and four-inch heels. To be honest, if I'd seen the picture of me in a magazine in that outfit, I would have thought, I will try that outfit! That looks *good* on her! And she has an arse a lot like mine, although a little bigger, hahaha!

That was just the frames, though: the one position it worked in. It took us 20 minutes, half an hour, an hour to find that one position the outfits looked good in. The rest of the time, it was dealing with the camel-toe here, the upper-arm fat there, the muffin-top bulge the other. The clothes were stretched, pegged, tied on with string; the lighting changed, the hair arranged; hats brought in, in an emergency, to balance cruelly proportioned shoulders. I felt like a pig. A clumpy, awkward pig out of her league. I was supposed to be selling these clothes by finding the "best" angle for them, fronting them, working them—but my tits were wrong, and my arse too big, and my arms helpless, heavy, and exposed. I left that studio, eight hours later, sweaty and in tears. It was the ugliest I'd ever felt. Without even the aid of being able to smile—"Look mysterious, and sexy. Kind of . . . vague"—I was reduced *entirely* down to the clothes on my back and how my body looked in them.

And in these styles, rather than the ones I've carefully collected as being "helpful" to me, I was a total failure.

I'm not stupid—I'd always known that the difference between models and normal women is that normal women buy clothes to make them look good; whereas the fashion industry buys *models* to make the *clothes* look good. Most clothes are helpless without models. They were certainly helpless on me. I could do nothing for this shit. I couldn't even stay upright in the heels.

"I'm so sorry—I bet all the models can do this for hours," I said gloomily, scrambling to my feet again, having keeled over sideways, ungainly, like a horse on its hind legs.

"Oh no," the stylist said cheerfully. "They fall over in them all the time, too. They're impossible to walk in. No one can walk in them. Hahaha!"

I thought again about my years of despair at not being able to walk in heels, despite "everyone" wearing them. Quite a lot of the "everyone," I now reflected, were in fashion shoots or on a red carpet, i.e., they weren't really wearing them as "shoes" to walk around in all day. They were just wearing them for the photographs. They *know* it's just for photographs. We—the customers—are the only ones who are buying this stuff and then trying to walk around in it all day; move in it; live in it.

So much of this stuff is just for tableaux—not real life, I finally realized. Although we use it as our major study aid, fashion does not, ultimately, help us get dressed in the morning. Not if we want to wear something we can walk around in without constantly having the hem ride up or picking the seam out of our crotches. Fashion is for standing still and being photographed. *Clothes*, on the other hand, are for our actual lives. And life is really the only place you can learn the most important lessons about how to get dressed and feel happy.

Here, then, is what I have learned about clothes—ignoring magazines and advertising campaigns and picking up the knowledge where it matters: (a) crying in a changing room in Topshop, while stuck in a pair of PVC leggings, (b) running down the street after someone who looks amazing and saying, "Where did you get that?" * or (c) my sister Weena coming into the bedroom, seeing what I'm wearing, going, "No," and walking out of the room again:

1) Leopard print is a neutral.
2) You can get away with nearly anything if you wear it with black opaque tights and boots.
3) Contrary to popular opinion, a belt is often not a good friend to a lady. Indeed, in many circumstances it acts merely as a visual aid to help the onlooker settle the question: "Which half is fatter—the bottom or the top?"
4) Bright red is a neutral.
5) Cellophane tape is NOT strong enough to mend a hole in the crotch of a pair of tights.
6) You should NOT buy an outfit if you have to strike a sexy pose in the changing-room mirror to make it look good. On the other hand, if you immediately start dancing the minute you put it on, buy it, however much it costs—unless it's lots, in which case, you can't, so don't. Fashion magazines will *never* say, "Actually, don't buy it if you can't afford it." Neither will your friends. I am probably the only person who will EVER say it to you. You're welcome.

---

* Sadly, the answer is almost always, "An amazing vintage shop in Rotterdam, four years ago, that has now sadly burned down in a fire, and which you wouldn't have been allowed in anyway," but I still haven't lost hope they might just point to M&S and say, "There. Ten minutes ago."

7) You should never describe your look as being "a mixture of high street and vintage." Remember how angry it makes you when Sarah Jessica Parker says it. Don't let the abused become the abuser.

8) You are very, very unlikely to look bad in an above-the-knee, fitted, 1950s-style dress with sleeves and a cardigan. Have you seen what Christina Hendricks—the stacked, hot Joan Holloway in *Mad Men*, the woman *Vanity Fair* recently christened "The Body"—looks like in modern combat trousers and a top? Awful. There's a lesson for us all there.

9) The most flattering trousers you'll ever have are some black running trousers with a fiercely high Lycra content. They make your thighs and arse look tiny. You spend over two years trying to pluck up the courage to wear them out with a pair of knee-high boots and a jacket, but always bottle it at the last minute. It is a source of lasting regret.

10) Silver lamé is a neutral.

11) Ditto gold sequins.

12) Instead of buying something that says, "Dry clean only," just put £50 in the garment's pocket and walk out of the shop, leaving both on the hanger. In the long run it will save you money, time, and the unedifying spectacle of you rubbing Sure Extra onto the armpits in an emergency, on a train on the way to a meeting.

And this is what I have learned about fashion.

CHAPTER 12

Why You Should Have Children

A Bad Birth

It was no surprise at all to me to discover I was terrible at giving birth. No surprise at all. All that I know about birth is what I've seen from my mother—returning after delivering every sibling as white as death; hobbling into the house seven times with a bad story: a breech, an emergency caesarean, a trapped nerve, a tangled cord. For her fifth—Corinne—the placenta didn't come away, and an inexperienced midwife simply took hold of the umbilical cord and pulled it, like a dog lead attached to a recalcitrant beagle. My mother hemorrhaged so badly they had to give her four pints of blood, and when they sent her home, it was like having someone return, shell-shocked, from a war.

I was 11—I carried the baby around like a cross between a doll and a baby monkey. We were all in fear of Mum suddenly collapsing again. She fainted in the supermarket, halfway up the stairs. It seemed like the baby was something that was essential to her and should have stayed inside. She seemed broken without it.

The next baby—Cheryl, two years later—was worse. Mum came back with a trapped nerve in her shoulder and couldn't move—she lay in the front room with the curtains drawn through a long hot summer, crying, as the house descended into a hot soup of mold, ants, and scared children. Thirteen now, I fed the family on tins of cheap hot dogs and crackers and jam, the new baby monkey in a cardboard box at my feet, along with the old one. It was awful until late September, when the hot weather broke and Mum finally started to walk around again, slowly; killing the ants with hot water and bleach.

So when I become pregnant at 24, I both know how to look after a baby—you put them in a cardboard box and eat tinned hot dogs—and dread one coming out. Frankly, I don't think I can do it. I don't know *how* you do it. I'm insanely, willfully ignorant. At my six-month checkup, I comment on an odd modern sculpture above the bed. In white plastic, it seems to show ten pupil-less eyes getting gradually wider, as if in alarm.

"What's that?" I ask cheerfully. "Is it a rip-off Jeff Koons?"

"It's the stages of cervical dilation," the midwife says, puzzled. "From nought to ten centimeters."

"The . . . cervix?" I say. "Why does the cervix dilate?"

"That's how the baby comes out," the midwife says, now looking like she's talking to a madwoman. "That's what labor is—the cervix gradually dilating to let the baby out."

"The cervix?" I repeat, wholly alarmed. "A baby can't come out of that! It's not a hole! I've felt it! That's a solid thing!"

"Well, that's why it's all a . . . bit of an effort," the midwife replies, as diplomatically as she can.

At that point, I know I can't have a baby. The me-math just isn't adding up. I can't open my cervix. I wouldn't even know where to start.

So all the way through pregnancy—through the jolly doctors and can-do midwives—I feel pityingly sorry for them every time they refer to my forthcoming labor. It's not going to happen, I say to myself. I feel as if they've all—nurses, obstetricians, my husband—been told that, in nine months' time, I am going to put on a magic show and will miraculously fly around the room like Peter Pan, or—almost literally—make monkeys fly out of my butt. The chairs are all set up and the audience is patiently waiting.

But I, of course, know I am not magic. I know I don't have one single half-ounce of enchantment in my entire body. I've tried everything I can to encourage magic to happen—the birthing pool is set up in the front room, surrounded by candles waiting to be lit. I have herbs and music and things to burn. I am ready to cast the spell—but as I go first one and then two weeks over my due date, I feel like a failed shaman pointing my staff at the sky, shouting, "BEHOLD! THE RAIN!" as the crops continue to wither in the fields and the womenfolk wail.

When my contractions finally start, they are painful yet useless. The baby is in the unfortunate posterior position—her skull grinds against my spine—and the midwives sadly explain that although the magic has started, I have accidentally, in my ignorance, called on bad magic instead: posterior labors are long, arduous and unsatisfying. After 24 sleepless hours, they suggest the hospital. I cry. They insist.

And in the brightness of the ward, confronted with the modern, sleek, beeping wonder of technology, the magic disappears completely. The shaman is revealed just to be an old man with a stick and shuffles away, never to be seen again; the contractions stop entirely.

A sour-faced Swedish midwife assesses me as I sit on the bed, weeping.

"This is what often happens with the mummies who say they want a home birth," she says with some satisfaction, as she opens my legs and inserts a hook—to monitor heart-rate—into my baby's head. Poor baby! Poor baby! I'm so sorry! This is not what I dreamed your first touch would be! "They end up having to come in here and get their tummies cut open."

Finally, I have met someone who realizes what I have known all along. This bitch sees me for what I am: incapable.

From Saturday night until Monday morning, the NHS slowly and dutifully goes through its list of actions to bail out failed women. My water is unbroken—they break it with a crotchet hook. My contractions have stopped—they jump-start them with a pessary. My cervix is unyielding—painfully, they sweep it, just as a contraction starts. It is a sensation a little like being diced, internally, at the start of slow murder.

They are helping me because they have to, of course: these are all things the female body is supposed to do, automatically and without fuss—like precipitation, or season change. My water breaking, my contractions starting—these are all things my body should have done itself, with its innards hidden, like a music box.

But due to my incompetence, they now have had to prise the casing off, and a roomful of increasingly worried doctors are playing each note by hand—strumming flatly on the teeth of the mechanism. My labor has no rhythm at all. Every beat is being forced.

Of course, after two days of this bad dance, the baby starts, very tentatively and apologetically, to die. On the monitor, her heartbeat sounds like a tiny toy drum. As each contraction squeezes her, you can hear the drum getting fainter—as if the Having a Baby parade was passing by in a distant street, or maybe moving away all together.

I know what comes next—intravenous oxytocin. The Drip. I have read about the Drip. Every book on childbirth teaches you to fear it. When you contract naturally, the body generally does it at a pace and intensity you can handle. The Drip, however, has no such compunction. It only has one speed: fast. It is a brutal machine—a metronome for the unrhythmic. An unstoppable atomic clock that makes you explode into contractions every minute, unfailingly. It is a pacemaker for the womb; like the red shoes in *The Red Shoes*. It makes you dance until you drop dead.

The pain was transformative—like going from agnosticism to evangelism in a single hour. The sky was suddenly full of God, and He had biblical pain for me. The breaks in between contractions were like licking a dripping tap in a burning house—a second of relief, but when you turned back, it was so hot that the moisture burned from your lips; the walls had gone up, and there had never been a door or window in the first place. The only way to get out was to somehow turn inside out, like an octopus, and fly out through the magic doorway in your bones.

But I was meat and pain, pinned in place by monitor wires, and my mother had never taught me how to turn inside out.

And in the end—because I wasn't magic and couldn't fly monkeys out of my butt, and I'd spent three days and nights in this place of failure—the doctors had to strap me down and cut me open. Instead of Lizzie coming out of me in a soft, spurting burst of magic and Milky Way, Dr. Jonathan de Rosa pushed my kidneys to one side and hauled her out of me, upside-down by her feet, like a shit-covered rabbit on a butcher's hook.

Of course, I haven't told you the half of it. I haven't told you about Pete crying, or the shit, or vomiting three feet up a wall, or gasping "Mouth!" for the gas and air, as I'd forgotten all other words. Or the nerve that Lizzie damaged with her face and how, ten years later, my right leg is still numb and cold. Or the four failed epidurals, which left each vertebra smashed and bruised, and the fluid between them feeling like hot, rotting vinegar. And the most important thing—the shock, the shock that Lizzie's birth would hurt me so much; would make me an animal with my leg caught in the trap of my own bones and leave me begging for the doctors to take a knife and cut me free.

For the next year, every Monday at 7:48 a.m., I would look at the clock and remember the birth, and tremble and give thanks it was all over, and marvel that we both survived.

Lizzie was born at 8:32 a.m.—but 7:48 was when they gave me the anesthetic, and the pain, finally, stopped.

Now, it's Monday morning. I am on my narrow hospital bed, with everything suddenly quiet and calm, and a saline drip in my hand, and a morphine shot in my leg, and my husband on a chair, and my daughter in an incubator, and not even flowers on the cabinet, it's still so early and new. My eyes are huge with morphine. When I look at the photographs later, I look gorgeous. Like Stevie Nicks, wasted on Mulholland Drive, but incongruously next to a baby.

Pete looks like shit. I didn't notice it at the time because, without pain, everything—even old, brown bloodstains and the punishing strip-lighting—looked beautiful; but the picture that Caz and Weena take of him when they arrive, ten minutes later, shows a man with cried-red eyes and pale green skin, from exhaustion and fear and drinking all my Lucozade.

His eyes are filled with tears; he can only look at me like I am going to die, and he is going to miss me more than he could ever explain.

"Pete," I say, putting my hand out to him. It has a drip in the back of it. Pete looks scared to touch it.

"Everything they did hurt you," he said, and started crying. Really awful crying, with his mouth all liquid, strings of spit between the lips. "I couldn't do anything. Every time I thought it was going to get better, they just did something that made you worse. When they put that thing in your back [the first of three failed shunts for the epidural], they were saying the pain would stop—but it went in wrong and you screamed and wet yourself. They ran with the trolley down the hall. You were making this terrible sound."

I look into the incubator and tap my finger on the side, like people do on goldfish bowls. Lizzie opens her eyes for a second and stares, with wrinkled monkey brow, at me. Her face looks red against the hospital sheet. She still looks like an internal organ. She has no white in her eyes—just black. Just huge pupils—two big holes in her monkey head that lead straight to her monkey brain. She stares at me. I stare back at her.

Pete and I look up at each other. We both know we want to smile at each other; but we cannot.

We look back at the baby.

Pain is transformative. We are programmed for it to be the fastest lesson we'll ever learn. I learned two things from the first baby I had:

1) That being very unfit, attending only two birth classes, and genuinely believing that I would probably die was *not* a good way to prepare for labor, all things told.
2) That once you have experienced that level of pain, the rest of your life becomes relatively easy. However awful an experience, it's really not wasted.

Because you know what you get along with 27 stitches in your belly, or seventh- to second-degree tears in your perineum? Perspective. A whole heap of perspective. I do not mean this in a—to use the technical term—"wanky way." But in many cases, a furious 24-hour dose of wildly intolerable pain sorts out many of the more fretful, dolorous aspects of modern life.

It is like a mental brush fire. You get rid of a lot of emotional deadwood. Do you currently get wound up about poor customer service, or ill-made sandwiches, or how your legs look? You won't when you've been dragged backward through the brightly burning gates of hell during a 48-hour labor!

In that respect, childbirth is far superior to Zoloft or therapy. Fairly early on in the event, you will have the most dazzlingly simple revelation of your life: that the only thing that *really* matters, in this whole goddamn crazy, mixed-up world, is whether or not there's something the size of a cat stuck in your cervix, and that any day when you do *not* have a cat stuck in your cervix will be, by default, wholly perfect in every way.

Around the time that a man with giant hands comes toward you with some forceps the size of barbecue tongs, you think, Perspective. Yes, yes, I do have some perspective now. I doubt that I will get angry about *Ghost Busters 2* being shit ever again.

To be frank, childbirth gives a woman a gigantic set of balls. The high you get as you realize it's all over, and that you didn't actually die, can last the rest of your life. Off their faces with euphoria and bucked by how brave they were, new mothers finally tell the in-laws to back off, dye their hair red, get driving lessons, become self-employed, learn to use a drill, experiment with Thai condiments, make cheerful jokes about incontinence, and stop being scared of the dark.

In short, a dose of pain that intense turns you from a girl into a woman. There are other ways of achieving the same effect—as outlined in chapter 15—but minute for minute, it's one of the most effective ways of changing your life. If I compare how I am now to who I was before I gave birth for the first time, the transformation is almost total. Opening my cervix opened my "doors of perception" more than drugs ever did—to be frank, all I learned from Ecstasy was that if you're caned enough, you can dance on a podium to someone saying, "Time to go home now, ladies and gentlemen" over and over again on a PA.

Birth, on the other hand, taught me a great many things. Before my first labor, here's a list of what I was scared of: The dark. Demons. UFO invasion. The sudden dawning of a new Ice Age. The often-reported phenomenon of the Hag—where sleepers wake up to find themselves paralyzed, with a hag sitting on their chest. Scary movies. Pain. Hospitals. General anesthetic. Insanity. Death. Going up or down a very tall ladder. Spiders. Speaking in public. Talking to people with very strong foreign or regional accents. Driving lessons—particularly changing gears. Cobwebs. Going bald. Lighting fireworks. Asking for help, unusually rapid incoming tides, and ever being sent, in a professional capacity, to interview Lou Reed—who is infamously very grumpy.

After I had the baby, here's what I was scared of: waking up and finding out that the baby had somehow got back inside me and needed to be heaved back out again. And that was it. Although I don't recommend that anyone have a three-day posterior labor, concluding in an emergency C-section, if you are going to have one, it's good to know it's really not a wasted experience. You basically come out of that operating theater like Tina Turner in *Mad Max: Beyond Thunderdome*, but lactating.

Child Rearing

Indeed, in the early years of motherhood, all the similes I could think of involved pugilism, battle, and mettle. Those with no children are apt to think of parenthood as some winsome idyll, primarily revolving around warm milk, bubble blowing, and hugs.

For those engaged in it, however, the language is often military, bordering, at times, on Colonel Kurtz in Vietnam. Many consider Marlon Brando's turn in *Apocalypse Now* as one of the bravura performances of Hollywood. Personally, I suspect he'd recently looked after colicky three-month-old twins for a week and based it on that.

The parallels to war are multiple: you wear the same clothes, day in, day out; you keep saying, hopefully, "It'll all be over by Christmas"; it's long periods of boredom punctuated by moments of sheer terror; you get repeatedly infested by vermin; no one seems to know what's really going on; you will only talk about the true realities of your experiences with other veterans; and you often find yourself lying in the middle of a field in France at 4 a.m., crying for your mother—although the latter tends to be because you've contracted mastitis on a Eurocamp holiday and realized you've only packed one sandal for the six-year-old, rather than because you can see your exploded, trousered leg 20 yards away, and know Wilfred Owen has already started writing a poem about you.

But while it's easy to slide into a gin-sodden, decade-long bout of Lego-stippled self-pity, I prefer to look at the whole business of being a mother from a more positive angle.

First, and most obviously, there is the sheer emotional, intellectual, physical, chemical pleasure of your children. The honest truth is that the world holds no greater gratification than lying in bed with your children, putting your leg on top of them in a semi-crushing manner, while saying sternly, "You are a poo."

Fifteen-thousand-pound bottles of vintage champagne; hot-air balloons flying over wildebeest migrations; sharkskin shoes with a diamond on the sole; Paris: these are all, ultimately, consolation prizes for those who don't have access to a small, ideally slightly grubby child whom they can mess around with, poke and squash a little—high on ridiculous love.

It's the silliness—the profligacy, and the silliness—that's so dizzying: a seven-year-old will run downstairs, kiss you hard, and then run back upstairs again, all in less than 30 seconds. It's as urgent an item on their daily agenda as eating or singing. It's like being mugged by Cupid.

You, in turn, observe yourself from a distance, simply astonished by the quantities of love you manufacture. It is endless. Your adoration may grow weary but it will never end: it becomes the fuel of your head, your body, and your heart. It powers you through the pouring rain, delivering forgotten raincoats for lunchtime play; works overtime, paying for shoes and puppets; keeps you up all night, easing cough, fever, and pain—like lust used to, but much, much stronger.

And the ultimate simplicity of it is awe-inspiring. All you ever want to know—the only questions that really matter—are: Are the children all right? Are they happy? Are they safe? And so long as the answer is "Yes," nothing, ultimately, matters. You come across this passage in *The Grapes of Wrath* and go cold at the truth: "How can you frighten a man whose hunger is not only in his own cramped stomach but in the wretched bellies of his children? You can't scare him—he has known a fear beyond every other."

There is a black-and-white picture in my hallway, of me, Nancy, and Lizzie in the bath, when Nancy was eight months old and Lizzie two-and-a-half. I am gently biting Lizzie. Nancy, in turn, is gumming my face. All eyes are on the person taking the picture—Pete, who was, as the slight camera-wobble shows, laughing. There we are—a tangle of half-shared DNA, all interlocking with each other; all being watched over by the one who loves us best. If I had to explain to someone what happiness is, I would show them this picture.

"It's biting some kids in a bath, as their dad shouts, 'Bite your mum's face! It's more sensitive there!' " I would say.

But it's not as if we don't know about the oozy, woozy sunrise love of becoming a parent. The spangled Care Bear world of mothering has long been documented. But—while the almost indescribable joys of selfless love are not to be underestimated—it does a woman good to ponder parenthood from this alternative angle, too: "What's in it for me? What's the good stuff? What am I going to get out of this?" Like you're mooching past the Shop of Sperm, ovaries in hand, wondering whether to go in.

Currently, ten years down the line, I can tell you what I've got out of it, so far. It's a surprisingly good deal.

No. 1: A superlative understanding of how long an hour is. Before I had children, I could spend an hour doing absolutely nothing. *Nothing*. Indeed, an hour was chickenfeed. I could spend whole *days* with absolutely no achievement at all. Ask me how my week had been, and I would puff my cheeks out and go, "Phew! I have been *flat out*! There is no rest for the wicked! It's end-to-end stuff! I am burning the candle at *both ends*, my friend"—when all I had really done was maybe write a single article and then halfheartedly start sorting out the kitchen drawers, before *Big Brother* came on and I left all the egg whisks on the floor for Pete to tread on.

Three days after having Lizzie, however, I suddenly realized the riches I had squandered. An hour! Oh man, what I could do with an hour now! Sitting on a rocking chair, holding a fitfully sleeping newborn—remote control tantalizingly out of reach—all I could do was watch the huge railway clock on the wall slowly ticking away each second; thousands of them, in which I could do nothing at all. Now, of course, all I could think of was how busy I would be if I could have my life back, and someone else were holding the baby.

Oh *man*, I could be learning French now, if I didn't have this baby, I would think dolefully. In an hour, I could learn how to order a coffee, a cab, and a pancake. Just an hour! If my mother wasn't so *sodding selfish* and simply gave up her life to come here and babysit, I could learn how to tie sailor's knots! Take in the exhibition of ancient maps at the British Museum! Finally buy a curtain for the bedroom instead of thinking it would be a "fun thing" to do "when the baby comes." WHY did I waste all that time before? OH WHY OH WHY? Now I'm not going to be able to do this for *years*. I will be 50 before I speak French. I am a fool.

This sudden, hurtling realization about the fleetingness of time often comes hand in hand with:

No. 2: A sudden, hurtling increase in ambition. Hey, work is for bread-heads and squares, I used to think before having kids. You won't find me selling out my soul to the Man! No—I am happy doing bare minimum and spending all my spare time on my fascinating hobbies of smoking marijuana, hand-making Christmas cards, fannying away nine hours a day in Internet chat rooms, having long breakfasts with friends, and watching *Cheers*. Stroll on, the Man—and take all your ephemeral trappings of success with you!

Within three weeks of having Lizzie, my opinions on this had taken a 360-degree turn. When people ask my children, "What does Mummy do?" I don't want them to look embarrassed and say, "She knows Cliff Clavin's mother's name," I thought sadly, looking down at Lizzie's soon-to-be embarrassed face. I want her to say, "She is the CEO of the international imagineering company that brought peace to the Middle East. *And* she knows Cliff Clavin's mother's name." Oh, Lizzie, I have let you down. I tell you what, little dude—if you just have a three-year-long nap, starting now, I'll sort it *all out*. I get it now. I have to *get on* with stuff. I am going to be a *high flier*.

So in the tiny windows of time that your child is asleep or someone else is looking after her, you find yourself becoming almost superhumanly productive.

Give a new mother a sleeping child for an hour, and she can achieve ten times more than a childless person. "Multitasking" doesn't come near to the quantum productivity of someone putting in an online grocery order, writing a report, cooking the tea, counseling a weeping friend on the phone, mending a broken vacuum—all within the space of a 3 p.m. nap.

The aphorism "If you want something done, ask a busy woman" is in direct acknowledgment of the efficiency boot camp parenthood puts you through. People with twins can even throw their voice into an adjacent room, while having an ostensibly uninterrupted conversation with an older child. It really is quite magic.

If you employ a parent in your place of work, yes, they may occasionally have to take the day off to nurse a child through dengue fever. But, my God, I bet they're the only people who know the correct way to kick the photocopier when it's broken and can knock you up a six-month strategy plan in the time it takes for the elevator to go from the 24th floor to the lobby.

No. 3: Nothing is impossible anymore. One thing's for sure: by the time your child is two years old, you will look back at what you were like before you had a child and regard yourself as a weak, spineless, dandified, pampered, ineffectual, shallow time-wasting dilettante.

Every parent has their particular moment where they realize that, since they've had a child, nothing really fazes them anymore. For me, it was the day that potty-training Lizzie went wrong, and I had to kick a poo across a falconry display in a marquee at Regent's Park Zoo. I had the left foot of Beckham, the icy composure of Audrey Hepburn on a catwalk, and the quick-thinking disposal nous of whoever it was that first thought of entombing radioactive material in concrete.

I can assure you, compared to that, the day I had only 27 minutes to get from my house in North London to 10 Downing Street to interview the prime minister—then received a phone call telling me the taxi was arbitrarily canceled—was *nothing*.

And, of course, I made the interview on time. And you know why? Because I'M A MUM. I technically outrank Barack Obama in at least nine categories.

A Good Birth

Two and a half years later, I'm doing it all over again: I've put a baby inside me, allowed its head to grow to an inadvisably large circumference, and now I have to trouble my cervix with that whole dilation thing.

This time around, though, I'm doing things differently. For starters, I haven't spent the last two months of my pregnancy thinking, Let Christmas last forever! Every morning can start with two mince pies, served with cream, six miniature heroes, and some Pringles! It's Crisp-mas! Hurrah for pregnant me!

As a result, I haven't put on forty pounds, and I'm capable of things like "walking," "standing," and "getting off the sofa without making an *Oooof*! sound." I've attended all my birth classes—including a birth visualization course, in which a hypnotically voiced woman repeatedly reminds me that my cervix really *is* a trapdoor, and that mentally jamming a chair against it while going, "Yeah—like *that's* going to happen" is not useful for anyone—least of all me. It's taken me until I'm 27 years old, but I now genuinely believe that a cervix really is a hole.

And finally, this time, I have acknowledged something that I just couldn't before: it's not going to kill me.

Deep down, this is what I really believed, the first time I was pregnant. That was the Kraken my birth was sunk by. I found labor and birth truly beyond imagining and—like a medieval peasant, denying anything beyond her conception—presumed this must mean that I would simply, and sadly, have to die when it happened. I was pleased—if incredulous—that other mothers managed to get through it alive; but nobly resigned to my own poignant gravestone in a churchyard: "Died in childbirth. 2001. Like Miss Melly in *Gone with the Wind*."

There is no such virgin fear now, though—no maudlin nine-month dreams of coffins, widowers, and wailing babies. I am not penning my own eulogy to myself—"She was a reasonably fair person, who could always accessorize well with gloves"—while weeping.

Now I know how birth works—now I've been talked through labor by that quiet-voiced woman—I feel I've finally been told what my task is. It's simple—so simple I'm amazed I didn't know it before. One morning I am going to wake up, and before I sleep again, I will have to tick off a long list of contractions, one by one. And when I get to the last one, I will have my girl. Each one of these will be a job in itself—a minute-long experience that would alarm anyone suddenly struck by it, without warning—but I know the one fact that makes it easy: there is nothing awry. Everything is as it should be. Unlike all other pain on earth, these don't signal something going wrong but something going right.

This is what I did not realize the first time, when I prayed wildly for the pains to stop. I didn't know then that these pains were actually the answer, and that their every alternative was much, much worse. Now I know what they are, and what they're for, I greet each one with calm cheer: 60 seconds to breathe through, as limp as a sleeping child, so that there is nowhere for this wash of sensation to snag—no tensed muscle it can get caught on. I am a clear glass of water, leaf-smoke blown sideways in the wind; empty space, for a moon to sail through.

By the time I get to the hospital, I'm contracting so hard I dramatically drop to my knees in the doorway and clutch at the nearest object—a life-size statue of the Virgin Mary. Four nurses have to run to stop it from toppling and crushing me.

For this birth, I don't lie on a bed, helpless—waiting for a baby to be delivered by room service. I've been told to walk, and I do—I pace miles and miles, like I'm on my way to Bethlehem. I use the hospital corridors like the world's slowest, fattest race track. I walk for four hours, nonstop. Oh, Nancy! I walk from St. Paul's to Hammersmith for you, barefoot, quietly sighing, from Angel to Oval, the Palace to the Heath. Your head is like stone against bone—a quiet pressure I can't stop now, and neither can you. Gravity is the magic I couldn't find before, strapped to the bed, two years ago. Gravity was the spell I should have invoked. I was looking in all the wrong grimoires.

After four hours of pacing, everything changes, and I know I have walked far enough. I climb into the pool and push Nancy out in five short bursts. As her face appears—a purple shar-pei puppy, with a lard-slicked 'fro—even I can see it's too late to go wrong now.

"That was easy!" I shout, the first words out of my mouth, before she has even left the water; as the midwives stand by with towels, waiting to wrap her. "That was easy! Why doesn't anyone tell you it's so easy!"

CHAPTER 13

Why You Shouldn't Have Children

Of course, while having children is hard work—a minimum 18-year commitment at full throttle; followed by another 40 years of part-time fretting, money lending, and getting on their nerves when you keep cutting their toast into soldiers, even though they're 38 and a neurosurgeon now—in many ways, it's the easy option for a woman. Why?

Because if you have children, at least people won't keep asking you when you're going to have children.

Women are always being asked when they're going to have children. It's a question they're asked even more often than "Can I help you, madam?" when they've just come in to a shop to make a mobile call somewhere quiet, or "Can't you trim those bangs back? You've got a *lovely* face," by their nan.

For some reason, the world really wants to know when women are having children. It likes them to have planned this shit *early*. It wants them to be very clear and up front about it—"Oh, I'd like a glass of Merlot, the clams, the steak—and a baby when I'm 32, please."

It is oddly panicked by women who are being a bit relaxed and "whatever" about it all: "But your *body clock*!" it is apt to shout.

"You need to be planning *at least* five years ahead! If you want a baby at 34, you need to be engaged by 29, *minimum*. Chop chop! Find a husband! Or you'll end up *like poor barren lonely Jennifer Aniston*."

And if a woman should say she doesn't want to have children at all, the world is apt to go decidedly peculiar:

"Ooooh, don't speak too soon," it will say—as if knowing whether or not you're the kind of person who desires to make *a whole other human being in your guts, out of sex and food*, then base the rest of your life around its welfare, is a breezy, "Hey—whatever" decision. Like electing to have a picnic on an unexpectedly sunny day, or changing the background picture on your desktop.

Women, it is presumed, will always end up having babies. They might go through silly, adolescent phases of pretending that it's something that they have no interest in—but, when push comes to shove, womanhood is a cul-de-sac that ends in Babies "R" Us, and that's the end of that. All women love babies—just like all women love Manolo Blahnik shoes and George Clooney. Even the ones who wear nothing but sneakers, or are lesbians, and really hate shoes, and George Clooney.

So, really, you're kind of *helping* them when you ask them when they're going to finally get on with it and have a baby. You're just reminding them to keep their eyes open—in case they see any sperm, when they're out and about. They might need it, later.

When I was 18, I presented, for one year, a late-night music show on Channel 4 called *Naked City*. If asked to summarize it in one sentence, I would say, "It was canceled after two series and no one ever remembered it."

Nonetheless, when it first launched, it had a bit of publicity around it, and I got to spend a couple of weeks being interviewed by Her Majesty's press and having my picture taken, during which

I would, unfailingly, do my "open-mouthed Muppet face," to the consequent and immense dispiritment of everyone involved.

While all the various sections of the press had their trademark angles on the interviews—the *Sun* asked me about my "boobs," the *Mirror* tried to get me involved in a "feud" with Dani Behr, the *Mail* wanted to know just how far back the Moran family had emigrated into the country and, therefore, how foreign I was—there was one common question, across the board:

"And so—do you want to have kids?"

The first time I was asked this, I laughed hysterically for three minutes.

The interview was being conducted in my shambolic Camden house—electricity still cut off, Saffron the stupid dog molting everywhere so badly that I'd had to put a sheet of newspaper down on the sofa for the interviewer to sit on, lest he leave wearing a pair of dog-hair chaps. I was in pajamas at 4 p.m., chainsmoking and serving out tots of Southern Comfort in a wineglass. They had come to interview someone whose job was presenting a late-night rock show on the "naughty" channel. I was 18. I was a child. But, still:

"And so—do you want to have kids?"

"Have kids?" I hooted. "Have kids? Dude, the mice in my kitchen have starved to death because I never have anything in. I can't even care for *vermin*. Have kids. HAHAHAHA."

So that was the first time—but not the last.

Of course, I understood why these journalists were asking me this question; when I was being a journalist, I was asking this question too.

I wasn't at *first*. When I interviewed, say, Björk or Kylie Minogue, the last thing on my mind was asking them if they wanted children. After all, I never asked Oasis or Clive Anderson if they did. But if you work for a glossy women's magazine—which I did, sporadically—when you filed your interview, more often than not, the editor would read it and then ring you, to have this conversation:

EDITOR: It's amazing. Reeeeeally lovely. Fabulous. Gorgeous. We love it. LOOOOOVE IIIIIIT. [PAUSE] Just two things, though. First of all—what was she wearing?

ME: I dunno. A top?

EDITOR: Whose top?

ME, confused: Her top?

EDITOR: No—*whose* top? Was it Nicole Farhi? Joseph? Armani?

ME, trying: It was gray . . .

EDITOR, briskly: Just ring her PR and ask, could you? And put it in the first paragraph. You know. "Kylie sits on the couch with her bare feet tucked under her, dressed down but elegant in a cashmere top by Joseph, trousers by McQueen, kicked-off Chloé shoes on the floor beside her." That kind of thing.

ME, bemused but willing: OK.

EDITOR: And second thing—does she want kids?

ME: I dunno!

EDITOR: Is she going out with someone now?

ME: I dunno! I didn't ask. We were talking about the album, and this party she went to, and how she cried when Michael Hutchence died . . .

EDITOR: Could you just do a quick phoner and ask her? Ask her when she wants to become a mother. I think the piece needs it . . .

Only with the women, though. I've never once been asked to do it with a male interviewee. You *never* get asked to ask Marilyn

Manson if he's been hanging around in JoJo Maman Bébé, touching tiny booties and crying.

The reason they don't ask men when they're having kids, of course, is because men can, pretty much, carry on as normal once they've had a baby. That's how the world's still wired. Millions of admirable men choose not to, obviously—they go, hand in hand, with their partners, and cut the sleeplessness and the fear and the exhaustion and the remorselessness of the birdlike squawking 50/50. As a result, I fancy them.

But when women are asked when they're going to have children, there is, in actuality, another darker, more pertinent question lying underneath it. If you listen very, very carefully—turn off all extraneous sound sources and press your finger to your lips, to silence passersby—you can hear it.

It's this: "When are you going to fuck it all up by having kids?"

When are you going to blow a four-year chunk, minimum, out of your career—at an age when most people's attractiveness, creativity, and ambition is peaking—by having a baby? When are you going to—as is the decent, right, and beautiful thing—put all your creativity and power on hold in order to tend to the helpless, minute-by-minute needs of your newly born? When are you going to stop making films/albums/books/deals? When do the holes start appearing in your CV? When do you get left behind and forgotten? CAN WE GET POPCORN AND WATCH?

When people ask workingwomen, "When are you going to have a baby?" what they're really asking is "When are you going to leave?"

And the question is always "When are you going to have kids?" Rather than "Do you want to have kids?"

Women are so frequently scared about their biological clocks—

"YOU'VE ONLY GOT TWO YEARS LEFT TO HAVE A BABY!"—that they never get the chance to consider if they actually care or not if the damn thing grinds to a halt. With female fertility being presented as something limited and due to vanish quite soon, there's a risk of women panicking and having a baby "just in case"—in much the same way they panic and buy a half-price cashmere cardigan two sizes too small in a sale.

On the one hand, they didn't really want it, but on the other they might not have the chance to get one again, so better safe than sorry.

It's not unknown for mothers to say at 2 a.m., gin-truthful, "It's not that I wish I hadn't had Chloe and Jack. It's just, if I could do it all again, I don't know whether I'd have kids at *all*."

But deciding not to have children is a very, very hard decision for a woman to make: the atmosphere is worryingly inconducive to saying, "I choose not to," or "It all sounds a bit vile, tbh." We call these women "selfish." The inference of the word "childless" is negative: one of lack, and loss. We think of nonmothers as rangy lone wolves—rattling around, as dangerous as teenage boys or men. We make women feel that their narrative has ground to a halt in their thirties if they don't "finish things" properly and have children.

Men and women alike have convinced themselves of a dragging belief: that somehow women are incomplete without children. Not the simple biological "fact" that all living things are supposed to reproduce, and that your legacy on earth is the continuation of your DNA—but something more personal, insidious, and demeaning. As if a woman somehow remains a child herself until she has her own children—that she can only achieve "elder" status by dint of having produced someone younger. That there are lessons that motherhood can teach you that simply can't be replicated elsewhere—and every other attempt at this wisdom and self-realization is a poor and shoddy second. Like mothers can graduate with honors from Harvard, while the best the childless can manage is a high school equivalency diploma.

Although I'm generally pro any rare anomaly in societal attitudes that values women's work highly—in this case, the belief that motherhood is some necessary, transformative event, without any parallel or equivalent—it is, ultimately, a right pain in the arse for women.

Part of this feeling that women can only become powerful elders in society when they have kids—the rise of the "yummy mummy" in the UK, or Sarah Palin's "mama grizzly" in the United States—is, I suspect, linked to the fact that women aren't valued when they actually *do* get old: essentially, the peak of your respectability and wisdom is seen to come in the years you're still fertile, holding down a family and, increasingly, a job at the same time. By the time you hit 55 you're being fired from the BBC and getting sniped at for being wrinkly. You don't have a glorious, eminent old age—where you're a bit like Blake Carrington, but a lady—to look forward to. *Your* big moment in society is during the breeding years. The inherent sexism—and stupidity—in this takes my breath away.

Because this injunction for all women to have children isn't in any way logical. If you take a moment to consider the state of the world, the thing you notice is that there are plenty of babies being born; the planet really doesn't need *all* of us to produce more babies.

Particularly First World babies, with their ferocious consumption of oil and forest and water, and endless burping-out of carbon emissions and landfill. First World babies are eating this planet like termites. If we had any real perspective on fertile Western women, we'd be jumping on them in the streets, screaming, "JESUS! CORK UP YOUR NETHERS! IMMUNIZE YOURSELF AGAINST SPERM!"

If we could remember this for more than ten seconds at a time, women would never be needled with "So—when are you going to pop one out?" again.

Because it's not simply that a baby puts a whole person-ful of problems into the world. It takes a useful person *out* of the world as well. Minimum. Often two. When you have young children, you are useless to the forces of revolution and righteousness for *years*. Before I had my kids I may have mooched about a lot but I was politically informed, signing petitions, and recycling everything down to watch batteries. It was compost heap here, dinner from scratch there, public transport everywhere. No Barclays Bank, no Kenyan beans—I paid my dues to the union, and to charity. I rang my mother regularly. I was smugly, bustingly, low-level good.

Six weeks into being poleaxed by a newborn colicky baby, however, and I would have happily shot the world's last panda in the face if it made the baby cry for 60 seconds less. The cloth diapers—"If we don't use cloth diapers, who will?"—were dumped for disposables; we lived on ready meals. Nothing got recycled; the kitchen was a mess. Union dues and widow's mites were canceled—we needed the money for the disposables and the prepared meals. My mother could have died and I would neither have known nor cared.

I had no idea what was going on outside the house—I didn't read a newspaper or watch a news report for over a year. The rest of the world disappeared. This world, anyway—with China, and floodplains, and malaria, and insurgency. *My* world map now was soft—made of brightly colored felt and appliqué: covered in the undulating turf of Teletubbyland and scattered with rabbits.

Every day, I gave thanks that both my husband and I were just essentially useless arts critics—in no way engaged in the general betterment of the world.

"Imagine if you and I had been hot-shot geneticists, working on a cure for cancer," I used to say gloomily, after another panicked day of shoddy, half-finished work, filled with the despairing cries of "Dear God, let the editor have pity on us!"

"And we were so exhausted that we had to simply give up the project—downgrade to something easier, and less vital," I continued, eating dry coffee granules for energy. "Lizzie's colic would be responsible for the deaths of billions. *Billions*."

Let's face it, most women will continue to have babies, the planet isn't going to run out of new people, so it's of no real use to the world for you to have a child. Quite the opposite, in fact. That shouldn't stop you having one if you want one, of course—a cheery cry of "Yes—but my baby might grow up to be JESUS. Or EINSTEIN! Or JESUS EINSTEIN!" is all the justification you need, if you actually *want* one.

But it's also worth remembering it's not of vital use to you as a woman, either. Yes, you *could* learn thousands of interesting things about love, strength, faith, fear, human relationships, genetic loyalty, and the effect of apricots on an immature digestive system.

But I don't think there's a single lesson that motherhood has to offer that couldn't be learned elsewhere. If you want to know what's in motherhood for you, as a woman, then—in truth—it's nothing you couldn't get from, say, reading the 100 greatest books in human history; learning a foreign language well enough to argue in it; climbing hills; loving recklessly; sitting quietly, alone, in the dawn; drinking whiskey with revolutionaries; learning to do close-hand magic; swimming in a river in winter; growing foxgloves, peas, and roses; calling your mum; singing while you walk;

being polite; and always, always helping strangers. No one has ever claimed for a moment that childless men have missed out on a vital aspect of their existence, and were the poorer and crippled by it. Da Vinci, Van Gogh, Newton, Faraday, Plato, Aquinas, Beethoven, Handel, Kant, Hume. Jesus. They all seem to have managed quite well.

Every woman who chooses—joyfully, thoughtfully, calmly, of her own free will and desire—not to have a child does womankind a massive favor in the long term. We need more women who are allowed to prove their worth as people, rather than being assessed merely for their potential to create new people. After all, half those new people we go on to create are *also* women—presumably *themselves* to be judged, in their futures, for not making new people. And so it will go on, and on . . .

While motherhood is an incredible vocation, it has no more inherent worth than a childless woman simply being who she is, to the utmost of her capabilities. To think otherwise betrays a belief that being a thinking, creative, productive, and fulfilled woman is, somehow, not enough. That no action will ever be the equal of giving birth.

Let me tell you, however momentous being a mother has been for me, I've walked around exhibitions of Coco Chanel's life work, and it looked a lot more impressive, to be honest. I think it's important to confess this. If you're insanely talented and not at all broody, why not just go and have more fun? As I'm sure we're all aware by now, there really are no prizes for drudgery. Jesus is not keeping a note of every tiny arse you've wiped in Jesus's Big Jotter of Martyrdom.

And if you're a nerdy girl, you've read enough books and seen enough films to know that being on a mission, saving the world, trying to get the band back together, or just putting on a play, right there, in a barn, really is a life well lived. Batman doesn't want a baby in order to feel he's "done everything." He's just saved Gotham again! If this means that Batman must be a feminist role model above, say, Hillary Clinton, then so be it.

Feminism needs Zero Tolerance over baby angst. In the 21st century, it can't be about who we might make, and what *they* might do, anymore. It has to be about who we are, and what we're going to do.

Plus—having decided to remain footloose, unimpregnated, and at the height of her creative potential—Caz is always available for babysitting for me. I'm going to get her an IUD for Christmas.

CHAPTER 14

Role Models and What We Do with Them

If there is one single thing that gives me hope for the future of female liberation, it has been, over the last few years, watching the fall, and rise, of various female icons. In many ways, it is within the pages of the glossy gossip magazines that the next chapter of feminism has slowly, and incongruously, been taking shape.

In the interregnum between female emancipation and female politicians, businesswomen, and artists finally coming into true equality, celebrity culture is the forum in which we currently inspect and debate the lives, roles, and aspirations of women. Tabloids, magazines, and the *Daily Mail* work by means of turning the lives and careers of a few dozen women into a combination of living soap and daily morality lesson—on the good side, responding to the gigantic desire to examine the modern female condition, but on the bad side, leaving the subjects ostensibly powerless to write their own narrative or express their own analysis of the matter. This is why any modern feminist worth her salt has an interest in the business of A-list gossip: it is the main place where our perception of women is currently being formed. That's my excuse for buying *OK!* anyway.

So in the absence of a female Philip Roth scrutinizing aging, death, and desire, we have the stories of "cougars" like Demi Moore, Kim Cattrall, and Madonna dating younger men and remaining surgically "youthful." We might not have a female Jay McInerney or Bret Easton Ellis—young, talented, and off the rails—but we do have Lindsay Lohan and Britney Spears becoming successful absurdly young and then self-destructing on a hundred sidewalks and at a thousand parties.

As these stories get endlessly discussed in the gossip rags, we form our own opinions of both the celebrities themselves ("Bloody idiot. And *horrible* hair") and the way the press treats them ("Everything they say about her is *vile patriarchal bullshit.* I wish to *GOD* Germaine Greer had a gun"). Until we get a proper female canon of artists, these minutely papped lives will have to do.

Perhaps the most notable case of all—while we still lack a coherent/populist fifth wave of feminist discourse—has been Katie Price, aka Jordan, who has come to embody a whole nexus of female issues.* In a capitalist society, Price is an undeniably successful businesswoman—but by dint of selling her personal life.

---

* Katie Price is the third most famous woman in Britain after Kate Middleton and Princess Diana who is, obviously, dead. A former glamour model turned reality TV star—imagine a cross between Snooki and Kim Kardashian, but incalculably less charming—Price has gained her fame by being willing to sell any and every aspect of her life to glossy magazines for a fat fee. Of course, in order to become the multimillionairess she is you have to have a lot of life to sell—and so Price's time on Earth has been spent ricocheting between various startled-looking husbands, lovers, and celebrity friends, while her alarmed-looking children trail behind her, blinking in the blinding burst of paparazzi flashbulbs.

To give a measure of the woman, one of her most notable life events was a £30,000 hairdo that went wrong. I'm sure Americans spend £30,000 on their hair all the time—but here in Britain that would buy you the

She is powerful—but by dealing in an outwardly old-fashioned notion of female sexuality. And she is independent—but defined and judged by her high-profile relationships. A few years ago, Price was being seriously touted as a feminist icon in broadsheet newspapers—I suspect because, at root, she simply confused cultural commentators to the point of panic. You can see her tits—but she also has her own line of bed linens. What's *that* all about?

I was one of those broadsheet journalists sent to find out whether or not she was a good feminist role model. In 2006 I spent half a week trailing around after her for a cover story for *Elle* magazine. I ended the whole thing reflecting that I have genuinely interacted with monitor lizards with more warmth than Price. The first time I met her, it was at the photoshoot for the feature. Greeting me with a smile that didn't reach her teeth, let alone her eyes—but then that's Botox for you—she was sitting at a mirror, having her makeup done.

"There's something I'd like to say," Price said. "I'd love to do a mascara ad. All the ones on television are false advertising—they use false eyelashes. But these are *real*. I would *love*," she reiterated, looking at me in a "make sure you put this in the feature" way, "to do a mascara ad." She prodded her eyelashes with her fingertips to show me how good they were.

Five minutes later her manager, Claire Powell, took me to one side. "We're thinking Katie's next move should be a cosmetic advertisement, makeup endorsement, that kind of thing. That's where we're moving to."

---

hair of EVERY LIVING PERSON IN THE COUNTRY, plus dibs on the pelts of most of our animals.

Please do not judge our country harshly on the basis of Price: we also invented a) the Beatles b) most cheeses and c) the suspension bridge. Underneath it all, we are good people.

Still, at least on this point if we were talking about her eye-lashes—Price had something to say. For the next three hours in the studio, every other attempted conversational tactic failed. Books, current affairs, television and movies—Price shrugged at each one. When I asked what she did in her spare time, she sank into silence for nearly a minute, and then offered that she liked to stick Swarovski crystals onto household appliances—"like the remote control."

It became very clear that unless it was a book she'd "written," current affairs she'd taken part in—such as selling exclusive coverage of her wedding for £1 million—or a television show she'd starred in, Price had absolutely no interest in it whatsoever. Her world consisted entirely of herself, her pink merchandise line, and the constant semicircle of paps minutely photographing this ongoing narrative of solipsism. No wonder her eyes were so blank—she had nothing to think about apart from herself. She's like the ouroboros—the mythical serpent, forever eating her own tail.

Perhaps because of this lucrative self-obsession, throughout our time together, she was never less than a charmless, basilisk-eyed tyrant, bossing her then-husband Peter Andre around as if he were a piddling puppy, squatting on her best shoes, and infusing every engagement with a world-weary contemptuousness—as if wearing dresses, riding in cars, and talking to people was the pastime of a cunt, and she was furious she'd gotten landed with it.

At one point she was so rude that Andre had to apologize to everyone in the room—"She'll wear anything apart from a smile, ha-ha!" he said, trying to make a joke of it—as I stood and marveled at the idea that someone whose sole career consisted of "being herself" was doing it so unappealingly and gracelessly. It was like watching an Olympic sprinter coming off the blocks sulkily, and then complaining about "getting sweaty," or a rabbit bellyaching about all the sex it was supposed to have.

There were some fun bits to the week—trying on Price's wedding ring, which was the size of a pork chop, larded with pink diamonds. And on the last night—at an awards ceremony dinner—Price had a glass of champagne and launched into a furious bitching session about other female celebrities: hissing "She's so false!" at Caprice and gleefully boasting about how Victoria Beckham had to hire "ugly nannies" in case David Beckham was "tempted. She can't trust him to keep his dick in his pants with anyone good-looking! I feel sorry for her. All my nannies are *gorgeous*," she boasted, flashing a crushing look at Peter Andre.

But after five days together, on and off, the only real novel "discovery" I'd made about Price was that she had, for years, worn the wrong bra size. "Marks and Spencer put me in a 34B!" she said. "And when I got measured I found out that I was really a 34GG all along!"

I know. It's scarcely Watergate. But given the rest of my interview, it was the best quote I had. I duly wrote up the piece—only to be emailed the next day by her management. "Would you mind not printing the thing about Katie's bra size?" her manager asked. "It's just, we really want to give that as an exclusive to *OK!*"

Flummoxed by a situation where news of a woman's bra size was literally currency, I capitulated.

I don't really mind one misguidedly thinking that Price is a good businesswoman—despite the fact that she has to rope her kids into her business to make money: something I always associate with desperate Third World families, rather than nice middle-class girls getting million-pound paychecks. At the end of the day, it's a busy, mixed-up world and we've all got to pick our fights.

But what I *do* find intolerable are the people who claim that Price is a feminist role model—simply because she has earned a lot of money.

The reasoning is this: men still have all the power and money.

But men have a weak spot—sexy women. So if what it takes to become rich and powerful is to sex up the blokes, then so be it. That's business, baby. You might be on all fours with your arse hanging out in "glamour" calendars, but at least you're making the rent on your enormous pink mansion.

Well, there's a phrase for that kind of behavior. It is, to quote Jamie, the spin doctor on *The Thick of It*, the majestic satirical British comedy series, being a "mimsy bastard quisling f***."

Women who, in a sexist world, pander to sexism to make their fortune are Vichy France with tits. Are you 34GG, waxed to within an inch of your life and faking orgasms? Then you're doing business with a decadent and corrupt regime. Calling that a feminist icon is like giving an arms dealer the Nobel Peace Prize.

"I'm strong," Price will say in another exclusive interview with *OK!* But by and large, strong people tend not to go quacking to the press every week about how they're "feeling" and how unfairly everyone's treating them, and what an arse their ex-husband's been.

As Blanche said in the long-running soap opera *Coronation Street*: "In my day, when something bad happened, you'd stay at home, get drunk, and bite on a shoe."

Price could learn much from this. This idea that Price is "strong" has come solely from the fact that she keeps saying "I'm strong," while doing really weak things, like appearing on *I'm a Celebrity Get Me Out of Here!* so that people can learn "the real me" and trying to get out of a dangerous driving fine by saying, "I'm just a typical woman driver."

There's a similar bit of neurolinguistic programming going on with her being a "great parent" and being voted Celebrity Mum of the Year.

"I take care of my kids," she says. "I love my kids."

Well, to quote comedian Chris Rock: "You're SUPPOSED to

look after your kids, you low-expectation-having motherfucker! What do you want—a cookie?" One of the most cheering things in the last few years has been Price hanging around long enough for all the terrible consequences of her decisions and attitude to play out in public. Any girl who—in 2007—thought it would be an admirable and viable career plan to start off in topless modeling, make a series of reality TV documentaries about her marriage, get her hapless children to model her clothing line, and persistently act like a craven, ungrateful, miserable, resentful, and hard-bitten curmudgeon—but with huge tits—would surely have rethought it all by 2010, when Price's public image rated just below that of the fox that bit those kids in North London.

Similarly, around the same time, the phenomenon of the footballers' WAGs—previously an equally aspirational role model for teenage girls—started to pall. As one footballer after another was revealed to have been serially unfaithful, suddenly the idea of aiming to do nothing but hitch your life and livelihood to a famous, wealthy man started to look at best tacky and at worst mentally perilous.

For as these marriages broke up, under intense scrutiny, the tone of the media coverage was "But what would a woman *expect* from these men? If you enter into a relationship so unequal—in which your only value and resource is your attractiveness—can you be surprised when your partner finds you so interchangeable with other similarly powerless, nonautonomous women he meets in dark nightclubs, gakked off his tits?"

But while Price—who has nothing to speak about or sell except herself—has waned, a whole generation of highly creative women have simultaneously begun to wax furious.

I've already discussed the concept of women being "losers"— admitting that as a sex, our achievements are modest compared to those of men and addressing the quiet, unspoken suspicion that this means that we really aren't as good as men, underneath it all. After all, if women's power and creativity had simply been suppressed by thousands of years of sexist bullshit, surely we should have knocked out *Star Wars* and conquered France within a year of getting the vote?

But, of course, on being freed, people who've been psychologically crushed don't immediately start doing glorious, confident, ostentatious things. Instead, they sit around for a while, going, "What the fuck was that?" trying to work out why it happened, trying—often—to see if it was their fault.

They have to work out what their relationship is with their former aggressors and come up with new command structures—or work out if they want command structures at all. There's a need to share experiences and work out (a) what "normal" is and (b) if you want to be it. And, above all, it takes time to work out what you actually believe in—what you think for yourself. If everything you have been taught is the history, mores, and reasoning of your victors, it takes a long, long time to work out what bits you want to keep, which bits you want to throw away: which bits are poisonous to you, and which parts salvageable.

In short, there is a long period of gently patting yourself, going, "Am I okay? Am I all right?" often followed by a long, long, thoughtful silence before any action gets under way.

But the action *is* getting under way now—and one of the places this is most apparent is in pop music. Pop is the cultural bellwether of social change. Because of its immediacy, reach, and power—no two-year turnover, like movies; no three-year writing process, like the novel; no ten-year campaigning process, like politics—any thought or feeling that begins to foment in the collective unconscious can be number one in the charts two months later. And as soon as a pop idea gets out there, it immediately triggers action and reaction in other artists, whose responses are equally rapid— leading to an almost quantum overnight shift in the landscape.

In 2009—13 years after the Spice Girls's *Wannabe* made them the biggest female band ever—the charts, finally, and for the first time ever, became dominated by female artists. La Roux—a lesbian! Florence and the Machine—a ginger! Lily Allen—a gobby ingénue! Beyoncé—a phenomenal, big-thighed icon! and, of course, Lady Gaga—a meat-wearing, bisexual, multimedia agent provocateur!—were the most written about, the most papped, the most in demand, and, of course, the most successful. Along with Katy Perry, Rihanna, Leona Lewis, and Susan Boyle, the onrush of women into the charts meant that male artists were dead in the water.

The conversations I'd had at *Melody Maker* 16 years previously—"Oh God, we've just got to get a bird in the paper!"—were turned on their head.

Now, at the Arts section of *The Times*, editors despair about having to cover male artists: "No one cares. Who wants to look at another picture of some dull bloke?"

In 2010, I went to interview the woman being touted as the next big feminist icon in the broadsheets: Lady Gaga. As an indicator of how quickly the landscape can change under the influence of just one prominent figure, the difference between her and the last mooted Big Feminist Icon—Price—couldn't have been more vast.

Price is a middle-class girl who'd risen to prominence via tittyshoots, with nothing to say—once she'd gained attention—except "Memememememe look at ME! And my Katie Price Pink Boutique iPod, 64GB, £399.99."

Gaga, on the other hand, is a middle-class girl who'd risen to prominence by writing three of the best pop singles of the 21ˢᵗ century on the trot ("Poker Face," "Just Dance," and "Bad Romance"), and with so much to say that she'd had to employ a multimedia art collective—the Haus of Gaga—to tour with her in order to express it all. Gaga's ticket was gay equality, sexual equality, political activism, tolerance, and getting shit-faced on the dance floor while busting some serious moves. And wearing a lobster on her head.

While it's always too early to call a career until it's ten years in, the sheer scope, scale, impact, and intent of Gaga's first two years as a pop star thrill me more than any female artist to emerge since Madonna. Indeed, much as I acknowledge, as a Western woman, my eternal indebtedness to Madonna—I would *never* have had the courage to paraglide with my muff hanging out or shag Vanilla Ice if it weren't for the pioneering work Madonna did in *Sex*—it should also be noted that Gaga ascended to the world stage wearing an outfit made of raw meat and protesting against the U.S. Army's homophobia, when she was just 24. At 24, Madonna was still working at a Dunkin' Donuts in Brooklyn.

And the thing about Madonna was that, as a teenage girl, she always kind of . . . scared me. She was cool, and hot, and amazingly dressed, and I could see that all her songs of empowerment were going to do me good, buried in my subconscious. But I couldn't get over the feeling that if she met me, she'd look me up and down—dressed in my jumble-sale boots, patched shirt, and straw hat—and then walk straight past me, to chat up Warren Beatty instead.

And fair enough—at the time, all I would have been able to offer Madonna, by way of conversation, was a long rant about how I believed the driver of the 512 bus in Wolverhampton was a pervert, how lonely I was, and how much I liked "Cool for Cats" by

Squeeze. If I were her, I would have gone and shagged Warren Beatty as well.

But this is why, if I were a bookish teenage girl in 2011 and I saw Lady Gaga, I'd feel like all my pop Christmases had come at once. Because Gaga is an international female pop star on the side of all the nerds, freaks, outcasts, intellectual pretenders, and lonely kids. If you go to one of her gigs, while the atmosphere is "club"—impossibly loud bass, mass frugging, poppers, and WKD—the audience consists of every awkward kid in the city. Kids dressed up with Coke cans in their hair—à la the "Telephone" video—with slogans scrawled on their faces, their arms draped around drag queens, and Morrissey look-alikes in glasses and cardigans. They're watching a woman with a quote from Rilke tattooed up her arm ("In the deepest hour of the night, confess to yourself that you would die if you were forbidden to write." Yes. It's quite a small font) who's performing on a custom-made, 14-foot-high piano made to look like the spider-legged elephants in Dali's "Temptation of St. Anthony," singing about doomed love through the metaphor of Alfred Hitchcock movies.

And while she undoubtedly deals in sexuality—if you haven't seen a close-up of Gaga's crotch in the last week, you simply haven't watched enough MTV—it's not the confident, straightforward animal sexuality of every other female pop star. Gaga's take on sexual mores is to examine female dysfunction, alienation, and sexual neuroses. When her debut album came out, she had to fight her record company, who wanted to put a straightforward, borderline soft-porn image of her on the cover.

"The last thing a young woman needs is another picture of a pop star covered in grease, writhing in the sand, and touching herself," she said. "I had to cry for a week to get them to change it."

By the time she played the 2009 MTV Awards, her performance consisted of a chandelier dropping onto her head, with Gaga slowing bleeding to death as she sang. The year before, Katy Perry had jumped out of a cake.

When I went to interview Gaga, we got on like a house afire. At the end of the interview, she invited me to "come party" with her at a sex club in Berlin.

"You know *Eyes Wide Shut?* It's like that," she said, swishing down a backstage corridor in a black taffeta, custom-made, one-off Alexander McQueen cape. "I can't be responsible for anything that happens, and remember—use a condom."

We went across Berlin in a blacked-out motorcade of 4x4s—her security effectively curtailing the trailing paps by simply standing in front of their cars and impeding their exit—and ended up in a disused industrial complex down an alleyway. To get to the dance floor, you had to go through a maze of corridors and past a series of tiny, cell-like booths, decked out with a selection of beds, bathtubs, hoists, and chains.

"For fucking," a German member of our entourage ex-plained—both helpfully and somewhat unnecessarily.

Despite the undoubted and extreme novelty of such a venue, Adrian—Gaga's British press officer—and I gave away our nation-alities instantly when we commented, excitedly, "Oh, my God! You can SMOKE in here." It seemed a far more thrilling prospect than . . . some bumming.

It was a small entourage: Gaga, me, Adrian, her makeup artist, her security guy, and maybe two others. We walked onto the small dance floor, in a club filled with drag queens, lesbians dressed as sailors, boys in tight T-shirts, girls in black leather. The music was pounding. There was a gigantic harness hanging over the bar. "For fucking." The same helpful German again.

Gaga headed up our group. Even, like, Keane would slope off

to a VIP booth at this point and wait for people to bring them drinks. Instead—cloak billowing, and looking very much like one of the Skeksis in *The Dark Crystal*—Gaga marched up to the bar and leaned on it in a practiced barfly manner. With a bellowed, "What does everyone want to drink?" she got the round in.

"I really love a dingy, pissy bar," Gaga said. "I'm really old-school that way."

We went into an alcove with a wipe-clean banquette—"For the fucking!" the German said again—and set up camp. Gaga took off her McQueen cloak and chucked it into a corner. I promptly stood on it, to the wincing horror of her makeup artist, who carefully removed its £10,000 worth of taffeta from under my feet. Gaga was now just in bra, fishnets, and knickers, with sequins around her eyes.

"Do you know what that girl at the bar said to me?" she said, sipping her Scotch and taking a single drag off someone's fag before handing it back. "She said, 'You're a feminist. People think it means man-hating, but it doesn't.' Isn't that funny?"

Earlier in the day, conversation had turned to whether Gaga would describe herself as feminist or not. As the very best conversations about feminism often will, it had segued from robust declarations of emancipation and sisterhood ("I am a feminist because I believe in women's rights and protecting who we are, down to the core") to musing on who she fancied. ("In the video to 'Telephone,' the girl I kiss, Heather, lives as a man. And as someone who does like women, something about a more masculine woman makes me feel more . . . feminine. When we kissed, I got that fuzzy butterfly feeling.")

We had concluded that it was odd most women "shy away" from declaring themselves feminists, because "it really doesn't mean 'man-hating.' "

"And now she's just said the same thing to me! AND she's hot!" Gaga beamed. She pointed to the girl—who looked like an androgynous, Cupid-mouthed, Jean Paul Gaultier cabin boy. "Gorgeous," Gaga sighed.

By 2 a.m., we had drunk a lot of vodka, and Gaga had her head in my lap. I had just come up with the theory that, if you have one of your heroes lying drunkenly in your lap, that's the time you tell them all the little theses you've come up with about them.

"Even though you wear very little clothing," I said slightly primly, gesturing to Gaga's bra and thong, "you're not doing all this as a . . . prick-tease, are you?"

"No!" Gaga replied, with a big, drunken beam. "It's not what straight men masturbate over when they're at home watching pornography. It's not for them. It's for . . . us."

And she gestured around the nightclub, filled to the brim with biker-boy lesbians and drag queens.

Because Gaga is not there to be fucked. You don't penetrate Gaga. In common with much of pop's history, and particularly its women—she's not singing these songs in order to get laid, or give the impression she wants to. She wishes to disrupt and disturb: sunglasses made of burning cigarettes, beds bursting into flame, dresses made of raw meat, calipers made of platinum, Gaga being water-boarded in a bathtub—eyes dilated with CGI so that she looks like her own manga cartoon. Her iconography is disconcerting, and it disarranges what we are used to seeing.

The end point of her songs is not to excite desire in potential lovers, but the thrill of examining her own feelings, then expressing them to her listeners, instead. Her gang—the millions-strong army of Gaga fans, who call themselves Little Monsters, and call her Mama Monster, the den mother of their alternative world. As a woman, Gaga's big novelty is not her theatricality, talent, or success but that she has used them to open up a new space for pop fans. And this—Gaga's gay-friendly, freak-friendly, campaigning facet—might be the most exciting thing about her of all. For women, finding a sympathetic, nonjudgmental arena is just as important as getting the right to vote. We needed not just the right legislation, but the right atmosphere, too, before we could finally start to found our canons—then, eventually, cities and empires.

Ultimately, I think it's going to be very difficult to oppress a generation of teenage girls who've grown up with a liberal, literate, bisexual pop star who shoots fireworks out of her bra and was listed as *Forbes* magazine's seventh most powerful celebrity in the world.

The week after I interviewed Gaga, a blurry fan's shot of her in the nightclub appeared in magazines across the world. You could just make out my gigantic, sweaty, back-combed hair behind her.

"GAGA HEALTH WORRIES!" the headlines shouted, claiming that "insiders" had been "worried" by her actions that night. I can assure you, they hadn't. They were up dancing with her on the banquette of the nightclub, having the time of their lives.

Here's one of the big pitfalls of the modern media's obsession with famous female role models. While it's thrilling that a career like Gaga's is front-page news all over the world—discussed in easy-to-access tabloid newspapers and magazines, rather than hidden away in textbooks, fanzines, or tiny nightclubs with bad wine, where only three determined, hard-core feminists, who don't really need it, will find it—there is a pitfall to most discourse on the state of modern womanhood taking place in these publications.

To wit: those deciding the editorial context of most of these magazines and newspapers are dispiritingly cretinous and mean-spirited, constructing fictional narratives about a series of entirely unconnected events or photographs and paying the unenlightened drones in Sector B of multinational publishing empires to write them. The underlying attitudes these stories on famous women reveal would make Kate Millett—or, indeed, anyone who's read *Psychology for Dummies*—put their head in their hands and sigh, "Oh, the *humanity*. How can we have allowed our stupidity to be so *obvious*?"

And that's the *positive* spin on the situation. The paranoid, suspicious part of me—which rises up at 2 a.m., after taking the crude cling-film bung off a bottle of red wine that was opened three months previously and ill-advisedly drinking the whole lot before looking for miniatures of Malibu—sometimes wonders if this kind of journalism is written with a darker and more purposeful intent.

Because the kind of media coverage our prominent women are given is hugely reductionist and damaging. Although the media attitude to all famous people has an underlying schadenfreude-y current of "Haha—wait until you show the slightest sign of weakness, and then we'll stick a chisel in it and work it a mile wide," female celebrities suffer disproportionately from this, because of the pivotal attention given to their appearance.

A "sign of weakness" for a male celebrity is being found to be unfaithful, or unkind to an employee, or having crashed his car while stoned out of his tiny mind. A "sign of weakness" for a woman, on the other hand, can be a single unflattering picture. Women are pilloried for wearing a single "bad" outfit—not just on the red carpet, where part of their job description is looking like some otherworldly apparition of beauty, no matter how busy, worried, unhappy, or genuinely unconcerned about the whole stupid crapshoot they are.

No—paps will take pictures of women going to the shops in jeans and a sweater, with no makeup on, and make it look like her world is on the verge of crumbling because she didn't have a blow-dry before she left the house.

Of course, in the real world, we know that women who always blow-dry their hair before leaving the house are freaks: any mother at the school gates with a glossy bob is subject to pitying looks from the other mothers, who can't believe she wasted 20 minutes, and a lot of upper-arm strength, zazzing her riah for any event less momentous than publicly announcing her engagement to Kiefer Sutherland at Cannes. But when we see, say, Kate Winslet in the paper, looking perfectly normal on her way to Waitrose, we've become so conditioned to the tabloid view of female appearance that even the most hard core feminists might find themselves having the trigger reaction of "Jesus, Winslet—your hair looked better when you were going down with 1,517 souls on the *Titantic*. Run a brush through it, love"—before they suddenly come round and shout up to the heavens, "DEAR LORD! *WHAT* have I *BECOME?*"

And that's just bitchiness about looking a bit drab. There's a whole other league of judgment heaped on single pictures—one frame, out of 24 per second—when it appears a woman's body has changed shape in any way. Again, I understand the interest in fluctuating physical statistics—men, worriedly, measure their willies; women, worriedly, measure their thighs. We all do it. We are fascinated by our bodies, and those of others, but it is surely ludicrous to load such significance onto such a tiny thing: like plonking an Acme anvil in a child's hammock. Just as William Blake claimed to see the world in just one grain of sand, we presume we can see a whole woman's life in just one shot of Eva Longoria's upper arm looking a bit squished in a T-shirt.

A picture of Catherine Zeta-Jones in trousers that are puckering, slightly, around the groin will be met with a hail of "Catherine EATER Jones" headlines and faux-concerned editorials about how Zeta-Jones has always "battled" with her weight. Alexa Chung is photographed in a pair of clumpy shoes that make her legs look smaller, and suddenly she's anorexic and on the edge of a nervous breakdown. They never blame the *clothes* in these pictures—stupid puckering too-tight clothes, or stupid baggy clothes. It must always be the woman's body that's at fault. Lily Allen, Angelina Jolie, Drew Barrymore, Jennifer Aniston, Michelle Obama, Victoria Beckham, Amy Winehouse, Mariah Carey, Lady Gaga, Madonna, Cherie Blair, Oprah Winfrey, Carla Bruni, the Duchess of York, Sarah Brown—there can't be a magazine-consuming woman in the Western world who's not been called upon to speculate on the mental and emotional health of these women on the basis of a single bad photo of her. I've read more about Oprah Winfrey's arse than I have about the rise of China as an economic superpower. I fear this is no exaggeration. Perhaps China is rising as an economic superpower *because* its women aren't spending all their time reading about Oprah Winfrey's arse. If I knew more about China, and less about Oprah Winfrey's arse, I could probably argue a direct cause-and-effect.

And the absolute randomness of this damaging, time-wasting speculation is perhaps the most pernicious and ludicrous thing of all. Journalists seem to choose who they're "concerned" about with the randomness of a roomful of people pulling names out of hats. I've seen shots of Mischa Barton in one publication faux-concernedly lamenting her "worryingly skinny frame"—and then the self-same shot in the magazine next to it on the rack, captioned: "Mischa Barton—celebrating her new curves."

Argh! "Celebrating her curves!" Is there any more evil sentence in modern celebrity journalism? "Celebrating her curves" is—as every woman knows—the codified way that magazines can accuse someone of looking fatter but without the celebrity being able to complain, lest they look like they're disapproving of women being "curvy." It's an engagingly evil paradox—the kind of mind-fucking a North Korean dictatorship would go in for, if they decided to suppress the proletariat using only cattiness and rampant body dysmorphia.

And so these celebrity women have to spend whole interviews listing what they eat—"I love toast!"—and engaging in a relationship with the media much like that between the teenage inmates of an eating disorders clinic and a stern nurse: constantly having to "prove" that they've been good and have eaten up all their shepherd's pie, rather than hiding it in the sleeves of their cardigan and dumping it in a plant pot when no one's looking. And what is the reason given for these gleefully run pictures of women in swimsuits on the beach, who are depicted not as people "on holiday," "doing some work," or "being with their family," but in the middle of a lifelong "struggle" with their "body issues"? It's "the human angle."

"Jennifer Lopez has cellulite—there is a God!" they will trumpet, next to a hatefully enlarged shot of Jennifer Lopez's thighs. "Celebrities—they're JUST like YOU!" they parp, next to a shot of some poor bitch from *EastEnders* wearing bad jeans that give her a muffintop—seemingly unaware of what an alarming statement this is. For a female reader, there's ultimately no comfort in seeing a picture of a famous woman, papped with a long-angle lens, with red "circles of shame" around her soft thighs, stretch-marked upper arms, or slightly swollen belly. Because what this ultimately tells a reader—usually young and impressionable, and still hopeful about the world—is that if she were a creative and ambitious woman who worked hard, got some breaks, and, somehow, managed to rise to the top of her profession and become as famous as these women in a still male-dominated industry, the paps would come for her and make her feel just as shitty as Paula Abdul. What a fucking depressing state of affairs.

Here's why I hate "the human angle."

1. I don't want my celebrities to be more human. Art should be an arena to reinvent and supersede yourself. I don't want a load of normals trudging around, moaning about water rates and blackheads. I want David Bowie pretending to be bent, and from space.

2. In the 21st century, any woman, succeeding in any arena, does not need "humanizing." There are absolutely no exceptions to this. Not even Margaret Thatcher. It's been a long, slow 100,000-year trudge out of the patriarchy. There are still parts of the world where women are not allowed to touch food when they're menstruating or are socially ostracized for failing to give birth to boys. Even in right-on America, or Europe, women are still so woefully underrepresented in everything—science, politics, art, business, space travel—that if *any* woman manages to construct a suitable persona for getting on in the world and achieves even a fraction of the eminence men take for granted, I absolutely want her to be able to keep her front up. Let her keep her work face on. Let her seem a little indomitable and distant. Let her acquire mystery, or foreboding, or outright terrorizing invulnerability, if she likes. When the world is overrun with Thatcher-faced Amazonian Illuminati, manipulating the world with a combination of nuclear weapons and sexual blackmail, then we'll really *need* to get in there and humanize them. In the meantime, Jennifer Aniston has simply released another happy-go-lucky rom-com. I don't think we need to start disassembling her fearsome iron mask just yet by asking her when she was last on the rag.

Even though female role models expand in their variety and their achievements by the month, there is one thing we need to ask ourselves: Is what we read about them, and say about them, "reportage" and "discussion"? Or is it just a global media acting like a total bitch?

CHAPTER 15

Abortion

I think I have polycystic ovaries. That's what I'm getting the ultrasound for. I've been to my GP three times with symptoms—acne, exhaustion, weight gain, disrupted menstrual cycle—and this is where they've referred me: the ultrasound unit at the Whittington Hospital.

Yes—with those symptoms, you think I'm pregnant, don't you? But I did a test six weeks ago and got nothing, and this is where my GP has sent me now. I'm eating two cans of tinned pineapple for breakfast and cry when I see a sad squirrel in an ad. Of course I'm pregnant. But the test said no. And I'm still breast-feeding. And I don't want to be pregnant. So I'm not.

I lie on the bed. The monitor is up on the wall, waiting to show me what's inside. I don't really know what polycystic ovaries look like, but I'm guessing I'll see circles, like oxygen bubbles. Or maybe something more visceral: clusters; bracts.

As the nurse washes her hands in preparation, the ultrasound screen looks like the view from the deck of the *Millennium Falcon*, when it's parked. Dark, black space, with occasional speckles of light. Still.

When they finally put the ultrasound to my belly, though, it's like the light jump: the whole solar system roars into life. Lines and whorls and kidneys and guts. Moons with asteroids circling. And then, at the center—low, deep, hidden—a pulsar. A signal. A clock that's ticking.

That is a heartbeat.

"You're pregnant!" the nurse says cheerfully. Nurses must be told to always say this cheerfully. They always do—however pale the client is, or however loudly the client has just said, "Fuck" and started shaking.

She is doing calculations with an on-screen tape measure.

"I would say you're around 11 weeks," she says, pushing the ultrasound monitor into my belly.

That really is it—there is nothing else that looks like a fetus. The curve of the spine, like an etiolated crescent moon. The astronaut helmet skull. The black, unblinking eyes, like a prawn.

"Oh, my God," I say to the baby. "Oh, you outrageous thing."

I am sure he is my gay son—the one I always wanted. His entrance is so showy—so jazz-hands, so "ta-da!" So sudden. So camp. An absolute blackout on prepublicity until he can make his first appearance like this, on TV; like it's fucking *Oprah* or something.

And his luck! This kid is clearly lucky—we only had one unprotected fuck; that night in Cyprus, in the 20 minutes both girls were asleep. This kid is going to buck odds all his life: he'll break casinos and befriend millionaires in the deli queue. He'll find gold the first time he pans the stream, and true love on the very day he decides he needs to settle down.

"I can't have you," I tell him sadly. "The world will fall in if I have you."

Because not even for a second do I think I should have this baby. I have no dilemma, no terrible decision to make—because I know, with calm certainty, that I don't want another child now, in the same way I know absolutely that I don't want to go to India, or be blond, or fire a gun.

This isn't who I'm going to be, again: another three years of being life support to someone who weeps for me and rages against me, and who knows, when he's ill, can only be relieved by resting his head on my belly and dreaming he's back inside. My two girls, whom I walk backward in front of—looking like I'm bowing down to them, keeping the wind off them, watching everything they do like a jealous camera—are all I want.

I used to fear their deaths—the car! the dog! the sea! the germ!—until I realized it need never be a problem: on the trolley, on the way to the mortuary, I would put my hands into their ribs and take their hearts and swallow them, and give birth to them again, so that they would never, ever end. I'll do anything for those girls.

But I will only do one thing for this baby—as quickly as I can, before it goes any further.

I thank the nurse, wipe the jelly from my stomach, and go outside to make a call.

In 2007, *Guardian* columnist Zoe Williams wrote a wholly clear-headed and admirable piece examining why women always felt compelled to preface discussion about their abortions with an obligatory, "Of course, it's terribly traumatic. No woman enters into this lightly."

She went on to explain that this is because, however liberal a society is, it assumes that, at its absolute core, abortion is wrong—but that a forgiving state must make legal and medical provision for it, lest desperate women "do a Vera Drake" down a back alley and make things even worse.

Abortions are never seen as a positive thing, as any other operation to remedy a potentially life-ruining condition would.

Women never speak publicly about their abortions with happy, relieved gratitude. There are no "Good luck with your morning-after pill!" cards. People don't make jokes about it despite the fact that all the truest jokes are about vexing topics and cover every other subject, including cancer, God, and death.

Additionally, there is the spectrum of "wrongness" to consider. There are "good abortions" and "bad abortions," like Chris Morris's sketch on *Brass Eye*, where he discusses "good AIDS" and "bad AIDS." Hemophiliacs who caught the virus from blood transfusions have "good AIDS," and deserve sympathy. Homosexuals who picked up the virus from casual sex, however, have "bad AIDS" and are accorded no solicitude at all.

A raped teenage girl seeking an abortion—or a mother whose life is endangered by the pregnancy—is having a "good" abortion. She still won't discuss it publicly or expect her friends to be happy for her, but these women get away with barely any stigmatization.

At the other end of the spectrum, of course, are the "worst" kind of abortions: repeated abortions, late-term abortions, abortions after IVF, and—worst of all—mothers who have abortions. Our view of motherhood is still so idealized and misty—Mother, gentle giver of life—that the thought of a mother subsequently setting limits on her capacity to nurture and refusing to give further life seems obscene.

For mothers must pretend that they are loving and protective of all life, however nascent or putative it might be. They should—we still quietly believe, deep down inside—be prepared to give and give and give, until they simply wear out. The greatest mother—the perfect mother—would carry to term every child she conceived, no matter how disruptive or ruinous, because her love would be great enough for anything and everyone.

Women who decide to continue with pregnancies that endanger their lives—"Doctors told me another pregnancy would kill me—but here's baby William!"—are written about in magazine features as admirable, the ultimate mothers. They are the truest embodiment of oxytocin, the pregnancy hormone of love and bonding that keeps the world full.

Women should be, essentially, capable of endless, self-sacrificial love.

I have problems with that assumption. For one thing, I believe something very elemental and, in the theological sense, non-Christian. One of the big dilemmas over abortion is trying to work out when "life" begins with a fetus—concluding that if abortion could occur before "life" begins, that would be a "right" kind of abortion. But given that both science and philosophy continue to struggle to define what the beginning of "life" is, wouldn't it be better to come at the debate from a different angle entirely? For if a pregnant woman has dominion over life, why should she not also have dominion over not-life? This is a concept understood by other cultures. The Hindu goddess Kali is both Mother of the Whole Universe and Devourer of All Things. She is life and death. In Sumeria, Inanna is the goddess of sex and fertility, but she also turns into Ereshkigal, goddess of the underworld. On a very elemental level, if women are, by biology, commanded to host, shelter, nurture, and protect life, why should they not be empowered to end life, too?

I'm not advocating stoving in the heads of children, or encouraging late abortions—but then, no one is. What I am vexed with is the idea that, by having an abortion, a woman is somehow being unfemale and, indeed, unmotherly. That the absolute essence of womanhood and maternity is to sustain life, at all costs, whatever the situation.

My belief in the ultimate sociological, emotional, and practical necessity for abortion became even stronger after I had my two children. It is only after you have had a nine-month pregnancy, labored to get the child out, fed it, cared for it, sat with it until 3 a.m., risen with it at 6 a.m., swooned with love for it, and been reduced to furious tears by it that you really understand just how important it is for a child to be wanted. How motherhood is a game you must enter with as much energy, willingness, and happiness as possible.

And the most important thing of all, of course, is to be wanted, desired, and cared for by a reasonably sane, stable mother. I can honestly say that my abortion was one of the least difficult decisions of my life. I'm not being flippant when I say it took me longer to decide what countertops to have in the kitchen than whether I was prepared to spend the rest of my life being responsible for a further human being, because I knew that to do it again—to commit my life to another person—might very possibly stretch my abilities, and conception of who I am, and who I want to be, and what I want and need to do—to breaking point. The idea that I might not—in an earlier era, or a different country—have a choice in the matter seems both emotionally and physically barbaric.

As Germaine Greer puts it in *The Whole Woman*, "to become a mother without wanting it is to live like a slave, or domestic animal."

Of course, there was every chance that I might eventually be thankful for the arrival of a third child. He might have arrived and forced me to discover new reserves of energy, dedication, and love. She might have been the best thing that ever happened to me. But I am, personally, not a gambler. I won't spend £1 on the lottery, let alone take a punt on a pregnancy. The stakes are far, far too high. I can't agree with a society that would force me to bet on how much I could love under duress.

I cannot understand antiabortion arguments that center on the sanctity of life. As a species, we've fairly comprehensively demonstrated that we don't believe in the sanctity of life. The shrugging acceptance of war, famine, epidemic, pain, and lifelong, grinding poverty show us that, whatever we tell ourselves, we've made only the most feeble of efforts to *really* treat human life as sacred.

I don't understand, then, why, in the midst of all this, pregnant women—women trying to make rational decisions about their futures and, usually, those of their families, too—should be subject to more pressure about preserving life than, say, Vladimir Putin, the World Bank, or the Catholic Church.

However, what I do believe to be genuinely sacred—and, indeed, more useful to the earth as a whole—is trying to ensure that there are as few unbalanced, destructive people as possible. By whatever rationale you use, ending a pregnancy 12 weeks into gestation is incalculably more moral than bringing an unwanted child into this world.

It's those unhappy, unwanted children, who then grew into angry adults, who have caused the great majority of humankind's miseries. They are the ones who make housing projects feel feral; streets dangerous; relationships violent. If psychoanalysis has, somewhat brutally, laid the responsibility for psychological disorders at parents' doors, the least we can do is to tip our hats to women aware enough not to create those troubled people in the first place.

But, of course, we don't. In the last two years, three bills have been tabled in the Commons seeking to curtail women's access to termination. *The Times* reported that "Unprecedented numbers" of doctors are opting out of terminations, dismayed by the increase in operations.

A great deal of the reason why antiabortion sentiment is allowed to hold ground is that the debate is just that—an ideological, religious, or sociopolitical debate on abortion. It is rarely discussed in terms of personal experience, despite record numbers of women—189,100 in the UK in 2009—having them. Every year, an estimated 42 million abortions occur worldwide—20 million occurring safely, with proper medical supervision, and 22 million occurring unsafely. Across the world, women are doing what they have always done throughout history: dealing with a potentially life-altering or life-threatening crisis, and then not talking about it afterward. In case anyone near to them—those people who are not bleeding, and who have not just had an abortion—get upset.

Women—always loath to talk about the more visceral elements of female reproductive physicality—are too ashamed, or unconfident in their reception, to discuss their terminations, even with friends or partners. This brings about the curious situation in which, while pretty much everyone must have someone dear to them who has had an abortion, the chances of them actually discussing it with their more conservative elders, or menfolk, are remote.

Consequently, we have a climate where antiabortionists can discuss abortion as something that "they" do, over "there," rather than the reality—that it has, in all likelihood, been a calm, rational, well-thought-out act, which has statistically occurred very close to home.

When I wrote about my decision to have an abortion in *The Times*, I was amazed at the reader response—more than 400 online comments, and over 100 letters and emails. By a rule of thumb, those who were antiabortion cited no experience of pregnancy or abortion, while those who were proabortion did.

The response that I found most surprising, however, was a wonderful letter from a well-known feminist columnist who said that, although she had written about abortion many, many times, she had never mentioned her own terminations.

"I always feared what would happen if I did. I presumed no one would forgive me. I thought it would—somehow—invalidate my argument."

And—as a woman reconciled in her own body—I feel I can argue with anyone's god about my right to end a pregnancy. My first conception—wanted so badly—ended in miscarriage, three days before my wedding. A kind nurse removed my wedding manicure with nail-polish remover, in order to fit a finger-thermometer for the subsequent D&C operation. I wept as I went into the operating theater, and wept as I came out. In that instance, my body had decided that that baby was not to be and had ended it. This time, it is my mind that has decided that this baby was not to be. I don't believe one's decision is more valid than the other. They both know me. They are both equally capable of deciding what is right.

I want to end the pregnancy as quickly as possible and go straight to see the consultant I had for my last birth. During an awkward five-minute consultation, he has to point out to me that the hospital we are in—St. John & St. Elizabeth's in St. John's Wood—is a Catholic hospital, and I have just, in effect, asked the Pope for an abortion.

Back home, the world's least-fun Google search suggests a consultant in Golders Green, followed by a "procedure" out in Essex. There are two viable options for the abortion itself—I can either be knocked out and wake up to find it all over, but then spend the night in hospital; or I can stay conscious but go home the same day. I am still breast-feeding my youngest—so staying conscious then going home it is.

There is the third option—the "medical abortion," where you take two pills and then miscarry at home—but, asking around, anyone who's experienced it says, "It tends to freak you out quite a lot. You just walk around your house bleeding for days. And there's a chance it won't work, and then you'll end up having to have a D&C anyway. Just go in and get it over and done with."

The clinic we go to is out in Essex, in an area that has that light suburban air of wife-swapping and neat brothels run by bosomy women. I suppose, given its air of offering harbor to humanity's shameful physical needs, this is the right place for an abortion clinic. Inside, it reminds me of a Victorian Youth Hostel—the atmosphere of the "clients" being up to no good, and the staff watching them quietly, from the landing above, purse-mouthed and disapproving.

In the waiting room, there are four couples, and two women on their own. The younger woman is from Ireland—she arrived here this morning and apparently—I gather, from what she is whispering to the receptionist—will go back on the ferry tonight.

The older woman looks in her late forties, maybe even early fifties. She cries without making a sound. She has the air of a woman who hasn't told a soul, and never will.

The couples are silent, too—all possible conversations have been had before you get here. My husband is red-eyed but solid, just as he was through two births and a miscarriage. He made his definitive statement on all this years ago: "It seems wildly unfair that, for *us* to reproduce, *you* have to go through all this . . . shit."

In the peerlessly unromantic conversation we had when I phoned him from outside the ultrasound clinic, there wasn't even a debate. He said, "What do you want to do?" I said, "No," and he said, "Yeah."

We knew how we both felt—God, we'd lain in bed the week before, after spending the day with friends and their newborn, going, "She's got that thousand-yard stare, and he looks half dead. You forget how much *attention* they need, don't you? How you're just . . . stuck."

The nurse calls my name, and I leave his hand to go to that room. As I walk, I levitate up, up, up into a panic attack, and in a telescopic rush, I know—coldly *know*—that I am making a terrible mistake, and that I must keep this baby, no matter what.

But I also know panic attacks, and I know they lie. Every single other thought you have had has brought you, unfailingly, here, I tell myself. This isn't a last-minute revelation. This is just fear. Tell it to stop.

I don't know what I thought abortion would be like. When I had a D&C after my miscarriage, they knocked me out—weeping—and I woke up—weeping—with it all over.

"Where's the baby?" I kept saying, off my face, as they wheeled me into a room and told me—as gently as possible—to shut up. The only real knowledge I had of that procedure was the aftereffects: sore, obviously, and aware of the pregnancy hormones leaving me, hour by hour. Taking away the estrogen floatiness, and making me feel heavy—my proper gravity—again: like when you stay in a bath, reading, as the water drains away.

This time, I'm awake for all of it. The whole thing is a bad surprise. I suppose I thought the one thing it would be was "clinical"—doctors just doing their job, coldly and quickly; procedure precise and fast. But as I lie on the bed—the last appointment of the day—the doctors have the air of people who've spent far too long doing unpleasant things in order to rectify the mistakes of others.

You wanted to become a doctor to help people and feel better at the end of your job, I think, watching them, as the nurse takes my hand. But I don't think you do feel better at the end of the day. You look like humans have constantly disappointed you.

The abortion itself is not what I had expected, in that it is both painful and seems fairly crude. The cervix is opened manually, with some manner of ratchet. Then a speculum is inserted, and they start to perform the abortion, which appears to be just smashing stuff up with a spoon. It's wincingly violent. Like breaking the yolk of an egg with a chopstick, I think, doing the breathing I learned for labor, which is, of course, a very bad joke.

It's quite painful—like labor, five hours in. The painkiller has been absolutely useless, but complaining about pain, given what you are doing, seems inappropriate. Even if you yourself don't believe you should experience pain while having an abortion, there's a distinct atmosphere that the staff here do.

"You're doing fine," the nurse says, holding my hand very hard. She is kind, but she is also, obviously, already putting her coat on and thinking about getting out the door. She can smell the weekend from here. She is already far away.

The doctor then uses a vacurette to hoover my womb out, which is pretty much exactly as you'd imagine having the contents of your womb vacuumed out to feel like. In the months after, it makes me repeatedly demur from the purchase of a Black & Decker Dustbuster.

The whole process has taken maybe seven minutes—it is brisk—but the longing for every instrument and hand to retreat from you and allow you to quietly knit back together, to heal, is immense. You want everyone to GET OUT of you. Everyone.

The doctor turns the vacuum off. He then turns it on again and does one last little bit: like when you're doing the front room, finish, and then decide to give the sofa cushions a once-over while you're at it.

Finally, he's done, and I let out an involuntary "Ahhh!" as his hand withdraws.

"See!" he says, with a firm smile. "Not too bad! All done!"

Then he looks down into the dish, which holds everything that was inside me. Intrigued by something, he calls his colleague over, from the sluice.

"Look at that!" he says, pointing.

"Haha—unusual!" the other says.

They both laugh, before the dish is carried away, and the gloves are peeled off, and the cleaning up starts. The day is now done.

I don't want to ask what it is they have seen. Maybe they could detect he was gay, even at this early stage.

The best thought is: perhaps she's hideously deformed, and I would have miscarried her anyway.

The very worst thought is: perhaps something was struggling to stay alive—perhaps he's running out his last piece of luck as I lie here, feeling pale as paper on the outside, and red and black on the inside, like bad meat. That's the worst bit. The very worst bit. I wish these doctors would shut up.

When they take you into the next room—the Recovery Room—you lie, wrapped in a terry cloth robe, on a reclining chair. They give you a magazine and a cold drink. There is a potted palm tree in the corner. It looks like the worst-ever remake of Wham!'s "Club Tropicana" video.

The girl from Ireland leaves after five minutes—she has to catch her bus, to catch her coach, to catch her ferry back home. She walks sore. It's blatantly obvious that she shouldn't have had to come to another country to get her life back on track. I wonder if the judges in Ireland have ever seen a woman as pale as this, counting out fifties onto the reception desk in a country where she doesn't know a soul, and then bleeding all the way from Essex to Holyhead. I wonder if her father approves of the law because he doesn't think it applies to her—and whether he would hate that law if he knew it did, and has brought her here.

The older woman—who was crying silently in the waiting room—is here now, still crying. We all seem to have agreed, at some point, to pretend that we're not here, so no one catches her eye. We just read the magazines until the 40 minutes' "recovery time" is up and the nurse says, "You can go."

And we drive away—with my husband driving dangerously, because he's holding my hand very, very tight—and I say, "I'm going to get the contraceptive version of Berlin Wall fitted, I think," and he says, "Yeah," and holds my hand even tighter. And that is the end of that day.

Given the subject matter, it seems odd to say that this is the happy ending—but it is.

All accounts of abortion that I have seen always had, as dolorous coda, how the procedure left a mark. However female-sympathetic the publication, there is a need to mention how the anniversary of the abortion is always remembered with sorrow—the baby's due date marked with a sudden flood of tears.

The narrative is that while a woman may tell herself, rationally, that she couldn't have that baby, there will be a part of her that does not believe this—which carries on silently marking the baby that should have come. Women's bodies do not give up their babies so easily, and so silently, is the message. The heart will always remember.

This is what I expect. But this is not how it is. Indeed, it's the opposite. I keep waiting for my prescribed grief and guilt to come—I am braced, chest out, ready—but it never arrives. I don't cry when I see baby clothes. Friends announcing pregnancies don't make me jealous, or quietly blue. I do not have to remind myself that sometimes you must do the "wrong" thing for the "right" reason.

In fact, it's the opposite. Every time I sleep through the night, I am thankful for the choice I made. When the youngest graduates out of diapers, I'm relieved there isn't a third one, following behind. When friends come round with their new babies, I am hugely, hugely grateful that I had the option not to do this again—and that that option didn't involve me lying on a friend's kitchen table, after the kids had gone to sleep, praying I wouldn't get an infection, or hemorrhage to death before I got home.

I talk to other friends about this, after a few drinks, and they agree.

"I walk past playgrounds thinking, If I'd gone through with the pregnancy, I'd still be sitting on that bench, fat, depressed, knackered, and just waiting for my life to start again," Lizzie says.

Rachel is, as always, brisker. "It's one of the top four best things I ever did—after marrying my husband, having my son, and getting a fixed quote on the loft conversion."

I suppose what I'd been given to believe is that my body—or my subconscious—would be *angry* with me for not having the baby. And that, additionally, their opinion on the matter would, in some way, be superior—more "natural," more moral—to the rational decision my conscious mind had made. That women were made to have babies, and that each one that is not brought to fruition must be accounted and mourned and repented for, and would remain unforgiven forever.

But all I could see—and all I can see now, years later—is history made of millions of women trying to undo the mistake that could then undo them, and then just carrying on, quiet, thankful, and silent about the whole thing. What I see is that it can be an action with only good consequences.

CHAPTER 16

Intervention

I am now 35, stacking up decades as casually as I stacked up weeks as a child. I'm stronger-minded and more flexible in my emotions, but these gains seem to have been made at the expense of my skin, which has taken on the slightly brittle qualities of taffeta. Perhaps the collagen is absorbed from skin into the heart, I think, dragging my finger over my arm and watching, fascinated, how the skin herringbones behind it. I palm Cocoa Butter into the pleats, and they disappear. Hours later, they're back again.

My skin is starting to be . . . needy.

It's not the only part of my body that's registering change. Hangovers now take on slightly ominous, depressive qualities. The awkward quarter-turn on the staircase makes my knee ache. My breasts start to need the underwiring equivalent of bodyguards—I must have my security around me at all times. I'm miles away from exhausted, and not even tired, but I don't feel I could spontaneously dance at any point, which I often felt before.

I'm just a little bit more interested in sitting down than I was before.

The first big reminder notes about mortality start to arrive. People's parents start to ail. People's parents start to die. There are funerals and memorials, at which I say comforting things to my friends—while secretly comforting myself that death is still a generation away. A suicide, a stroke, cancer, these are all still happening to the grown-ups above me. They do not encroach on my generation just yet.

But I watch the older mourners at the graveside, in the church, in the crematorium that looks oddly like a municipal sauna, by way of instruction on a future event. Soon it will be me, dealing with these awful good-byes.

Soon I, too, will look down at my hands and realize they are the hands of my nana, and that the ring that went on shiny all those years ago has—without me doing anything about it—become an antique. I have finished being truly young. There will be a holding period, a decade or so of stasis, and then the next thing that will happen is I will start to be old. That is what is happening next.

A month later and I am at an awards ceremony in London.

This is where the great and the good of the media industry gather for an evening of celebration, before going back to the grind of being great and good again.

The pavement outside has a semicircle of photographers, lighting up the doorway with their epilepsy flashes. Trying to get through that doorway when you are not someone they want to photograph is a complex and embarrassing experience: it is vital that you walk toward it with a casual, humble-yet-busy gait—exuding the vibe, I am not a Famous. Stand down your weapons. You may safely ignore me.

Should you misjudge your gait and walk too confidently, you will suffer the terrible indignity of thirty photographers half-raising their cameras as you approach them only to lower them again, disappointedly, when they realize you're not Sadie Frost. Sometimes they even shout at you.

"Fucking timewaster," one yelled once, when I rocked up in a fake-fur coat that accidentally looked too real. I have learned since—a nice duffle coat is better. Paps never bother looking at someone in a duffle. A duffle is safe.

Inside, and I'd never been in a room with so many eminent people before. Their power exuded a low hum, like a BMW engine, a hum muffled further by the good quality of their clothes. The cloth was thick and well-cut. The coats were Prada, Armani, Dior. Calfskin leather from the bags and shoes; hand creams in vetiver and rose petal. The whole room smelled wealthy. It embodied quiet, unshakable English privilege. I had expected all of that.

But what I hadn't expected was the faces—the women's faces. The men's faces are just as you would expect—famous and nonfamous alike, the men just look like, well, men. Men in their forties and fifties and sixties. Well-to-do, well-cared-for, largely untroubled men. Men who holiday in reliably sunny places, and like gin.

But the women: oh, the women *all look the same*.

The few women in their twenties and early thirties are exempt. They look normal. But as soon as the ages creep to 35, 36, 37, the first aspects of homogeneity start to appear. Lips that haven't worn down in quite the way one would expect—lips that appear to puff upward and outward, illogically, in Elvis pouts. Tight, shiny foreheads. Something indefinably—but definitely—wrong around the cheeks and jaw. Eyes pinned wide open—as if they were in Harley Street and have just been given the final bill for it all.

There is an air that the Eastern European maid had washed and ironed their dress, coat, and face, all in one go. That in the laundry room, at 11 p.m., these women's faces have hung from rosewood coat hangers, spritzed with verbena linen spray, sleeping.

As I look across the room, it reminds me of that scene in *The Magician's Nephew*, when Polly and Digory find a banquet hall where an entire court—dozens of kings and queens, all crowned— sit around a long table, frozen in stone, by magic.

As the children walk down the table, the faces gradually change—from "kind, merry, friendly" expressions at one end, through a middle section of anxiety, unease, and shiftiness, and ending, at the extreme right, in people whose faces are "the fiercest—beautiful, but cruel."

And this is what the women look like. Except they don't seem cruel, or cold, or calculating.

As you progress through the decades—from the jolly, untroubled gals in their twenties toward the grande dames in their forties, fifties, and sixties—the women in the room just look more and more scared. To be as privileged and safe as they are—but to still go through such painful, expensive procedures—gives the impression of a room full of fear. Female fear. Adrenaline that had taken them all the way to a surgeon, and a ward full of bandaged faces.

I don't know what exactly they are scared of—their husbands leaving them, the younger women in the room superseding them, the cameras outside the room judging them, or just the quiet, tired disappointment of the bathroom mirror in the morning—but they all look unnerved. They've spent thousands and thousands of pounds to look, literally and figuratively, petrified.

So that was the day I finally knew, knew inside my bones, that surgery wasn't the sane or happy thing to do. I stared at the results and they looked both unhealthy and unholy. Because not only do all these women look like they've done something very extreme and obvious out of fear, but their husbands and partners and brothers and sons and male friends seem oddly oblivious to the whole thing. *They* haven't had this stuff done. They stand right next to them, live alongside them, but clearly in a wholly different world. Something ails—deeply ails—these women, something that their men have brushed off like bugs. As I have said, in the same way that you can tell if some sexism is happening to you by asking the question "Is this polite, or not?" you can tell whether some misogynistic societal pressure is being exerted on women by calmly enquiring, "And are the *men* doing this, as well?"

If they aren't, chances are you're dealing with what we strident feminists refer to as "some total fucking bullshit."

Because the real problem here is that we're all dying. All of us. Every day the cells weaken and the fibers stretch and the heart gets closer to its last beat. The real cost of living is dying, and we're spending days like millionaires: a week here, a month there, casually spunked until all you have left are the two pennies on your eyes.

Personally, I like the fact that we're going to die. There's nothing more exhilarating than waking up every morning and going, "WOW! THIS IS IT! THIS IS REALLY IT!" It focuses the mind wonderfully. It makes you love vividly, work intensely, and realize that, in the scheme of things, you really don't have time to sit on the sofa in your undies watching *Homes Under the Hammer.*

Death is not a release, but an incentive. The more focused you are on your death, the more righteously you live your life. My traditional closing-time rant—after the one where I cry that they closed that amazing chippy on Tollington Road, the one that did the pickled eggs—is that humans still believe in an afterlife. I genuinely think it's the biggest philosophical problem the earth faces. Even avowedly nonreligious people think they'll be meeting up with nana and their dead dog, Crackers, when they finally keel over. Everyone thinks they're getting a harp.

But believing in an afterlife totally negates your current existence. It's like an insidious and destabilizing mental illness. Underneath every day—every action, every word—you think it doesn't *really* matter if you screw up this time around because you can just sort it all out in paradise. You make it up with your parents and become a better person and lose that final 14 pounds in heaven. And learn how to speak French. You'll have time, after all! It's eternity! And you'll have wings, and it'll be sunny! So, really, who *cares* what you do now? This is really just some lackluster waiting room you're going to be in for only 20 minutes, during which you will have no wings at all and are *forced* to walk around, on your feet, like pigs do.

If we wonder why people are so apathetic and casual about every eminently avoidable horror in the world—famine, war, disease, the seas gradually turning piss-yellow and filling with ring-pulls and shattered fax machines—it's right there. Heaven. The biggest waste of our time we ever invented, outside of jigsaws.

Only when the majority of the people on this planet believe—absolutely—that they are dying, minute by minute, will we actually start behaving like fully sentient, rational, and compassionate beings. For while the appeal of "being good" is strong, the terror of hurtling, unstoppably, into unending nullity is a lot more effective. I'm really holding out for us all to get the Fear. The Fear is my Second Coming. When everyone in the world admits they're going to die, we'll *really* start getting some stuff done.

So. Yes. We're all dying. We're all crumbling into the void, one cell at a time. We are disintegrating like sugar cubes in champagne. But only women have to pretend it isn't happening. Fifty-something men wander around with their guts flopped over their waistbands and their faces looking like a busted tramp's mattress in an underpass. They sprout nasal hair and chasmlike wrinkles, and go "*Ooof!*" whenever they stand up or sit down. Men visibly age, every day—but women are supposed to stop the decline at around 37, 38, and live out the next 30 or 40 years in some magical bubble where their hair is still shiny and chestnut, their face unlined, their lips puffy, and their tits up on the top third of the rib cage.

Why can't we just loosen our belts, take off our heels, and cheerfully rot, like the boys?

My Subconscious Conspiracy Theory about age denial is that women are, as I've said, generally deemed to start going "off the boil" in their midthirties. This is the age fertility declines, and the Botox and the fillers start to kick in. This is when women go into their savings accounts and start spending all their pension to remove these signs and pretend they're 30 again.

Given this, my Subconscious Conspiracy Theory would like to point out that your midthirties—by way of a *massive* coincidence—is the age that women usually start to feel confident.

Having finally left behind the—let's be frank—awfulness of your twenties (You had sex with Steve. Steve! "Beaver-face" Steve! You had that job where you were so bored, you hid in a cupboard and ate small pieces of paper! THERE WAS THE SUMMER OF CULOTTES); your thirties are the point where the good stuff finally kicks in.

You're probably doing pretty well at your job by now. You've got at least four nice dresses. You've been to Paris and experimented with anal sex and know how to repressurize your boiler and can quote bits of *The Wasteland* when you're making Whiskey Macs.

How odd, then, that as your face and body finally begin to display the signs (lines, softening, gray hairs) that you've entered the zone of kick-ass eminence and intolerance of dullards, there should be pressure for you to . . . totally remove them. Give the impression that, actually, you *are* still a bit gullible and incompetent, and *totally* open to being screwed over by someone a bit cleverer and older than you.

I don't want that. I want a face full of frown lines and weariness and cream-colored teeth that, frankly, tells stupid and venal people to FUCK OFF. I want a face that drawls—possibly in the voice of James Cagney, although Cagney from *Cagney & Lacey* will do—"I've seen more recalcitrant toddlers/devious line managers/steep mountain passes/complicated dance routines on Parappa the Rapper/bigger sums than you'll ever see in your *life*, sunshine. So get out of my special chair and bring me a cheese sandwich."

Lines and grayness are nature's way of telling you not to fuck with someone—the equivalent of the yellow-and-black banding on a wasp, or the markings on the back of a black widow spider. Lines are your weapons against idiots. Lines are your "KEEP AWAY FROM THE WISE INTOLERANT WOMAN" sign.

When I get "old" (59—I reckon 59 is old), I personally intend to bomb around town with white hair fully two feet wide, looking like one of the Wild Women of Wonga, SHOUTING about how I can feel my cells dying and ordering doubles to help me forget it. I'm not going to spend £50,000 on dying my hair, pumping up my tits, resurfacing my face, and pretending I'm a dewy virgin shepherdess, off to seek my first tumble at the bridal fair.

Because there is an unspoken announcement commensurate with that look. Women who've had the needle, or the knife, look like they're saying: "My friends are not my friends, my men are unreliable and fainthearted, my lifetime's work counts for nothing, I am 59 and empty-handed. I'm still as defenseless as the day I was born. PLUS, I've now spunked all my yacht money on my arse. By any sane index, I have failed at my life."

*

But what of the aesthetics? While it's shooting frozen fish in a barrel to dismiss the women who've spent £30,000 on bad procedures and who now look like astronauts experiencing g-force in a wind tunnel, there are some women—celebrities we can't name, because they sue, BUT WE ALL KNOW WHO THEY ARE, who've had the really expensive, subtle kind of interventions. They just look kind of . . . young, and fresh, and sparkly. Amazing. Thousands and thousands and thousands of dollars' worth of amazing. Surely the *subtle* interventions are okay? You're not trying to look 27 again. You're just trying to look like an *amaaaaaaazing* 52. In some ways, to advance a moral case against plastic surgery seems surreally nebulous. After all, we seem to have stopped having discussions about the morality of arms-dealing years ago—and that's about killing people, in some cases quite severely. Plastic surgery, on the other hand, is about slightly dumpy women wanting to have their noses look like Reese Witherspoon's—something that most of us, I'm sure, would agree is not quite in the same league as blowing a Somali orphan's leg off.

But the thing is, they're not subtle. We're still noticing it. We're all commenting on the "good" intervention, just as much as we would if it were "bad." We still observe that Time appears to have suddenly swerved off to the right when it approached them, and left their faces unmarked. We still notice the 30-something cleavage on top of the 50-something heart. Even though it looks natural, we know—we know, because we can see the date on the calendar, and our own faces—that it is unreal. That it is in denial of the fact we are dying. An unsettling, fundamental rerouting of perception. That only—only—only women are having to conspire in. THERE IS NO SUCH THING AS "SUBTLY" LOOKING DRAMATICALLY AND ILLOGICALLY MUCH, MUCH BETTER THAN EVERYONE ELSE.

Sigh. Look: I love artifice and fantasy and escapism as much as the next person—I love drag and makeup and reinvention and wigs and make-believe and inventing yourself from the floor up, as many times as you need to. Every day, if you want. At the very end of all this arguing, women should be allowed to look how they damn well please. The patriarchy can get OFF my face and tits. In an ideal world, no one would ever criticize women for how they look—however it is. Even if that look is "I have a bulldog clip under my hair pulling my face this tight." A woman's face is her castle.

But this is all under the provision that how women look should be fun, and joyful, and creative, and say something amazing about us as human beings. Even though a five-foot-eight drag queen— tottering through Birmingham city center at 4 a.m., in pinchy-winchy shoes and inch-thick lippy—will have suffered pain and spent a great deal of money, and is in TOTAL denial of reality (i.e., that he has a penis), he hasn't done all that out of fear. On the contrary, the bravery involved is off the scale.

But women living in fear of aging, and pulling painful and expensive tricks to hide it from the world, does not say something amazing about us as human beings.

Oh, it makes women look like we were *made* to do it, by big boys. It makes us look like losers. It makes us look like cowards. And that's the last thing we are.

That's the very, very last thing women are.

POSTSCRIPT

London, October 2010

So do I know how to be a woman now? The pat, self-deprecating thing would be to say, "No. No, I still don't have a clue! I'm just still the same schlumpy, well-meaning idiot I was at 13. I'm still just a chimp in a frock with a laptop, setting fire to saucepans, falling down staircases, saying the wrong thing, and feeling like an insecure child inside. I'm a buffoon! A div! A numbnut!"

Because, of course, there *are* still ways in which I don't know how to be a woman yet. I've not had to deal with teenage children, or family bereavement, or menopause, or losing my job. I still can't iron, do math, drive a car, or—and I must be frank here—100 percent reliably remember which is "left" and which is "right" in an emergency. I am responsible, when navigating, for a lot of screeching U-turns and swearing. There's still a million things I have left to learn. A billion. A trillion. In terms of how much better I potentially *could* be, I've barely even been born yet. I'm still an egg.

But then, on the other hand, I distrust this female habit of reflexively flagging your own shortcomings. Not the breezy, airy witticism in the face of a compliment—"Lost weight? No. We're just in a larger room than usual, darling." "You think my children are well mannered? I have wired them with small electrodes, and every time they misbehave, I punch the BAD KID button in my pocket." That's fine.

No—I'm talking about the common attitudinal habit in women that we're kind of . . . failing if we're not a bit neurotic. That we're somehow boorish, complacent, and unfeminine if we're content.

The way women feel that they are not so much well-meaning human beings doing the best that they can but, instead, an endless list of problems (fat, hairy, unfashionable, spotty, smelly, tired, unsexy, and with a dodgy pelvic floor, to boot) to be solved. And that, with the application of a great deal of time and money—I mean, a *great deal* of time and money. Have you *seen* how much laser hair removal is?—we might, one day, 20 years into the future, finally be able to put our feet up and say, "For nine minutes today, I *almost* nailed it!"

Before, of course, starting up the whole grim, remorseless, thankless schedule the next day, all over again.

So if I was asked, "Do you know how to be a woman now?" my answer would be, "Kind of *yes*, really, to be honest."

Because if all the stories in this book add up to one single revelation, it is this: to just . . . not really give a shit about all that stuff. To not care about all those supposed "problems" of being a woman. To refuse to see them as problems at all. Yes—when I had my massive feminist awakening, the action it provoked in me was a . . . big shrug.

As it turned out, almost every notion I had on my 13th birthday about my future turned out to be a total waste of my time. When I thought of myself as an adult, all I could imagine was someone thin, and smooth, and calm, to whom things . . . happened. Some kind of souped-up princess with a credit card. I didn't have any notion about self-development, or following my interests, or learning big life lessons, or, most important, finding out what I was good at and trying to earn a living from it. I presumed that these were all things that some grown-ups would come along and basically tell me what to do about at some point, and that I shouldn't really worry about them. I didn't worry about what I was going to *do*.

What I *did* worry about, and thought I should work hard at, was what I should *be*, instead. I thought all my efforts should be concentrated on being fabulous, rather than doing fabulous things. I thought my big tasks were discovering my "Love Style" via questionnaires in *Cosmopolitan*, assembling a capsule wardrobe, learning how to go from day to night with the application of heels and lipstick, finding a signature perfume, planning when to have a baby, and learning how to be mesmerically sexually proficient—but without getting a reputation as a total slag. While, at the same time, somehow losing a whole load of character traits that would blow my whole "pretending to be a proper woman" cover—talking too fast, falling over, arguing, emitting smells, getting angry, being quite excited about the idea of a revolution, and wanting to be a guest star on *The Muppet Show*, in a plot where Gonzo fell in love with me. Even though they'd stopped making *The Muppet Show* seven years previously.

I presumed that once I'd cracked being thin, beautiful, stylishly dressed, poised, and gracious, everything else would fall into place. That my real life's work was not a career—but myself. That if I worked on being pleasing, the world would adore and then reward me.

Of course, this supposition that women are supposed to just "be," while men go out and "do," have been argued as inimically sex-tied traits. Men go out and do things—wage wars, discover new countries, conquer space, tour *Use Your Illusion I* and *II*—while women inspire them to greater things, then discuss afterward, at length, what's happened: like the Golden Girls around Blanche's table.

But I don't know if I believe "being" *is* an innately female thing to do—that that's just how we're wired. Going back to my previous argument—about so many suppositions about "femaleness" actually coming down to us having been "losers" for so long—I would suggest that when you've spent millennia not being allowed to do anything, you *do* tend to become more focused on being self-critical, analytical, and reflective because there's nothing else you *can* do, really, other than (a) look hot and (b) turn inward.

Would Jane Austen's characters have spent pages and pages discussing all the relationships in their social circle if they'd been a bit more in control of their own destinies? Would women fret themselves half to death over how they look and who fancies them if this wasn't the main thing they were still judged on? Would we give so much of a shit about our thighs if we, as a sex, owned the majority of the world's wealth, instead of men?

When I think of everything about womanhood that had hamstrung me with fear when I was 13, it all came down, really, to princesses. I didn't think I had to work hard to be a woman—which is scary but, obviously, eventually achievable. I thought I had to somehow, magically, through superhuman psychic effort, transform into a princess instead. That's how I'd get fallen in love with. That's how I'd get along. That's how the world would welcome me. The books; the Disney films; the most famous woman in the world being, when I was a child, Princess Diana: while there were other role models around, the sheer onslaught of princessalia every girl is subject to wedges its way into the heart, in a quietly pernicious way.

In the last decade, the postfeminist reaction to princesses has been the creation of "alternative" princesses: the spunky chicks in *Shrek* and the newer Disney films, who wear trousers, do kung-fu, and save the prince. Possibly as a reaction to the life, and then death, of Diana, princesses have had to be reconfigured to acknowledge that we all now know that being a real princess isn't all about wafting around in a castle, being beautiful and noble. It's about eating disorders, loneliness, Wham! mix-tapes, shagging around, waging a pitched battle with the royal family, and, eventually, the incredible fascination that you hold over others conspiring to kill you.

It's interesting to note that, since the death of Diana, women have generally lost interest in the idea of actually being a *real* princess. Princesses have forfeited a great deal of their currency. When Prince Charles was of marriageable age, he was the subject of worldwide perving from the ladyfolk: treated as a cross between James Bond and Prince Charming. And when Diana married him, women across the world sighed over the dress, the ring, the diamonds, and the dreamlike life she was marrying into.

When Prince William announced *his* marriage to Kate Middleton, on the other hand, womenfolk were united in their sentiments: "Poor cow. Jesus Christ, does she know what she's let herself in for? A lifetime of scrutiny, bitching, pap-shots of her thighs, and speculation on her state of mind. Rather you than me, darling."

No—the dream now for women still set on "being," rather than "doing," is to become a WAG* instead. Marry a footballer and you get a princess's wealth, glamour, and privilege—plus the same implicit acceptance that your powerful husband is going to

---

*WAGS—or "Wives and Girlfriends"—are the latest British celebrity obsession. They are the useless pretty, usually jobless girls tasked with spending the multimillion-pound paychecks of their superstar soccer-playing husbands. At first, they appear to enjoy being papped coming out of nightclubs at 4 a.m.—fake-tanned, Manolo-heeled and dripping in gold.

Then they get papped coming out of their mansions, weeping, after their partners are revealed to have been unfaithful, and the deal looks less sweet.

cheat on you and that you just have to accept that—but without the expectation that you also have to be demure, upstanding, and good at a banquet. The WAG is the 21st-century princess.

But whether it's a WAG in Dolce & Gabbana at Mahiki, or Ariel in her fishtail under the sea, the tropes of "princess women" are still the same. The residual hold they have over female ability to imagine our own future is sneakily harmful.

What is it about the princess that is so wrong? Well, I know that—from personal experience—the thing that has given me the most relief and freedom in my adult years has been, finally, once and for all giving up on the idea that I might secretly be, or will one day become, a princess. Accepting you're just some perfectly ordinary woman who is going to have to crack on, work hard, and be polite in order to get anything done is—once you've gotten over the crippling disappointment of your thundering ordinariness—incredibly liberating.

Let me list my aspects of nonprincessiness—acknowledgment of each gained with terrible initial sadness and loss.

1) I can't sing. Admitting that to myself was a massive sorrow—all princesses sing. All women are supposed to be able to sing. They can calm the birds in the trees as soon as they start trilling. By way of contrast, I sound like the noise gigantic 16-wheeler trucks make, just before they smash into a police roadblock. HONK HONK. SCREEEECH. "Oh, my God—no one will come out of that alive."

2) I don't taste sweet—like cake, or honey. I can't tell you the amount of filthy books I've read that led me to believe that, when a man went down on you, he was basically lapping away on a Sherbet Dip Dab. The first time someone commented—positively, mind—that I

tasted like "a lovely pie," I cried hysterically for two hours afterward. What kind of stompy, sweaty, beefy item was I? It was supposed to be like tiramisù down there . . . some kind of sweet, milky paradise; junket pudding. Not some hearty peasant main course. A hog roast. But we are, of course, sweaty, fleshy lady-animals—all fur and umami. Of course we don't taste like a Bird's Strawberry Trifle—*like a princess would.*

3) I'm not going to be worshipped by some powerful, loaded, sword-wielding man who will change my life if I marry him. Because that is Aragon, son of Arathorn, and he doesn't exist. I don't *want* some alpha-y patriarchal brute—some confident man of action, who will treat me like "his woman." When P. J. O'Rourke said, "No woman ever dreamed of being thrown on a bed and ravished by someone dressed as a liberal," I wished to cry, "Speak for yourself, dear! *You* are scarcely qualified to judge. When were *you* last in All Bar One in your Spanx, eyeing up the ass?" In the modern world, this old-fashioned notion of what makes men desirable to women is useless and outdated, as evidenced by the fact that it's usually only people over the age of 40 who ever go on about it. For most people under that age, they see that this is a time when what *really* makes a man "alpha" is avoiding pugilism (the legal system is a drag, plus expensive), being amusing (we're sitting on top of 50 years' worth of amazing sitcoms. If you haven't picked up a couple of techniques for cracking a joke by now, you look a trifle slow-witted), and, as a bonus, knowing how to reinstall Adobe AIR when Twitter goes down on your laptop. Speaking for all my lady friends, we all want some geeky, nerdy, polite, and ri-

diculous mate whom we can sit at home with, slagging off all the tossers, and waiting for our baked potatoes to be ready. Who, obviously, is additionally so hot for us he regularly crawls across the front room on his hands and knees, croaking, "I must have sex with you now, or go literally insane." Compared to that, Prince Charming looks like a total donk.

4) Princesses never run in gangs. They never have any mates. There's no palling around. Princesses never spend the day wandering round the Natural History Museum with their sisters, arguing about their favorite mineral or stone (mine is the piece of peridot that landed here in a meteor. Weena's is feldspar: "It's sensual"). Princesses never sit outside a pub with a couple of princes on a crisp autumn afternoon, putting their favorite Beatles vocal performances into order of preference. Princesses never go away with a couple of other families on holiday, get a bit wankered, and end up doing "The Nudie Run" around a tree on the lawn, as their children watch—disapprovingly—from an upstairs window. Princesses don't enliven a dull day in the office by playing the game "I Am Burt Reynolds." (A person is chosen to be "it." They must think of a celebrity. All the other players must take it in turns to ask as many questions as possible in order to guess the identity of the celebrity, until—finally—someone asks, "Is it Burt Reynolds?" It is always Burt Reynolds. This game can be played for hours.)

Anyway, by 16, I had a new idea. I didn't want to be a princess. Princes were dull. I was all about the artists instead. They were the guys to be hanging with. I wanted to be a muse. I wanted to be a muse quite badly. To be so incredible that some band wrote a song about me, or some writer based a character on me, or a painter produced canvas after canvas of me, in every mood, that hung in galleries across the world. Or even a handbag. Jane Birkin inspired a handbag. By way of contrast I would happily have settled for my name on a plastic H&M bag.

It's not like I was the first ambitious girl to think this was how to make my way in the world. In an interview in *Please Kill Me*, Patti Smith—by all accounts a feminist goddess—recounted how, when she was growing up in New Jersey, "the coolest thing in the world was to become the mistress of a great artist. The first thing I did on leaving home was to [move to New York and] become [legendary photographer] Robert Mapplethorpe's lover."

Of course, in the end, when Mapplethorpe turned out to be very gay, Smith was left with no other option than to go off and write *Horses* and grow the world's most influential lady mustache instead. Her hand was forced into productivity.

Inspired by Smith, when I started attending after-show parties, drunk, I would stand around—trying to look so potent with mystery that someone would be compelled to write a song about how cool I was. Like a lady Fonz, but sexy. And when that plan abjectly failed, and there were no songs about me, and I got a little drunker, I just took a more direct route: tipsily berating friends in bands to immortalize me in a song.

"It doesn't have to be a big single," I would say reasonably, fag in my mouth the wrong way round. "I'm not *that* demanding. It could be the first track on the album instead. Or the final, anthemic one, I suppose. The one that builds to an affirmative chorus about how nothing's going to be the same, now that you know me. Come on—how long would it take—five minutes? Write a song about me. WRITE A SONG ABOUT ME. BE INSPIRED BY ME, YOU FUCK!"

It wasn't purely out of egotism. "It would be good for womankind as a *whole* if you wrote a song about someone like me," I would explain nobly, as they quietly ordered a cab on their mobile. "All the songs about girls are about some boring model that Eric Clapton knew, or some groupie with an 'inner sadness.' Don't you think women would be happier if 'Layla' had a whole chorus about Eric Clapton watching Patti Boyd trying to climb over a park fence, pissed, in order to retrieve a shoe she threw in there for a bet? You'd be breaking new *ground*, man—muse-wise, it would be as revolutionary as the sonic introduction of the electric guitar! WRITE A SONG ABOUT A GOBBY BIRD! WRITE A SONG ABOUT MEEEEEEEE, YOU FUCK!"

As the years went on—and my friends kept persistently not writing novels, or West End musicals, about me—I gradually realized that I'm just not the muse type. Girls like me don't inspire people.

I'm just not muse material, I finally thought sadly on my 18th birthday—looking at a world wholly noninspired by me. "I'm not a princess. I'm not a muse. If I'm going to change the world, it's not going to be by endorsing a land-mine charity in a tiara, or inspiring the next *Revolver.* Just 'being' me isn't enough. I'm going to have to *do* something instead."

And in the 21st century, being a woman who wants to do something is not hard. At any other point in time, Western women agitating for change would be at risk of imprisonment, social ostracization, rape, and death. Now, however, women in the Western world can bring about pretty much whatever change we want by writing a series of slightly arsey letters, while listening to Radio 4 and drinking a cup of tea.

Whatever it is we want the future to be like, no one's going to have to die for it. While we may still essentially be crying, "Up the purple, white, and green!" we can now put together an outfit in whichever colors we choose, should purple, white, and green look "clashy." We do not have to throw ourselves under that horse.

Simply being honest about who we really are is half the battle. If what you read in magazines and papers makes you feel uneasy or shitty—don't buy them! If you're vexed by corporate entertaining taking place in titty bars—shame your colleagues! If you feel oppressed by the idea of an expensive wedding—ignore your mother-in-law and run away to a justice of the peace! And if you think a £600 handbag is obscene, instead of bravely saying, "I'll just have to max my credit card," quietly say, "Actually, I can't afford it."

There's so much stuff—in *every* respect—that we can't afford and yet we sighingly resign ourselves to, in order to join in and feel "normal." But, of course, if *everyone* is, somehow, too anxious to say what their real situation is, then there is a new, communal, median experience that is being kept secret by everyone being too embarrassed to say, "Don't think I'm a freak, but . . ."

Anyway, it's not like this is all just about, and for, the ladies. If women's liberation truly comes to pass—as the slow, unstoppable gravity of social and economic change suggests it must—then it's going to work out pretty peachy for the men, too. If I were the patriarchy I would, frankly, be *thrilled* at the idea of women finally getting an equal crack of the whip. Let's face it—the patriarchy must be *knackered* by now. It's been 100,000 years without even so much as a tea break: men have been flat-out ruling the world. They have been balls to the wall.

Faced, then, with the option of some manner of flextime— women ruling the world *half* the time—the patriarchy could finally take its foot off the gas a bit; go on that orienteering holiday it's been talking about for years; really sort the shed out, once and for all. The patriarchy could get stuck into some hard-core paint-balling weekends.

Because it's not as if strident feminists want to *take over* from men. We're not arguing for the *whole world*. Just our share. The men don't really have to change a thing. As far as I'm concerned, men can just carry on doing pretty much whatever they like. They don't really need to stop at all. Loads of stuff they're doing—iPads, and the Arctic Monkeys, that new nuclear arms deal between America and Russia—is cool. And they're funny, and I am friends with lots of them, and they're good for having sex with, and they look great in reproduction World War 2 uniforms, or reversing into tight parking spaces.

I don't want men to go away. I don't want men to stop what they're doing.

What I want, instead, are some radical market forces. I want CHOICE. I want VARIETY. I want MORE. I want WOMEN. I want women to have more of the world, not just because it would be fairer, but because it would be better. More exciting. Reordered. Reinvented. We should have the lady-balls to say, "Yeah—I like the look of this world. And I've been here for a good while, watching. Now—here's how I'd tweak it. Because we're all in this together. We're all just, you know. The Guys."

So, in the end, I suppose the title of the book is a bit of a misnomer. All through those stumbling, mortifying, amazing years, I *thought* that what I wanted to be was a woman. To be some incredible amalgam of Germaine Greer, Elizabeth Taylor, E. Nesbit, Courtney Love, Jilly Cooper, and Lady Gaga. Finding some way of mastering all the arcane arts of being female, until I was some witchery paragon of all the things that confused and defeated me at the outset, in my bed, in Wolverhampton, at the age of 13. A princess. A goddess. A muse.

But as the years went on, I realized that what I really want to be, all told, is a human. Just a productive, honest, courteously treated human. One of "the Guys." But with *really* amazing hair.

www.how-tobeawoman.com

ACKNOWLEDGMENTS

When I had my first ever meeting with my agent, Georgia Garrett, and she asked me what I wanted to do, I found myself saying, "I want to write a book about feminism! A funny, but polemic, book about feminism! Like *The Female Eunuch*—but with jokes about my knickers!"

It was as much a surprise to me as it was to her—I'd gone in to pitch her some "Eat, Pray, LOLcatz" stocking filler, and/or my long-term project: a gay reworking of *Oliver!* But her immediate, "I get it! Write this book! Now!" enthusiasm—coupled with the fact I figured that writing a book meant I had a legitimate reason to take up smoking again—meant I ended up writing *How to Be a Woman* in an urgent five-month blur. Man, I smoked a lot. By the end, my lungs felt like two socks full of black sand. But all the way through, she was the main cheerleader and rant-inspirer, and I thank her from the bottom of my tobacco-trashed heart.

My brilliant editor, Jake Lingwood—and all at Ebury—were similarly *"Wooo!"* about the whole thing—even at the stage where I was campaigning for the front cover to be my naked belly flopped out on a table, with "This is what a REAL woman's stomach looks like" written underneath in angry, red capital letters. Thank you, dudes. Particularly for the money. I spent it on a new stove and a handbag. Yeah! Feminism! Wooo!

In America, my amazing editor Jennifer Barth proved to be the PERFECT person to take the book across the Atlantic from the moment she took me out in London, and got me so hammered on mojitos I dropped my eyeliner in the toilet, and had to make a survival-style pair of rubber gloves, out of a plastic bag, to get it out. She also displayed incredible patience during the protracted and amazing process of explaining what a "Womble" is. Her team of Jonathan Burnham (publisher), Amy Baker and Erica Barmash (marketing), Gregory Henry (publicist), and Dalma De León (production editor) all made the whole thing a joy from beginning to end—thank you all SO MUCH my American cousins.

Thank you to Nicola Jeal, Louise France, Emma Tucker, Phoebe Greenwood, and Alex O'Connell at *The Times*, who displayed hot, sexy patience over a summer where I kept ringing up, saying, "Can I drop a column this week? I'm writing a book about FEMINISM, for God's sake, don't try to SHACKLE me to my CONTRACTUALLY AGREED WORD COUNT, get off my BACK, the Man," even though they are all women and were insisting I take the time off and being totally reasonable about the whole thing.

My family were, as always, both game for me to plunder their lives for laughs and very good at taking me to the pub when I got stressed, insisting I get shit-faced and then pretending they'd left their wallets at home. My sisters—Weena, Chel, Col, and Caz— are the most hard-core feminists this side of Greer, and were always very good at reinspiring my ardor for the project—mainly by reminding me that Carl Jung's favorite party trick was to whip people with a tea towel until they punched him. I don't know why that was particularly inspiring, but it was. And my brothers— Jimmy, Eddie, and Joe—are also my sisters in "the Struggle," apart from when they wrestle me to the floor, screaming, "It's time for a gimping!"

Endless thanks to the redoubtable Alexis Petridis, who— during a whole summer of me ringing him, weeping, "I appear to be writing an impossible book! Write it for me, Alexis! Even though you are part of the patriarchy!"—never once pointed out that he did actually have a job that he needed to be getting on with, and that I was hiccupping too much for him to make sense of what I was saying anyway.

The Women of Twitter—Sali Hughes, Emma Freud, India Knight, Janice Turner, Emma Kennedy, Sue Perkins, Sharon Horgan, Alexandra Heminsley, Claudia Winkleman, Lauren Laverne, Jenny Colgan, Clare Balding, Polly Samson, Victoria Coren, and particularly the awe-inspiring, and frankly terrifying, Grace Dent—who daily reminded me that funny women with a well-informed point are a dime a dozen, and I really needed to up my ante if I was going to pretend to compete with them. Thank you also to the Honorary Women of Twitter—Dorian Lynskey, Martin Carr, Chris Addison, Ian Martin, David Quantick, Robin Turner, and David Arnold—for being the best imaginary office-mates in the world; and especially Jonathan Ross and Simon Pegg, for their blockbusting quotes. And Nigella, whose comment made me *squeeeee*.

"Lizzie" and "Nancy"—I love you to bits, and I'm so sorry Mummy was away for a whole summer but, to be fair, Uncle Eddie is better at playing Mario Kart with you than I am, and once I'd taught you to say "Damn you, the Patriarchy!" every time you fell over, you'd had the best of me as a parent, to be honest.

Finally, I would like to dedicate this book—like I'm standing on a stage or something, about to play "Paradise City"; rather than just typing on a laptop with absolutely no one watching—to my husband, Pete Paphides, who is the most Strident Feminist I've ever met, to the point where he actually taught me what feminism is, or should be, anyway: "Everyone being polite to each other." Darling, I love you very much. And it *was* me who broke the back door handle that time. I fell on it when I was drunk and pretending to be Amy Winehouse. I can admit that now.